Locked Up, Locked Out

Locked Up, Locked Out

Young Men in the

Juvenile Justice System

Anne M. Nurse

Vanderbilt University Press

Nashville

This book is printed on acid-free paper.
Manufactured in the United States of America

Library of Congress Cataloging-in-Publication Data
Nurse, Anne, 1968–
Locked up, locked out : young men in the juvenile justice system / Anne
M. Nurse. — 1st ed.
p. cm.
Includes bibliographical references and index.
ISBN 978-0-8265-1711-1 (cloth : alk. paper)
ISBN 978-0-8265-1712-8 (pbk. : alk. paper)
1. Juvenile justice, Administration of—United States. 2. Juvenile detention
homes—United States. 3. Juvenile delinquents—United States. 4. Young
men—United States. I. Title.
HV9104.N873 2010
364.360973—dc22
2009045466

Contents

Locked Up, Locked Out

Chapter 1

An Introduction to the Juvenile Justice System

In the summer of 2002, Charles, a seventeen-year-old male, was arrested for assault in Cleveland, Ohio. He, like many juveniles arrested in the state, was taken to his county detention home to be held until a hearing before the juvenile court. Because of the seriousness of the offense and a previous arrest record, the judge decided to commit him to the Department of Youth Services (DYS), the state-level juvenile correctional system. He arrived at the DYS intake center in the fall to begin serving his twelve-month sentence.

We know the facts of this Cleveland case because they are a matter of public record; the details of the youth's arrest and sentence appeared in his local paper. The same information was also available in the arrest and incarceration statistics collected by local and state officials for the year. Beyond this minimal information, however, the public was told little about the young man, the circumstances that brought him to juvenile court, or what happened to him after he was released. We did not learn about the family he left behind when he entered the DYS system, nor did we hear about his experiences in juvenile detention. His post-release attempts to find a job and stay out of trouble were also invisible.

Each morning more than ninety-four thousand youth wake up in detention centers (Livsey, Sickmund, and Sladky, 2009). This translates to hundreds of thousands of young people passing through the gates of these facilities each year. Some of them are housed in institutions that offer real assistance. Many, however, awaken in dangerous and underfunded facilities that do little more than warehouse them for the length of their sentence. Recent investigations have revealed the existence of endemic violence, abuse, and other serious problems in many of these facilities (Cohen, 2008; Krisberg, 2003; U.S. Department of Justice, 2008). The public's lack of knowledge about these conditions, or about the residents themselves, is a matter of concern. It prevents us from engaging in informed debate or adequate oversight. Instead, juvenile correctional facilities and their residents become the subject of speculation and stereotyping. Without an understanding of their lives, it becomes easy to characterize incarcerated youth—like the Cleveland youth described above—as "gangsters" or "super-predators."

There has never been a better time, or a more important one, to set aside stereotypes and focus on the reality of our nation's correctional system. Over the past thirty years America has engaged in an "unprecedented imprisonment binge" that has put our incarceration rate well ahead of any other industrialized country (Austin and Irwin, 2001, 1). In addition to the youth in juvenile facilities, there are 2.3 million inmates in our adult prisons. As a result, with only 5 percent of the world's population, our country is home to 25 percent of the world's prisoners (Liptak, 2008). The financial and social costs associated with this massive incarceration are immense. By 2006, direct expenditures for the U.S. correctional system topped sixty-eight billion dollars annually (Bureau of Justice Statistics, 2008). Incarceration also exacts a grave human toll as families deal with the absence of parents, children, and siblings. When prisoners return home, they face significant challenges including social stigma and barriers to employment. African Americans, who are overrepresented in the prison system, shoulder a particularly large share of this emotional and financial burden. A high incarceration rate can also have widespread (and sometimes surprising) societal effects, like an increase in racial inequality (Western, Petit, and Guetzkow, 2002). It can even have an effect on election outcomes when large numbers of people are unable to vote because they are in prison (Maurer, 2002).

Today's record level of incarceration—and the significant social effects associated with it—have spurred an explosion of research on prisons. Researchers, however, have focused most of their attention on the adult system. While it is tempting to turn to this literature to gain insight into juvenile correctional facilities, there are compelling reasons to consider the two systems separately. As I describe later in this chapter, reformers created the first juvenile prisons because they believed that juveniles were more amenable to rehabilitation than adults. Although this rehabilitative zeal has waned in recent years, its impact on the juvenile system remains. For example, incarcerated juveniles generally serve shorter sentences with more flexible release dates than adults. Juvenile facilities differ from those for adults in architecture, size, programs provided, and inmate conduct policies. There are also important differences between the adult and juvenile systems in terms of parole rules and reentry issues. These differences are reflected in the official language used to refer to institutions in the two systems. While the term "prison" is freely applied to adult facilities, juvenile institutions are usually called "correctional facilities" or "detention centers."

In addition to structural differences, juvenile and adult correctional facilities differ in the populations they house. Research from both psychology and sociology suggests that juveniles are significantly different from adults—developmentally, socially, and financially. In terms of developmental differences, psychologists have found that adolescents tend to be less able to use reason under stress. They are also more susceptible to peer influence and more tolerant of risk (Scott and Steinberg, 2008). These characteristics are likely to have a unique effect on how youth respond to the highly stressful and dangerous prison environment. Life course theorists suggest that there are also social differences between adults and youth that may make the prison experience different for the two groups. They argue that the timing of significant life transitions has an effect on other transitions. For example, the age at which a person marries can have long-term repercussions on their career, lifestyle, education, and childbearing decisions. Similarly, the age at which a person is incarcerated is likely to have an important effect on post-release decisions and subsequent life changes. In other words, time served as a juvenile may have a different impact on employment, school, and social relationships than time served as an adult. The fact that juveniles have few financial resources and are often dependent on their parents also makes their experience quite different from that of adults.

It is important that researchers, policy makers, and the public focus their attention on juvenile justice issues with the recognition that juvenile correctional facilities are not simply smaller adult prisons. Juvenile detention has become an increasingly common experience in the United States. Between 1991 and 2003, for example, the population of juvenile correctional facilities grew 27 percent (Snyder and Sickmund, 2006, 199). Research on the juvenile justice system is necessary to help policy makers and academics interested in reforming this system and improving outcomes for our nation's youth. Such research also has the potential to help change the adult prison system. Recidivism rates as high as 50 percent indicate that many youth leave juvenile correctional centers only to reappear as prisoners in the burgeoning adult system (Juvenile Justice Digest, 2006; Texas Youth Commission, 2003; Ohio Department of Youth Services, 2008). Thus, it may be possible to reduce the population in adult prisons by reshaping the way we approach juvenile corrections. Increasing our knowledge of juvenile corrections is also important because it has implications for a number of areas of sociology including life course theory, social network theory, and critical race theory.

This Book

This book is designed to enhance understanding of the juvenile correctional system by providing detailed information about the day-to-day experiences of youth who reside within it. It also provides a broad overview of the system itself. Chapter 1 begins with information about history, facility organization and design, funding, court structure, and demographics of incarcerated youth. Although individual states exhibit great variation in their systems, I focus on the commonalities while highlighting any states that are exceptional. The information contained in this first chapter is applicable to both males and females in the juvenile justice system. In the chapters that follow, however, I offer a detailed look at how young men experience incarceration and reentry. My focus on males is useful because they currently compose the majority (85 percent) of the population in youth detention (Snyder and Sickmund, 2006, 206). It is important to note, however, that females compose a growing segment of the juvenile justice system, and research (as well as juvenile justice policy) all too often overlooks them. I am hopeful that their unique experiences will be the subject of future study and policy.

The next section of this book delves into the world of the male juvenile correctional facility. In Chapter 2, I introduce the forty young men whose experiences form the basis for the rest of the book. These youth were all first-time admissions to the Ohio juvenile correctional system in 2002, and I interviewed them three times over the next two and a half years. Chapter 3 explores the formal structure of the correctional facility—the way institutions are organized to rehabilitate, punish, and keep youth under control. Here I pay substantial attention to the programs offered to youth in custody, including those focusing on education, anger management, job training, and parenting skills. Chapter 4 explores the informal structure of the facility with a particular emphasis on the social organization and status systems the youth create and maintain. Chapter 5 looks at contact between incarcerated youth and the outside world and also explores the impact of incarceration on families. This discussion is enhanced by interview data with fifteen parents and other relatives of the Ohio youth.

In Chapter 6, I follow the study's youth as they are released from correctional institutions and return to their communities. I focus on their experiences of parole, schooling, and employment but also explore the effects of incarceration on their relationships with family and friends. The final chapter of the book, Chapter 7, pulls together the information presented in the previous chapters to consider the theoretical and policy implications of the study.

A Brief History of the Juvenile Justice System

Until the 1800s, juveniles and children as young as seven were tried in the same courts and served prison terms alongside adults. By the end of the century, however, new attitudes about youth, crime, and urbanization created an opening for reformers to reshape the way juveniles were handled by the justice system. First, the public began to accept the idea of adolescence as a unique developmental stage. Juveniles came to be seen as less culpable and more receptive to rehabilitation efforts than adults (Schlossman, 1995). This idea went hand in hand with the notion that adolescent crime and poverty were primarily caused by environmental and developmental factors rather than by individual traits (Bernard, 1992). Consequently, reformers became concerned about the ways that bad parenting, poverty, and urbanization might be linked to criminality in youth.

These new attitudes about youth and crime paved the way for development of an innovative model of juvenile corrections. Wayward youth needed to be removed from negative home environments, but they also needed to be kept away from the dangerous influence of adult prisons. One judge described adult prisons as "a fruitful source of pauperism, a nursery of new vices and crimes, a college for the perfection of adepts in guilt" (quoted in Bernard, 1992, 36). For this reason—and because of high levels of abuse and deprivation in adult penitentiaries—some judges became unwilling to send youth accused of minor offenses there. The solution, it seemed, was to create new institutions that would provide a healthy environment specifically tailored for juveniles. The New York House of Refuge was the first institution in the United States to attempt to answer this call. Founded in 1825 by the Society for the Reformation of Juvenile Delinquents, it was conceived as a way to remove youth from the influence of the streets, adult criminals, and abusive or neglectful parents. Other states quickly followed New York's lead and created their own houses of refuge. Residents in these early institutions engaged in hard work and were exhorted to adopt a strict moral code.

While some of the children confined in houses of refuge had committed criminal acts, most were simply poor, and officials perceived them to be at high risk of later pauperism and criminality (Bernard, 1992). This policy went largely unquestioned until 1838, when a writ of habeas corpus was filed on behalf of a girl named Mary Ann Crouse. Mary Ann had committed no crime but was confined in the Philadelphia House of Refuge on the request of her mother. Her father, however, objected to her confinement and requested that the state justify and explain the grounds on which his daughter was being held. He believed that Mary Ann's institutionalization was illegal since it represented the imposition of a punishment without a crime. The

Pennsylvania Supreme Court ultimately ruled that Mary Ann's confinement was legal because it was designed to help her, not punish her. The decision invoked the doctrine of parens patriae, which gives the state the role of "parent of the country." This doctrine provided the state with justification for taking measures to ensure the welfare of children, including removing them from their homes.

Bolstered by the outcome of the Crouse case, states and private groups continued to open and operate juvenile institutions. By midcentury, however, houses of refuge began to fall out of favor, and reform schools became more popular. The difference between the two was primarily semantic, but reform schools were usually run by states rather than by private groups. Reform schools also tended to house larger proportions of children who had been accused of crime (McShane and Williams, 2007). The reform schools served multiple purposes—they allowed children to receive special rehabilitative programming, they removed more children from dangerous and overcrowded adult prisons, and they provided housing for neglected and needy children. Although the goals of the founders were primarily charitable, the creation of the early schools may also have been in response to high levels of immigration that began in the last half of the nineteenth century. Many of the new immigrants were impoverished and seen as morally deficient. The reform schools were envisioned as a way to control and socialize the children of these immigrants (Rothman, 1971).

Daily life at both houses of refuge and reform schools was organized around work, often the work required to run the institution itself. Many reform schools also provided limited academic and vocational training, and some even helped youth obtain apprenticeships after their release. Over the course of the century, however, the number and size of reform schools grew quickly, and it became difficult to provide comprehensive educational or vocational training. The apprenticeship system was largely abandoned, and schools began to release youth back into the community with no supervision (Schlossman, 1995). As the population of juvenile institutions continued to grow, so too did abuse and neglect (Bernard, 1992).

Separate juvenile correctional facilities became well established during the first half of the nineteenth century, but it was not until the very end of the century that the idea of a separate juvenile court system took hold. The first juvenile court was established in Cook County, Illinois, in 1899. Advocates for the creation of this system argued that children were less culpable than adults and more amenable to treatment. They envisioned the juvenile court as a place in which fatherly judges could help guide both criminal and neglected youth to better lives. Criminality and neglect were seen as two sides of the same coin; a criminal child was, by definition, a child who needed attention. At the same time, a neglected child was viewed as a criminal waiting to happen. These arguments were compelling enough that by 1925 almost every state had a separate juvenile court system. In line with the idea that judges should have wide discretion to help misdirected youth, the courts were set up to be quite informal and did not have the same legal protections as adult courts.

The early juvenile courts were unique in their emphasis on treatment and the "whole child." To help them assess and meet children's needs, courts developed innovative psychological clinics and extensive probation programs. The first of these clinics opened in Chicago in 1909, and other cities quickly followed Chicago's lead (Glueck and Glueck, 1934/1965). Staff in the court clinics conducted intensive psychological testing of each child referred to them by the court. They also took a social history. The clinics' goal was not therapeutic; rather, they were responsible for helping the court develop a plan to address a child's needs. Juvenile courts also developed probation programs that allowed them to supervise youth without placing them in detention. While probation had been used in the criminal justice system for about fifty years, its systematic use in the juvenile court helped to popularize and formalize it. (For a fascinating history of these clinics and probation programs, see Levine and Levine, 1970).

The years between 1925 and 1960 were relatively quiet ones for juvenile justice, with no major changes or challenges to the system. During this time, however, a number of states did begin to experiment with new treatment and rehabilitation techniques. Most notably, reform schools were encouraged to put more emphasis on individual classification and treatment of youth. Several states, including California and Texas, created a "Youth Authority" system intended to use scientific principles to diagnose and treat behavioral disorders. This quiet period of juvenile justice ended abruptly in the 1960s with the filing of a number of due process lawsuits against states. The most famous of these involved a fifteen-year-old named Gerald Gault who was committed to a state reform school on charges of making lewd phone calls. The U.S. Supreme Court, in the 1967 decision *In re Gault*, found that Gerald's rights were violated because, among other things, he had not been allowed legal representation in court and he was precluded from appealing the court's decision. The resolution of this case forced states across the nation to institute due process protections in their juvenile courts. Some of the more notable new protections resulting from *Gault* included a juvenile's right to counsel, the right to confront witnesses, and the right against self-incrimination.

The *Gault* decision marked the beginning of a wave of litigation that dramatically remade the juvenile court system. The verdict in the Supreme

Court case *In re Winship* (1970), for example, required courts to have "proof beyond a reasonable doubt" to convict juveniles. In another Supreme Court decision, *Breed v. Jones* (1975), youth were granted the same ban on double jeopardy as adults. This case was particularly important because it held that delinquency proceedings were similar to criminal trials (Feld, 2000). These cases and others formalized the juvenile court process and moved it in the direction of the adult criminal courts. As scholar Barry Feld commented, "By emphasizing criminal procedural regularity in the determination of legal guilt, the Supreme Court shifted the initial focus of juvenile courts' delinquency proceedings from paternalistic assessments of a youth's 'real needs' to proof he or she committed a crime" (2000, 514).

The most significant changes to the juvenile justice system of the 1960s and 1970s occurred in the area of due process, but there were other changes as well. For example, there were new laws designed to keep low-level offenders out of court and ensure that juveniles were not housed in adult facilities. Community treatment options were also expanded during this time (Snyder and Sickmund, 2006). The 1980s and 1990s, however, were marked by a dramatic reversal of this rehabilitative ethos. In 1974, Robert Martinson authored a meta-analysis of prison rehabilitation programs. His well-publicized (although methodologically flawed) conclusion that "nothing works" was quickly picked up by the public and policy makers and used as a justification for reducing funding to rehabilitative programs in prison. Public fears of crime also increased during this time, justifying the creation of a more punitive juvenile justice system (Callahan, 2004). Lawmakers lengthened sentences and made additional categories of youth eligible for incarceration. These new sentencing policies, combined with increasing rates of crime, led juvenile detention populations to reach record highs by the end of the century.

Today, juvenile corrections has entered a period of uncertainty and change. Since the 1980s, the system has experienced unprecedented growth. This rapid growth has led to overcrowding, staffing shortages, and insufficient funding for institutional programs. In 2002, a coalition of rights groups filed a lawsuit on behalf of eleven youth held at the California Youth Authority. The extensive investigation prompted by the lawsuit found that there were serious problems in the state's juvenile correctional system, including a lack of educational and treatment programs, inadequately trained staff, and high levels of violence (Krisberg, 2003). Speaking about the lawsuit and the findings of the investigation, Governor Arnold Schwarzenegger commented, "California is wrong. We made mistakes and therefore we should settle it" (Murphy, 2004). The lawsuit was ultimately settled out of court when the state agreed to institute dramatic reforms. Since then, California has closed two large facilities and has nearly halved the number of youth in state custody (White, 2009).

Ohio faced its own lawsuit in 2004, filed against the DYS by the Children's Law Center of Kentucky. It alleged abuse of female inmates at the state's juvenile intake center. In 2005, the Law Center expanded the lawsuit to include conditions in both male and female correctional facilities across the DYS system. The parties agreed to allow a fact-finding commission to investigate before the case went forward, and an independent consultant was hired. The consultant's report, released in early 2008, was damning; it cited, among other things, overcrowding, lack of proper medical and dental care, mistreatment of youth by poorly trained staff, and lack of educational programs (Cohen, 2008). In May 2008, a settlement was approved by a U.S. district court that required Ohio to hire 115 new correctional officers and other staff, improve care and programming at its facilities, put low-risk offenders in community placements, and design a new method of arriving at release dates.

The California and Ohio lawsuits provided important evidence that our juvenile correctional system faces significant challenges. Lawsuits and investigations in a number of other states, including Texas and Arizona, confirmed that the problem is national in scope. In January 2010, the Department of Justice released a report showing widespread sexual abuse at juvenile detention facilities around the nation (Associated Press, 2010). At the same time, there are also signs that the juvenile justice system is moving in a positive direction. Missouri, for example, has created a system that boasts small facilities, strong staff training, and extensive aftercare services. It appears that this program is achieving notable success in lowering recidivism rates and in helping youth to earn high school credits (Moore, 2009; Missouri Youth Services Institute, 2009). A number of other states, including Florida, Illinois, and Louisiana, have adopted elements of the Missouri model. Additionally, the Annie E. Casey Foundation has developed recommendations to help juvenile court systems keep youth out of secure confinement. These methods have been implemented successfully in counties in both New Jersey and California (Moore, 2009). Finally, a number of states and localities are experimenting with other promising new programs to stem violence in institutions, increase youth's educational and employment outcomes, and connect youth with support services outside prison.

Our current juvenile justice system can only be understood in the context of its history. While the historical account included in this chapter is brief, it effectively illustrates the cyclical nature of juvenile justice. In his book *The Cycle of Juvenile Justice*, Thomas Bernard (1992) argues that juvenile justice practices move in a circle from harsh punishment to rehabilitation. During a period of punishment, judges are allowed only a few severe sentencing options and, simultaneously, conditions in juvenile correctional facilities are permitted to deteriorate. Judges then become unwilling to sentence youth to detention—especially those who have committed minor crimes. This means that some youth receive no punishment at all while others receive very serious sanctions. Eventually, the public realizes that this harsh punishment model has not resulted in a decrease in juvenile crime rates. They become willing to accept a more treatment-oriented system that eliminates the "forced choice" between harsh punishment and doing nothing. As time passes, however, the cycle turns back to punitive policies as it becomes clear that the more rehabilitative system has not solved the juvenile crime problem.

Bernard believes that we can see this punitive-rehabilitative cycle in operation across the history of juvenile justice, with rehabilitative peaks in the early 1900s and the 1960s through 1970s, and punitive peaks in the late 1800s and the 1980s. His work provides an important historical perspective on the juvenile justice system. It cannot, however, be taken as a complete explanation for today's historically harsh juvenile sentences and record levels of incarceration. A comprehensive discussion of the topic is beyond the scope of this book, but researchers who study growth in the adult prison system suggest that we must look at a wide range of factors including racism, politics, and nationalism (see for example, Bosworth, 2009; Gottschalk, 2006; Simon, 2007; Wacquant, 2000). Nonetheless, it is clear that the punitive period of the 1980s–1990s has had a profound effect on today's juvenile justice system. As Bernard predicts, however, there are also indications that a rehabilitative ethos may be reemerging.

The Road to the Juvenile Prison

The most typical starting point on the road to a juvenile correctional facility is when a youth is arrested as a suspect in a crime. There are two distinct types of crimes handled by the juvenile justice system. The first type, "delinquent offense," is an act that would be considered criminal regardless of whether the offender was an adult or a juvenile. Charles, the Cleveland youth described at the beginning of the chapter, was convicted of the delinquent offense of assault. Other delinquent offenses include burglary, murder, and drug dealing. The second type of crime that can send a juvenile to prison is a "status offense." Status offenses are acts that are only considered criminal if committed by juveniles. The most common status offenses are truancy, liquor law violations, and running away (Snyder and Sickmund, 2006, 192).

Once an arrest has taken place, the police must decide whether the matter is serious enough, and the evidence strong enough, to warrant a youth's referral to the courts. In about a quarter of all cases, the police make the decision to either drop the matter or handle it informally (Sickmund, 2003, 2). Most of the remaining cases are sent on to juvenile court or, in a few instances, sent directly to adult court. In many jurisdictions, juvenile court officials—like the police—have the ability to drop cases or to handle them informally. About 42 percent of the cases referred to the court are resolved in this way (Snyder and Sickmund, 2006, 171). Such informal arrangements are popular because they enable police and court staff to work with youth in developing a personalized plan to pay restitution, get treatment, or engage in community service. Some localities regulate these types of agreements through official "diversion programs." Diversion programs are usually limited to first-time nonviolent offenders who indicate that they are willing to participate in treatment. Under such an arrangement, a young person might agree to attend therapy or drug treatment instead of going through the traditional court process. If they fail to meet the requirements specified in the diversion process, the youth can be brought back to court on the original charges. When these programs are overseen by the probation department, they are sometimes called "informal probation."

Informal handling is reserved for minor or first-time offenses. In the case of more serious or chronic offenses, juvenile court officials have two options: they can hold a special hearing to determine whether a case should be moved to adult court, or they can schedule a trial (called a delinquency hearing) in juvenile court. While youth wait for their court appearances, they can be required to stay in a detention home. These facilities (colloquially called a "DH" or "juve") are usually reserved for short-term stays. Generally, only youth awaiting trial ("detained youth") or youth awaiting placement stay in these facilities. In some states, however, youth serving sentences ("committed youth") can be housed there as well. Charles, for example, served fifteen months as a committed youth at his local DH for a crime that took place before his 2002 assault charge. He later returned to the DH as a detained youth while he waited for his assault trial. Because some rural counties do not have juvenile holding facilities, some detained youth are held for short periods of time in adult jails.

Juvenile Court Jurisdiction

Over a century ago, the nation's first juvenile court was given a clear charge: they were to hear all cases involving children under the age of sixteen. This simple jurisdictional rule no longer exists. Instead, each state has its own complex set of laws regarding juvenile court jurisdiction. In addition to the various state systems, the federal government runs its own court and prison system. Youth who violate federal laws (such as immigration, trafficking, or any crime committed on a reservation) are sometimes diverted to the federal court system and, if found guilty, can be committed to the Federal Bureau of Prisons (BOP). The federal government does not run a separate juvenile justice system, but they must still comply with laws precluding juveniles from being housed with adults. For this reason, the BOP contracts with private prisons or with state-run juvenile facilities to house youth convicted of federal crimes. The federal system handles very few juvenile cases, however. In 2001, only one hundred juveniles were committed to federal prisons while over 75,000 were committed to state juvenile facilities (Snyder and Sickmund, 2006, 118, 197). The vast majority of arrested youth are accused of violating state laws and thus remain in the state-level system.

Youth in the state court system must meet a number of criteria to be charged in juvenile court. First, their age at the time of the alleged crime must fall within the limits of juvenile court jurisdiction. Most states, including Ohio, place the dividing line between the adult and juvenile systems at eighteen. In ten states, however, the juvenile court only has jurisdiction through age sixteen, and in three states—North Carolina, New York, and Connecticut—the maximum age is fifteen (National Center for Juvenile Justice, 2006). In addition to defining maximum age for juvenile court jurisdiction, some states also define minimum age. Of the sixteen states that have such statutes, North Carolina has the lowest minimum age of six years. Eleven states define the minimum age as ten years. Other states use case law or common law to determine the age at which children are too young to be sent to court (Snyder and Sickmund, 2006, 103). Children who are deemed too young for juvenile court are generally diverted to the state welfare system or to child protective services. Those over the maximum age limit are moved into the adult court system (also called "criminal court").

Age is the primary, but not the only, criterion used to decide court jurisdiction. All fifty states have laws that allow youth who are within the ages for juvenile court jurisdiction to be transferred to adult court. The most common type of transfer law—judicial waiver—has been in existence since the beginning of the juvenile court system. Early court judges made waiver decisions on a case-by-case basis using a standard of the "best interests of the child and the public" (Snyder and Sickmund, 2006, 94). This process was very subjective, and youth who were transferred to criminal court had little legal protection. This changed in 1966 when a Supreme Court ruling—*Kent v. the United States*—forced states to apply procedural protections when making waiver decisions. Morris Kent, the subject of the lawsuit, was sixteen and already on probation when he was arrested in the District of Columbia on charges of robbery and rape. The juvenile court judge transferred his case to criminal court without a hearing, claiming that he had conducted a "full investigation." The reasons behind the judge's decision were never made clear, and Morris Kent went on to be convicted in criminal court.

Once Morris's criminal trial concluded, his lawyer filed both an appeal and a writ of habeas corpus. The Supreme Court ultimately heard the case and ruled that states must hold a hearing before allowing a judicial waiver. In addition, a youth's counsel must receive access to his or her records, and the court must reveal the reasons for any transfer decisions. In the appendix of the decision, the court included a list of factors (taken from the District of Columbia policy memorandum) that states could use when making transfer decisions. These factors included the seriousness of a crime, whether the crime was against a person or property, the weight of the evidence, the maturity and previous criminal history of the youth, public safety, and the youth's potential for rehabilitation. While states are not required to use these factors, many have chosen to do so (Clausel and Bonnie, 2000).

Today, forty-six states use three different types of waiver laws to transfer youth to adult courts (Benekos and Merlo, 2008, 30). The most common, found in forty-five states, is a discretionary waiver. During discretionary waiver hearings, the assumption is that a case should stay in the juvenile system. The prosecution bears the burden of proving otherwise, and juvenile court judges make the final decision about whether to transfer eligible cases to adult criminal court. Presumptive waivers, by contrast, assume that eligible cases should be handled by the adult court unless a youth is able to prove otherwise. For example, in some states, a juvenile could argue against a transfer on the grounds that he or she is amenable to treatment and would benefit from remaining in the juvenile system. Fifteen states, including Alaska and New Hampshire, have presumptive waivers. Mandatory waiver, the final type of judicial waiver, simply requires that all cases deemed eligible be transferred. Fifteen states, including Indiana, South Carolina, and Connecticut, have this type of waiver law. (See Griffin, Torbet, and Szymanski, 1998, for a more detailed description of the different types of waiver laws.)

In the 1980s and 1990s, many states changed their laws to expand the categories of juveniles eligible for transfer to adult court. Some of these laws reduced the age at which transfers could take place, and others increased the range of crimes requiring or allowing adult court jurisdiction. These changes in law helped to raise the number of juvenile waivers from 7,200 in 1985 to 12,300 in 1994—an increase of 83 percent (Snyder and Sickmund, 2006, 186). After 1994, however, the number of waivers began to decline. This decline was partly in response to lower rates of violent crime, but it can also be explained by the increased use of direct filing and statutory exclusion, two other types of transfer mechanisms (Benekos and Merlo, 2008).

Under a direct filing system, jurisdiction for certain types of crime is granted to both the juvenile and adult courts, leaving it up to the prosecutor to decide where to file a particular case. States provide sets of guidelines to help prosecutors make this decision. Some states emphasize a youth's age, others focus on his or her criminal history, and still others prioritize the severity of the crime (Griffin, Torbet, and Szymanski, 1998). Direct filing does not require a hearing, and it therefore accords a great deal of power to prosecutors. Fifteen states currently have direct file provisions. Statutory exclusion laws—found in twenty-nine states—automatically send certain categories of serious offenders to adult court (Benekos and Merlo, 2008, 30). For example, Arizona has a statutory exclusion law requiring that any murder case involving a suspect over the age of fourteen be filed in criminal court. In recent years, states have increased their use of both direct file and statutory exclusion provisions, in part because they save the time and expense of a waiver hearing.

When a case is transferred to adult court through waiver, direct filing, or statutory exclusion, the youth is considered an adult and is sentenced accordingly. A transfer to adult court can, in some states, mean that a youth is considered an adult for all (or some) future violations. Thirty-four states have these kinds of "once an adult, always an adult" statutes. Because of the serious effects of a transfer on a youth, many states give criminal courts the power to send cases back to juvenile court. These provisions, called reverse waiver, are available to criminal court judges in twenty-five states (Benekos and Merlo, 2008, 30).

Sentencing and Juvenile Court

Once juvenile court jurisdiction of a case has been established, a youth is required to make an appearance before a judge. As described, most youth are ordered to appear in court as the result of an arrest and a subsequent referral from a law enforcement official. In fact, a full 84 percent of delinquency cases that went through the juvenile court in 2000 came from this type of referral (Snyder and Sickmund, 2006, 104). Some youth, however, are ordered to appear in juvenile court based on a referral from an individual in the community, like a parent or a school staff member. Often, these community referrals involve low-level or status offenses.

Juvenile court hearings are much like those for adults, but there are several important differences. First, juveniles generally appear before a judge rather than a jury. This practice was upheld in the 1971 U.S. Supreme Court case *McKeiver v. Pennsylvania*, when the court ruled that delinquency procedures are not equivalent to adult criminal trials. This decision was somewhat anomalous because it came during the time when courts were expanding due process rights to juveniles based on the idea that delinquency proceedings and criminal trials were similar. Today most states continue to follow the practices specified in *McKeiver*. A 2008 decision in the Kansas Supreme Court (*In re L.M.*), however, required all juvenile courts in the state to provide jury trials upon request. In their decision, the court found that the juvenile system does closely resemble the adult system and that both should have the same legal protections in place. This ruling could have profound consequences for the future of the juvenile court. Today, however, few juveniles in the nation receive jury trials.

A second key difference between the juvenile and adult court involves the way verdicts are worded. In adult court, the judge (or jury) is asked to make a finding of guilt or innocence. By contrast, juvenile court judges must decide whether or not to adjudicate a youth "delinquent." Being declared delinquent is like being found guilty, but it limits the impact of a juvenile record. Employers, for example, are allowed to ask prospective employees whether they have been convicted of a crime but not whether they have ever been declared delinquent. More often than not, the youth whose cases are handled formally through the juvenile court end up being adjudicated delinquent—in 2002, for example, seven out of ten cases resulted in a delinquency adjudication (Snyder and Sickmund, 2006, 172).

Once a youth has been adjudicated delinquent, the judge is able to impose a range of sanctions. By far, the most common sanction is formal probation. In 2005, a full 48 percent of youth who received a sanction in juvenile court were put on probation (Office of Juvenile Justice and Delinquency Prevention, 2008b). Probation varies widely across states and localities but generally involves monitoring, programming, and restrictions. For example, youth on probation are often required to meet regularly with a probation agent. They are also given a set of conditions they must meet. This can include curfews, the completion of programs, payment of restitution, or the avoidance of certain activities (like drug use). Because it is used so frequently, probation is sometimes called the "workhorse of the juvenile justice system" (Office of Juvenile Justice and Delinquency Prevention, 2008b). When a judge decides that probation is not appropriate, he or she has the option of requiring residential placement at a treatment center or a correctional facility. In 2005, about 22 percent of adjudicated delinquents were ordered into residential placement (Puzzanchera and Sickmund, 2008, 58).

Some youth who are sent to residential placement are told how long they will be held there. This type of sentence is called a determinate sentence (for example, a typical determinate sentence might require a youth to spend twelve months in custody). Much more common, however, is an indeterminate sentence, which does not specify an exact release date but instead allows for flexibility based on behavior or other considerations. In these cases, correctional facilities can hold youth until they complete institutional programming or post-release planning, and they can also continue to hold youth who exhibit serious behavioral problems. Some adult courts also use indeterminate sentences, but they are much more common at the juvenile level. This is, in large part, because of the juvenile court's historic emphasis on rehabilitation. Indeterminate sentences allow the court to supervise a youth until they are deemed reformed and no longer worthy of the "delinquent" label.

Indeterminate sentences give a good deal of power to the court and juvenile correctional authorities in establishing release dates. At the same time, this power is limited by state laws setting a maximum age for custody and parole. Most states have a mandated release age that is set higher than their maximum age for eligibility into the system (this is called "extended jurisdiction"). For example, in Ohio, most youth are eligible to go through the juvenile system if they commit a crime prior to their eighteenth birthday. The juvenile prison system, however, is allowed to hold them until their twenty-first birthday, ensuring that a sentence of at least three years can be served before mandatory release. The majority of states (thirty-two plus the District of Columbia) share Ohio's maximum release age. At the low end, seven states set the age limit for extended jurisdiction at the eighteenth birthday, and at the upper end, four states set the age limit at the twenty-fourth birthday (King and Szymanski, 2006).

Until recently, the sentencing of juveniles was a fairly straightforward process. Depending on the state, youth received either a determinate or indeterminate sentence and served their time in a juvenile facility (unless they were transferred to adult court). This picture is considerably more complicated today as judges in twenty-six states have the option of applying a "blended sentence" to certain categories of youth (Cheesman and Waters, 2008). Depending on the state, blended sentences can be imposed by either a juvenile court judge or—when a youth is transferred to adult court—a criminal court judge.

Under the most common type of blended sentencing (an "inclusive blend"), a juvenile is given both an adult and a juvenile sentence, but the adult sentence is suspended if a judge decides that the youth has completed the juvenile sentence successfully. In other words, a youth with a blended sentence serves the juvenile portion of his or her sentence, and at its conclusion, a judge holds a hearing to decide whether the youth is rehabilitated.

Youth who are declared rehabilitated are able to leave juvenile prison without serving any adult time. Those who have behaved badly in prison or who have not provided evidence of rehabilitation are required to serve the adult portion of their sentence. Kentucky, Connecticut, Minnesota, and Ohio are among the states that have this type of sentencing. Another type of blended sentence (called a "contiguous blend") allows juvenile court judges to sentence youth past the state's age of extended jurisdiction. For example, a youth in a state with an extended jurisdictional age of twenty-one could receive a sentence lasting until his or her twenty-fifth birthday. Youth with contiguous sentences are usually housed in a juvenile facility until they reach the maximum age for juvenile court jurisdiction and are then transferred to an adult facility. Texas, Rhode Island, and Colorado are examples of states that employ contiguous sentences. A third type of blended sentence, known as an "exclusive blend," gives a juvenile court judge the option to order an adult sentence or a criminal court judge the option to order a juvenile sentence. New Mexico is the only state to allow juvenile court judges this power, but a number of states, including California, Florida, and Virginia, have exclusive blended sentence options in adult criminal court (Cheesman and Waters, 2008, 3–4).

Blended sentences have become popular because they allow judges to impose strict sentences on youthful offenders while providing for leniency in the event of rehabilitation. Advocates argue that they provide an incentive for youth to behave well and participate in rehabilitative programming while in the juvenile prison. Critics point out, however, that there are ethical problems associated with blended sentences. In some states, youth receive their blended sentence in a juvenile court where, as described, there are fewer legal protections than in an adult court. As a result, some youth are sentenced to adult time without adult legal protections.

The Juvenile Correctional Facility: Organization and Funding

When a youth appears in a juvenile court, it is unlikely that he or she spends much time thinking about the organization and funding of the juvenile justice system. At the same time, these largely invisible arrangements have an important impact on the youth's sentencing, institutional placement, and day-to-day life in prison. States organize their juvenile justice systems in a variety of ways. Some, like Alaska, South Carolina, Kentucky, and New Hampshire, have centralized systems with one state-level agency responsible for all delinquency services. Decentralized states, like Ohio, California, and

Illinois, share the responsibility for delinquency services between state and localities. A popular type of decentralized arrangement gives counties the responsibility for running residential centers for youth with short sentences or those awaiting trial. States take responsibility for housing and rehabilitating more serious or chronic offenders.

Both centralized and decentralized systems face significant funding challenges because of the high cost of incarcerating youth. In fiscal year 2006, for example, Ohio estimated that incarcerating one youth for a year cost $73,584 (Sheridan, 2007, 6). California's and Illinois' estimates for 2006 were similar, at $71,700 and $70,827, respectively (California Department of Rehabilitation and Correction, 2008; Illinois Department of Juvenile Justice, 2007). South Carolina's expenses were somewhat lower at $54,750 per year (University of South Carolina, 2006). In centralized arrangements, the state must pay the entire bill for juvenile corrections. Decentralized systems, by contrast, divide the bill between counties and states. Counties tend to have more constrained budgets and are able to provide fewer services to incarcerated youth. County-level drug treatment, for example, is limited and often has long waiting lists. Because of these budgetary problems, states sometimes provide assistance to counties, generally through grants, to help them provide services.

The division of responsibilities in decentralized states can produce complex—and sometimes problematic—relationships between states and counties. For example, in the past a number of states allowed counties to waive financial responsibility for juveniles committed to state-level institutions. This put pressure on judges in cash-strapped counties to commit youth to the state rather than house them in local facilities. These judges felt additional pressure when their counties were unable to provide the kinds of treatment for substance abuse and mental health problems that the state system could afford. As a result, some counties committed large numbers of youth to the state, resulting in overcrowding. This was exactly the case in Ohio prior to 1995. County-level judges decided which youth to send to the DYS and which to keep in the community. They frequently chose the "free" DYS system, particularly when communities had no services to offer. As a result, DYS facilities were operating at 180 percent of capacity in the early 1990s. Then, in 1995, the state began to charge counties a percentage of the cost of housing each youth they sent to the DYS. The state also agreed to help fund community-based treatment options (Office of Juvenile Justice and Delinquency Prevention, 2008a).

In addition to Ohio, four other states (Pennsylvania, California, Wisconsin, and Illinois) have recently changed the way they structure funding to juvenile corrections. In Pennsylvania, for example, the state now pays 80 percent of the bill when a county provides treatment, and a county pays 40 percent of the expenses incurred if a youth is sent to the state system. This arrangement obviously serves as a strong incentive for counties to provide their own treatment services. Prior to 1996, California charged counties twenty-five dollars a month for each committed youth. Today, they charge a sliding scale based on the severity of the offense, with minor offenses being more costly to counties. This system encourages counties to reserve the state system for the most serious offenders (Tyler, Ziedenberg, and Lotke, 2006, 3). The financial changes made in these states have been effective in reducing juvenile prison populations.

The new funding rules in states like California and Ohio were designed to encourage counties to house youth in local facilities or to provide supervision and services to youth while they live at home. Legislators hoped this would meet two goals: to reduce overcrowding in state-level facilities, and to reduce overall costs. Research shows that these types of community-based options are considerably less expensive than placing youth in state-level institutions (Tyler, Ziedenberg, and Lotke, 2006). The potential savings generated by a shift toward community corrections was appealing to states facing increasingly high budget deficits. Another way states have tried to control the costs of juvenile corrections is through the use of privatization. Private juvenile correctional facilities are run by either a corporation or a nonprofit, and states pay a per diem rate to house youth in their facilities. The prison corporation provides all services and staffing at the facility, but states retain the ability to monitor the operations. Sometimes the private groups construct new facilities, while other times they simply get a contract to run an existing facility. Advocates argue that allowing the state to have a monopoly on correctional facilities has created a disincentive for innovation or cost saving. The introduction of privatization is designed to create competition and force the entire system to be more efficient and less expensive.

Private detention facilities are not a new phenomenon in juvenile corrections; they have been in existence from the beginning of the system. Today, twenty-three states and the District of Columbia contract with private corporations to run parts of their juvenile systems. There are more private than public juvenile facilities, but because private facilities tend to be smaller, they house fewer youth overall (Snyder and Sickmund, 2006). There are two major corporations providing private juvenile prisons: the Corrections Corporation of America (CCA) and the Corrections Services Corporation (CSC). Both of these corporations are publicly traded. This book's focus on state juvenile correctional facilities precludes a lengthy discussion of privatization. Suffice it to say that private prisons are highly controversial and do not appear to offer substantial cost savings, at least at the adult level (Pratt and Maahs, 1999). In addition, a number of private juvenile facilities have closed in recent years in response to allegations of abuse and violence. Two well-publicized examples are the High Plains Juvenile Facility in Colorado, closed in 1998, and the Shelby Training Center in Tennessee, which closed in 2008.

Arrival at a Juvenile Facility: Size and Design

Newly admitted youth and their visitors sometimes find it hard to believe that they are approaching Ohio's maximum-security juvenile facility because it is dwarfed by the Wal-Mart Supercenter and associated mini-mall across the street. It is a low-lying building surrounded by a large barbed wire fence. The front lobby is very plain, and it contains a metal detector and a desk where the security guard sits. This guard is in charge of processing everyone who enters or exits the facility. Once staff, visitors, and newly arrived youth clear security, they enter the administrative portion of the building. Here the superintendent and other high-ranking administrative personnel have offices. Staff sometimes joke that this is where the "carpet people" work, since this is the only section of the facility with a rug. This administrative section ends at a locked door. Behind this door is a short corridor leading to a second locked door. Incoming people must be buzzed through the first door, then wait until the door closes completely behind them. Security personnel then buzz them through the second door and into the main part of the facility. Behind these doors are residential wings, where youth are housed in groups of twenty-five. Most of these wings are general housing, but some can house special populations like high school graduates or youth with mental health issues. The wings each contain common space with games and a television, and private rooms accommodating two people.

The description of Ohio's maximum-security juvenile correctional facility fits many other juvenile detention institutions in the United States. Most are fairly nondescript institutional buildings containing housing, classrooms, offices, a kitchen and cafeteria, and laundry facilities. Some also have vocational areas where youth learn a trade. Another common architectural design is the "cottage model," in which small groups of youth share a building with adult caretakers, allowing them to live in a more family-like setting. This model can be traced back to the Mettray Colony for Boys in France, opened in 1840 (Johnston, 2000). We see this model today in Massachusetts as well as Missouri.

Most juvenile facilities are fairly small, with only seventy facilities in the

United States housing more than two hundred juveniles (Armstrong and MacKenzie, 2003). This stands in contrast to adult facilities, which frequently house upwards of a thousand inmates. It should be noted, however, that there are some very large juvenile institutions. One of these is the Garden State Correctional Facility in New Jersey, which houses about eighteen hundred youth. Of the two institutions studied in this book, one (which I call Oak Hill) is average size, with a population hovering around two hundred. The second (which I call Perry Point) is larger, housing about five hundred young men. Like many states, Ohio sends youth to different facilities based on the type and severity of the offense.

While there is considerable variation in the interior design of juvenile correctional facilities, most juvenile residents live in rooms with one or more roommates or in large communal dormitories. Most juveniles do not sleep in traditional cells, although some facilities do employ heavy doors with small barred windows. The design of most juvenile facilities also allows for the separation of some youth from others. By the mid-1900s, correctional officials were beginning to separate youth on the basis of offense type, gender, and even level of measured intelligence (McGuire and Booth, 1998). They made these divisions in an attempt to maintain control and protect certain classes of youth. Today, we continue to divide males and females, usually in entirely separate institutions. Within institutions, sex offenders are often given their own separate residential areas. This is to protect them from harassment and also to make it easier to provide them with targeted therapeutic programming. Some states also house drug addicts in special wings or cottages. In an attempt to lower the level of violence in their facilities, the California Division of Juvenile Justice has, at various times, segregated members of rival gangs in different wings or different institutions. Most juvenile correctional facilities also employ special management areas for youth who cause trouble or who are considered to be vulnerable. These areas generally have single rooms, few windows, and very severe restrictions.

Research suggests that prison architecture is important because it has an effect on security as well as on inmate mental health. Richard Wener and Richard Olsen (1980) point out that prison design has particularly dramatic effects on inmates because they are confined there for months or years. Outside prison, people move between a number of different environments each day. Because inmates experience only one environment, features of prison design may have magnified effects. I was able to witness the strong effect of a fairly minor architectural change at Oak Hill. During the course of my study, a new school building was constructed across a large courtyard from the residential units. Prior to this, classes were held in the same building as the housing, and during bad weather, youth were sometimes not allowed to go outside for long periods of time. The new school location required students to go outside every day, regardless of the weather. Youth told me over and over again how much less depressed they felt after this change was made.

The Youth in Juvenile Prisons

Virtually all the information we have about the population of youth in custody comes from data gathered by the federal Office of Juvenile Justice Delinquency and Prevention. This agency conducts two large-scale surveys: the Census of Juveniles in Residential Placement and the Juvenile Residential Facility Census. These surveys are conducted on alternate years, and both are one-day counts, taken at all juvenile custodial facilities in the country on the fourth Wednesday of October. All youth under the age of twenty-one who are being held because of contact with the justice system are included in the count. Thus, the number includes both detained and committed youth. Because these are one-day counts, they do not distinguish the number of youth who are in facilities for short periods of time (and thus underestimate the total number of youth in custody over the course of a year). They also exclude youth held in federal custody, in adult facilities, or in substance abuse treatment centers. In general, however, these data are the best available counts of the juvenile incarcerated population.

The data show that the number of youth in custody increased a dramatic 36 percent between 1991 and 1999, and then decreased 13 percent between 1999 and 2003 (Snyder and Sickmund, 2006, 199). This decline can be attributed to a number of factors, but a decreasing rate of violent crime is one important explanation. It should be noted, however, that incarceration rates vary greatly by state. On average, states incarcerate 307 youth for every 100,000 in the population, but individual state incarceration rates range from a low of 72 in Vermont to a high of 625 in the District of Columbia. States also vary in custody trends. Only half of the states experienced the national decline in juvenile incarceration that occurred between 1997 and 2003. Many states, like Texas, Idaho, and South Dakota, actually experienced increases in their custody populations during that period (Snyder and Sickmund, 2006, 201–2).

While there is tremendous diversity among the incarcerated youth in our country, it is possible to make a number of generalizations about them. First, and most obviously, youth in custody are overwhelmingly male. In 2003, males represented 85 percent of the incarcerated juvenile population. This gender disparity was even greater in secure detention facilities, where males constituted a full 90 percent of the population (Snyder and Sickmund, 2006, 206). Females were underrepresented in these secure facilities because they were more likely to commit status offenses and be sent to shelters and group homes.

Data from 2003 indicate that crimes against people were the most frequent reason for the incarceration of youth (34 percent). The most common types of crime within this category were sexual assault, aggravated assault, robbery, and simple assault. About 28 percent of young men in custody were held for property crimes including, in order of prevalence, burglary, theft, and auto theft. Public order offenses and drug crimes resulted in the incarceration of another 10 and 8 percent, respectively. The rest of the youth in custody (20 percent) were there as a result of technical violations of parole or status offenses. The offense profiles of incarcerated females were similar to that of males, although they were 5 percent less likely than males to be incarcerated for crimes against people and 8 percent less likely to be incarcerated for crimes against property. Much of this difference was made up in the status offense category. While most states try to avoid placing status offense cases into custody, about 5 percent of incarcerated males and 12 percent of incarcerated females were imprisoned on status offense charges in 2003. Here again there was tremendous variation by state. For example, less than 1 percent of the youth incarcerated in Florida had been convicted of a status offense compared with a full 22 percent of New York's caseload (Snyder and Sickmund, 2006, 203, 210).

As in the adult prison population, U.S. juvenile correctional facilities house disproportionately large numbers of blacks and Latinos. Based on the racial/ethnic composition of fifteen-to-nineteen-year-olds in the United States, we would expect to see about 15 percent black youth and 16 percent Latino youth in the juvenile prison population (U.S. Census Bureau, 2000). Instead, blacks made up about 38 percent of the 2003 custody population, and Latinos made up about 19 percent. While these numbers are disturbing, they do reflect some good news. Between 1997 and 2003 the incarceration rate dropped more quickly for black youth than for any other racial/ethnic group. In fact, the decrease for blacks (10 percent) was twice that for white youth (Snyder and Sickmund, 2006, 209, 211). This can be explained, at least in part, by a significant decrease in the number of arrests of black youth for violent crimes.

The disproportionate incarceration of minorities has been the subject of a great deal of attention and research. While we do not have a complete explanation for the disparity, group differences in levels and types of delinquency appear to be a factor (Huizinga and Elliot, 1987). At the same time, there is considerable evidence that the overrepresentation of blacks and Latinos in prison is a result of poverty and racism. Minority youth tend to be poorer than white youth and less able to pay for lawyers and alternatives to prison like private treatment centers (Bishop and Frazier, 1996). Police also tend to patrol more frequently and aggressively in poor and minority neighborhoods (Kempf-Leonard, 2007). Finally, researchers have uncovered evidence of discrimination in both law enforcement and court practices (Bishop and Frazier, 1996). Because this discrimination happens at several stages in the juvenile justice process, minority youth tend to accrue disadvantage as they pass through the system (Pope and Feyerherm, 1993; Snyder and Sickmund, 2006).

In the early 1990s, the Office of Juvenile Justice and Delinquency Prevention pushed states to take action on the issue of disproportionate minority confinement. As part of this initiative, states were required to evaluate racial patterns in confinement and propose solutions. States that did not meet this mandate risked losing part of their federal funding. While there were some limited successes, political resistance and the complexity of the issue prevented real change (Leiber, 2002). Today the issue of disproportionate minority confinement continues to be of critical importance. High levels of incarceration of African American and Latino youth have devastating effects on individuals as well as on families and communities.

Release and Parole

In states that use determinate sentencing, getting out of prison is a matter of waiting for a release date to arrive. Youth with indeterminate sentences, however, face a more complicated process. As described, indeterminate sentences specify both a minimum and maximum release date. A more specific release date is not determined until a youth arrives at the state-level intake center, where staff review his or her criminal history and make an assessment of treatment needs. During the course of incarceration, release dates can be changed if a youth causes behavioral problems or fails to complete programming. States with indeterminate sentencing have various arrangements to determine a final release date, but about three-quarters allow the juvenile correctional agency to make the decision while the others leave the decision up to parole boards or judges (Binder, Geis, and Dixon, 2001).

When a release date arrives, youth usually leave the facility with a parent or guardian or they are given a bus ticket to return to their home community. Most newly released young people, unless they have aged out of the system, are placed on parole (called "aftercare" in some states). Parole allows a youth to live in the community while still being under the supervision of the correctional system. A parolee is required to meet with his or her parole agent soon after being released. At that first meeting, the agent goes over the conditions of parole and sets up a regular meeting schedule. Parole conditions are generally determined by an agency separate from the juvenile correctional agency. For example, many states have release authorities or boards of parole. In theory, parole conditions are individually tailored to help a youth stay out of future trouble. In addition to periodic meetings with an agent, typical conditions include curfews, bans on drugs and alcohol, and requirements relating to school or work. Sometimes parole conditions specify where a youth must live. Parolees are also exempt from the normal legal protections against search and seizure and must submit to such searches if a law enforcement official requests one.

Parole is a conditional state—it is set up as a privilege that can be revoked or modified if a youth violates the terms of his or her parole. There are two categories of violations: the commission of a new crime and the violation of a parole restriction (this latter category is called a "technical violation"). There are many potential technical violations, such as coming home after curfew, hanging out with other parolees, or turning in a positive drug test. Parole agents have several options in dealing with such violations. They can choose to ignore them, or they can note them in the file but take no action. They also have the power to strengthen the conditions of the youth's parole—for example, they can add a new required class or tighten curfew restrictions (Travis, 2005). The most serious option agents can pursue is a revocation hearing. At this hearing a board (whose membership varies by state) discusses the youth's case and decides whether the technical violation is serious enough to warrant his or her parole being revoked. When parole is revoked, the youth is returned to custody for some specified length of time (sometimes until the youth reaches a certain age, other times for a set number of days or months).

The parole revocation process at the juvenile level is conducted in such a way that people outside the system know little about it. We do know that many states fail to uphold the same due process safeguards given to adults who face parole revocation. In general, parole officers bear the burden of proving that a youth violated the conditions of his or her parole, but parole hearings do not have the same rigorous standards of evidence and process that exist for adults. There is, for example, variation across states in the rules about youth retaining a lawyer for revocation hearings.

There appears to be change in the air, however, in terms of parole revocation. In 2006, a class-action suit was filed in California arguing that the state should be required to provide the same due process and representation to juveniles facing revocation as is afforded adults. Prior to this suit, youth could be held for months without being told their charges and were not eligible for representation when the hearing was ultimately held. Today in California, under the terms of the settlement, all youth have a right to representation at revocation hearings, the timing for hearings is clear and fairly rapid, and youth are given other due process protections. Given the success of this class-action suit in California, it is likely that other states will choose (or will be forced) to make changes in their revocation policies.

Until policy changes are put into effect, we can expect to see large numbers of youth returning to prison on technical violations. In 2003, 23 percent of the youth detained in institutions and 11 percent of youth committed to institutions were there on a technical violation. Like so many aspects of the juvenile justice system, however, there is variation by state. Connecticut, for example, had the highest percentage (58 percent) of parole violators among detained youth, and Wisconsin the lowest (3 percent) (Snyder and Sickmund, 2006, 204–5). This variation probably has little to do with the actual behavior of youth—instead, it occurs because some states place more youth on parole than others and some states more aggressively investigate and punish parole violations (Travis and Lawrence, 2002).

Confidentiality of Juvenile Records

One of the problems adult prisoners face as they return to society is that potential employers and others have access to their criminal records. This can complicate their efforts to get a job or join the military. Historically, this was not an issue for juveniles. Juvenile records were sealed, and youthful offenders, except those who were convicted as adults, did not have to report having a record or having been incarcerated. This policy was originally developed with the belief that juveniles could be rehabilitated and should be sent back into society with a clean slate. As a result, all but one state provided for the sealing or expungement of juvenile records once a youth had shown that he or she was rehabilitated (Teasley and Doyle, 2003). States generally did not fingerprint juveniles, and no lasting records were kept.

The laws regarding juvenile records are markedly different today. Expungement now frequently requires that a petition be filed with the court, and even if the petition is successful, it can be limited by provisions that keep the record open for law enforcement or reopen sealed files if a youth commits another crime (Teasley and Doyle, 2003). Notably, fifteen states have done away with or severely limited their expungement statutes for juveniles. As juvenile records come to be more widely used, states have needed to create repositories for them. Depending on the state, these records can be accessed by an increasingly long list of parties including prosecutors, police, victims, potential employers, and schools (Teasley and Doyle, 2003). In Texas, for example, employers and educational institutions can access juvenile records until a youth is twenty-one. If the youth commits no new crimes between ages seventeen and twenty-one, the record then becomes off-limits other than for criminal justice purposes. Another example of changing policy occurred in Virginia, where DNA samples are collected from all convicted felons over the age of fourteen. There are similar changes in policies regarding juvenile confidentiality at the federal level. In 1993, the FBI began accepting state-submitted juvenile fingerprints. States choose to participate and can send fingerprints from individuals who have been arrested, convicted, or both. They can also choose which offense types to include. Once a juvenile has fingerprints sent to the FBI, the record is treated as if it came from an adult (Bishop, 1997).

Further compromising juvenile confidentiality, a 2001 study of employers in Los Angeles indicated that about half of potential employers bypassed governmental background checks and relied on those provided by private firms (Holzer, Raphael, and Stoll, 2007, 135). These private firms, of which there are now hundreds, are not subject to the same kind of regulations as governmental agencies (Bushway et al., 2007). Therefore, they may be able to obtain and include juvenile records. In fact, some private firms already claim to include them. This is of concern because it lessens the confidentiality of juvenile records and because the record accuracy of private companies is generally lower than that of the government (Bushway et al., 2007).

Conclusion

This chapter provided a broad overview of the juvenile justice system and the process that youth pass through from the time of their arrest to parole. In the next chapter, I narrow my focus to describe the study on which the rest of the book is based. I also introduce the forty young men who shared their thoughts, experiences, and stories with me. We already met one of these young men at the beginning of this chapter—Charles, the Cleveland youth arrested for assault in the summer of 2002. Although originally sentenced to twelve months, Charles was actually held in a correctional facility for well over two years in order to provide him with the substance abuse treatment the DYS felt he needed. Charles hated incarceration but told me excitedly about his new sobriety and his progress toward a high school diploma. Because he had dropped out of school in the ninth grade, he had given up hope of ever getting a diploma, but incarceration gave him an opportunity to return to school. He told me that after his release, he hoped to find a job and live with his grandmother and girlfriend. He was quite clear that his plans did not include any future criminal activity. Two years after he was released, however, Charles received a three-year sentence in adult prison for another assault charge. In the pages that follow, we delve into the world of the juvenile correctional system to understand youth's experiences of incarceration, parole, and—as in Charles's case—recidivism.

Chapter 2

Incarcerated Youth and Their Worlds

PROFILE: NICK

I liked Nick from the minute he walked into the room, although it was obvious he didn't trust me. He had a quick smile and an even quicker wit. Prior to his incarceration at the Department of Youth Services (DYS), he was living with his grandmother, whom he clearly adored. His father was in prison. His mother, deep into drug use, had disappeared years before. Nick was sporadically attending life skills classes, attempting to get a diploma. He spent most of his time, however, dealing drugs in the very poor urban neighborhood in which he lived. Later, when I visited him at home, it became clear that he was not a low-level dealer but rather operated a small neighborhood network. He lived rent free with his grandmother but helped her with money when she needed it.

PROFILE: TIM

On my third day of interviewing, I asked to see Tim, the next name on my list. The DYS staff liaison hesitated at my request, saying that Tim had serious mental issues and might be difficult to work with. I assured her that I wanted to meet with the full range of youth entering the DYS system. Although her hesitation concerned me, the interview went well. Tim was enthusiastic and appeared pleased to be there. He seemed considerably younger than his eighteen years. When I explained the project to him, he was eager to participate. As the interview progressed, however, it became clear that he had no boundaries or sense of social conventions, and I could see that he had serious mental and developmental disabilities. His early life had been traumatic. His father was arrested after attempting to shoot seven-year-old Tim and his mother, and was subsequently incarcerated with a life sentence. Tim's mother disappeared soon after the shooting, and Tim became a ward of the state. He was bounced from foster home to jail to group home. There were numerous violent outbursts, the most recent of which was an assault on a group-home staff member. As a result of this assault, he was sentenced to six months at the DYS.

Nick and Tim were two of forty young men I came to know during the course of a longitudinal study on juvenile incarceration and parole. My research sample was drawn from first-time offenders arriving at juvenile correctional facilities in Ohio. These facilities were run by the Department of Youth Services (DYS), the state-level agency responsible for supervising youth convicted of serious or repeat offenses. In 2002, when the research began, the agency housed about two thousand youth in eleven institutions. I selected the sample of youth from two of these facilities: Oak Hill, a maximum-security prison housing about two hundred young men, and Perry Point, a medium-security prison with about five hundred male residents. My sample's distribution reflects the different sizes of the two institutions: twenty-seven of the youth were housed at the larger Perry Point facility, and thirteen were at Oak Hill. These institutions were ideal for this study because they were not intended for youth who had committed any particular type of crime (for example, sex offenses) and they drew young men from across the state. Both institutions housed the full range of ages found in the DYS—from twelve to twenty-one years.

To enable me to contact youth for the study, the DYS provided lists of all first-time admissions assigned to either Oak Hill or Perry Point. I received a new list every two weeks for three months. I chose to limit the sample to first-time admissions because I was interested in following youth from their first impressions of the system through their release. There may be differences, however, between my sample, who were new to the system, and youth who were reentering it. For this reason, care should be taken in generalizing my findings to the whole DYS population. Throughout the text, I try to point out areas—like adjustment to institutional life—where differences are likely to exist between first-time and repeat admissions. Nonetheless, I believe that most elements of institutional life, as well as reentry to the outside world, are common to all youth who serve time in the DYS.

A challenge I encountered during the initial stages of sampling was the state requirement that researchers obtain parental permission before asking any incarcerated youth under the age of eighteen to participate in a study. Therefore, I had to send out letters and consent forms to parents and guardians. Not surprisingly, this task proved to be difficult. In many cases, parents had moved by the time the letters arrived, or they received their letters and chose not to respond. When I failed to receive a response I attempted to call those parents for whom the DYS had a telephone number, but the numbers were frequently incorrect. Ultimately, I received permission from 20 percent of the parents I tried to contact. This low response rate raises concerns about sample bias. Although I do not have conclusive evidence, I suspect that those parents who were the least educated and poorest may have been more suspicious and unwilling to allow their sons to participate.

Fortunately, 100 percent of the youth whose parents signed forms agreed to participate. In addition to these youth, the final sample included youth who were eighteen years old when I received their names. These young men (who composed 50 percent of the final sample) were serving time in the juvenile system because they had committed crimes as seventeen-year-olds. Several weeks or even months can elapse between the commission of a crime and a youth's arrival at a correctional facility; thus a substantial number of seventeen-year-olds had turned eighteen by the time their names appeared on my sampling list. It proved to be much easier to interview these youth because I was not required to contact their parents. As with the younger age group, all of the youth I spoke with agreed to participate in the study. Therefore, despite the possible bias among the younger participants, I am confident that the eighteen-year-olds in the study reflect the full diversity of first-time admissions to the DYS.

Meeting the Youth

My first interviews took place at the Perry Point facility. A social worker, who seemed to have more important things to do, was put in charge of me. She located each young man, escorted him to me, and then went back to her office. I quickly grew used to the youth standing awkwardly with their hands "checked" (held clasped behind their backs, as they are required to do) until I came over, shook their hands, and invited them to sit down. We met in the relative privacy of an open-doored classroom. Interviews at Oak Hill were similar but took place in a conference room in the administrative wing of the building.

During this first interview, it was important to establish quickly who I was and why I was there because, as several young men told me later, I look like I could be a DYS social worker or psychologist. The youth are assessed and interviewed frequently in correctional facilities, and I did not want to appear to be yet another person trying to figure out what was "wrong" with them. To that end, I quickly told them to call me by my first name (a practice forbidden in the DYS, where titles and last names are used), and I stressed my affiliation with The College of Wooster. The College served as a great opening topic because many of the youth had college aspirations and were excited to meet a "real professor." Additionally, as I discuss in later chapters, location is an important status and group marker in prison, and Wooster's rural location provoked funny conversations as some youth tried to figure out where it was and whether it was near anything "real" (like a city).

I spent a good deal of time telling each young man about the study and making sure that they understood the longitudinal nature of the project and the fact that they would receive no benefit from participation (except lunch if I interviewed them outside of the facility in later interview rounds). I explained that if they did not want to participate, I would simply tell the prison staff that I had discovered that they did not fit the eligibility criteria for the study. Because none of the staff in the facilities knew what the eligibility criteria of the study were—and none ever asked or seemed to care—I planned to say something vague about the youth's age or his parole region if the situation ever arose. Fortunately, this never became necessary. Finally, I told the youth I would never give the tapes or transcriptions to the DYS, but that I might write a book using some of their words and stories. I expected that this might make some of the youth nervous, but as it turned out, their major complaint was about my policy of using pseudonyms for the individuals in the study ("Wait, I want my real name in the book!").

I had several goals in the first interview. First, and most important, I wanted to establish a relationship and gain the youth's trust. Second, I wanted to collect some basic information about their lives prior to incarceration. As part of this, I asked about relationships on the outside with family and friends. Third, I wanted to learn about their initial experiences in the DYS and their expectations for the future. While there was clearly some mistrust, it seemed that most of the youth enjoyed having somebody listen to them. The fact that I told them that I didn't care what type of language they used (which they understood to mean that they could go ahead and curse) seemed to please them and further differentiated me from others at the DYS. Also, in an effort to bolster my claim that this study was not about what was "wrong" with them, I did not ask them about their crimes. I used a semi-structured interview schedule, altering the order of the questions as the interview progressed. This resulted in a somewhat conversational tone and an ability to follow trains of thought.

It would be naive to think that who I am had no effect on the interviews. The effect, however, is difficult to measure. For example, the fact that I am female probably influenced the youth's responses to at least some of the questions. Research on this topic is somewhat contradictory but generally suggests that the strongest effect of an interviewer's gender occurs in questions about sex or gender issues (Macaulay and Kane, 1993). Although the construction of masculinity was certainly an important part of this project, I do not think that the youth were aware that it was a focus. I am hopeful that this allowed them to speak freely on the topic. Somewhat surprisingly, my occupation seemed to be an advantage in interviewing since it gave me some credibility and, as described, the youth saw me as a way to learn about college (in fact, over the course of the study, I provided application materials for three of the young men). My race (white) probably played out in more complex ways. Research suggests that people are more willing to talk about racial issues with someone of their own race (Schuman and Kalton, 1985), so it is possible that I got more accurate answers about this topic from whites. Fortunately, the blacks in the sample seemed very comfortable talking about racial topics, and I think that any bias was minimal. My background in corrections (having worked as a researcher at the California Youth Authority and having conducted a research project on incarcerated fatherhood) was another advantage because it gave me a familiarity with the population, the language, and some of the issues youth in prison face.

Meetings Two and Three

PROFILE: ETHAN

Ethan was one of the most troubled youth in the study. He was from a large city in southern Ohio and, prior to his arrest, had been working in a restaurant and living with his girlfriend and baby daughter. Ethan had spent a lot of time at his county-level detention home for various run-ins with the law—he estimated that he had been there thirty times. Although Ethan was never angry at me, his rage fills every page of his interview transcript. I tried to contact him after his release from prison but could not reach him. Finally, I went to his house and knocked on the door. He lived in a very poor, run-down section of town, and although no one answered, I sensed someone was home. By the third interview, Ethan was in adult prison serving six years for robbery. I asked him why I could not reach him while he was out, and he confessed that his girlfriend had torn up my letter in a jealous rage because she did not believe I was a researcher.

The second round of interviews took place nine months after the first. Because the youth in this study were first-time admissions to the DYS, their sentences were relatively short, and the majority (twenty-nine of the forty) had been released to parole by the time of the second interview. The eleven interviews that took place with still-incarcerated youth focused on their prison experience and contact with family and friends outside. Interviews with these young men took place under much the same circumstances as the first round except that three had been moved to a DYS therapeutic community facility and drug treatment center in Central Ohio. Interviews there took place in a private corner of the library. One youth, Chad, was back at the DYS intake center after being released and having his parole revoked. He was not entirely sure why this had happened, but he thought that someone might have told his parole officer he was doing drugs. Three other youth were not technically incarcerated but were housed in supervised living arrangements with strict rules governing their comings and goings. These three group homes were privately owned but contracted with the DYS to house newly released youth who needed further treatment or who had no other place to go.

The meetings with the paroled youth took place in a variety of locations in their communities but generally occurred in a restaurant of their choice. Youth took time to decide on a restaurant—they seemed to want to choose a place that was not too expensive and where we would both feel comfortable. Darius had me drive miles out of his predominantly black neighborhood to go to a Perkins in a white neighborhood. When I asked him why, he said that he thought I would feel more comfortable there. I suspect that he also did not want his neighborhood friends to see him with me, although he did not say this. One of the more memorable interviews was with Casey. He insisted that we eat standing up outside a Taco Bell because it was his favorite restaurant and he wanted to smoke while he ate. Fortunately, the other youth's choices were more conducive to thoughtful (and easily recordable) conversation. It was clear that the paroled youth were surprised to hear from me and pleased to be taken out to lunch. I also found it useful to see the youth in their homes and neighborhoods, and it gave me an opportunity to meet (and often interview) their families. During these interviews I focused my questions on reentry experiences and parole, although I also asked the young men about their final few months in prison.

The second round of interviews was far richer, longer, and more relaxed than the first. Youth even felt comfortable enough to challenge my language when it did not fit their experiences. For example, it quickly became clear that they found the terms "correctional facility" and "institution" unwieldy and inaccurate, preferring to say that they were "in prison" or "locked up." Instead of talking about "life outside prison," they would refer to being "on the outs." Out of respect for their experiences, I also use this terminology throughout the rest of the text. During this round, I ultimately reinterviewed thirty-five of the youth (88 percent). Ethan was one of the missing five. The others included Jamal, who was AWOL from parole, and Tony, who scheduled two appointments with me but failed to keep them. Matthew had been an enthusiastic participant when he was locked up, but once he was released, his mother refused to let him participate. In a fairly angry phone conversation, she told me that she hated the DYS, she associated me with them, and she would not allow her son to have anything to do with me.

Joseph, the fifth missing youth, simply refused to participate. This saddened me but was not surprising. He had been quiet and somewhat hostile when I interviewed him in the institution. I remember being concerned that he was not participating voluntarily and had reminded him several times that his participation was not mandatory and would not benefit him. At the time, he had insisted that he wanted to go forward. Joseph's story is a reminder of the difficult ethical terrain involved in prison interviewing. In a situation where inmates have virtually no power, they will jump at opportunities that they believe might benefit them. I think that Joseph wanted to get out so desperately that he would do whatever staff asked, even talk with me. While researchers can do everything in their power to ensure that inmate respondents are there voluntarily, I am not clear that true consent can be obtained in cases like Joseph's.

The final round of interviews was similar to the second. I continued to ask each youth about his life, family, friends, and future plans. I was able to interview thirty-four of the original forty. As mentioned, Ethan reappeared for the third interview, but another youth, David, had disappeared. At the second interview, David had been in legal trouble and was living with his mother and her new boyfriend in a large housing complex. He was particularly enthusiastic about this project and gave me six contact phone numbers. When I called these numbers nine months later, all had been disconnected. I went back to his housing complex, but the neighbors said the family had left and they did not know where they had gone. Anthony, the final missing youth, refused a third round interview. He had just been released to parole, and I met him at the parole office on a day he was supposed to take a class. As I arrived, I heard him arguing with his agent about the number of parole requirements he had. By the time I was able to talk with him, he was completely fed up and told me he wanted to quit the project and anything else remotely related to the DYS.

Although longitudinal researchers hope to be able to report a 100 percent retention rate in their studies, it rarely happens. In this study, I felt lucky to have an 85 percent retention rate over almost three years. The parolee population is particularly transient because of their youth, their poverty, and the instability of their family arrangements. Staff at the DYS told me that they had been betting on less than 50 percent by the second round. While I am pleased that the rate was considerably higher, it is likely that the missing youth were different from those who remained in the sample. In particular, it was clear that the youth who were most angry at the DYS were more likely to drop out. Even though I was not directly affiliated with the DYS, I was a reminder of the agency and the youth's prison experiences.

Family Interviews

Although my main focus in this project was on the experiences of the youth, I also conducted interviews with fifteen of their family members. Twelve of these family members were mothers, two were grandmothers, and one was a father. These informal meetings usually occurred when I went to a young man's home to pick him up for an interview. If any family members were home, I asked the youth if he minded my speaking with them. In a few cases, I conducted phone interviews with family members when I called to talk to a youth. The sample was not as complete or systematic as the youth sample, but I do think that the group was both random and diverse. I use these interviews in this chapter and in Chapter 5 to talk about the families' perceptions of the incarceration of their sons and grandsons. The family interviews were also useful as a way to check some of the youth's accounts. As it turned out, the parental accounts generally matched those of the youth, although it did appear that youth may have exaggerated their accomplishments somewhat. For example, Nick told me that he provided significant help to his grandmother so she could pay the rent. His grandmother, by contrast, reported that Nick would give her twenty to forty dollars every month or so.

Inside Outside Exchange Program

In addition to the forty youth in this study, I am indebted to three other groups of incarcerated young men who helped me to think through the material for this book. In 2004 I trained to be an instructor with Inside Outside, a unique program housed at Temple University. College instructors organize classes inside prison with half incarcerated students (the "inside" students) and half students from their home institutions (the "outside" students). Between 2006 and 2008 I taught one criminology course per year at a DYS facility. The point of Inside Outside is to provide a unique educational experience for both inside and outside students, not to provide a research opportunity for instructors. Consequently, I occasionally use anecdotes from the classes to illustrate a point, but I do not use the classes as a source of data. Over the three years, however, I ran my ideas for the book by the three classes and talked to them about what I was working on. Spending four hours a week in the prison also allowed me to watch interactions and daily life and to refine my own thinking about the culture of the prison.

Description of the Youth

In describing the young men in this study—or any prison population—it would be easy to reduce their lives to tales of woe. As the author of a fact-finding report about the DYS comments, the juvenile prison draws from a "damaged population" (Cohen, 2008, 1). The lives of incarcerated young men are filled with troubles introduced by poverty, family illness and separation, and educational deficiency. At the same time, the youth refuse to be defined by these challenges. They come across as human beings bursting with life and with all sorts of interests, plans, and relationships. I liked many of the young men in the study and, over time, developed close relationships with them. More than a few of them reminded me of the students I teach at my college. Some of the young men, however, were so deeply troubled that it was difficult to connect with them at all. Two (including Tim) had serious mental health problems, and several more were so angry at the world that it was hard to spend time with them.

As a group, the youth I interviewed were an average of seventeen years old at the beginning of the study. Sam, at fourteen, was the youngest, and Matthew, at nineteen, was the oldest. The sample's average age was slightly higher than that of the population at the DYS (sixteen years), and it was clearly higher than the average of first-time admissions to the system (Ohio Department of Youth Services, 2009). This disparity is, in large part, a result of the difficulties I encountered in obtaining permission to interview youth under the age of eighteen. It is also worth noting that youth incarcerated in juvenile facilities in Ohio are younger, on average, than comparable youth in some other states. This is because of differing definitions of the age of minority and majority. For example, California detains some youth in its correctional facilities until they are twenty-five. Thus the average age of their juvenile prison population is higher than the states (like Ohio) whose age of majority is twenty-one.

In terms of race and ethnicity, Ohio is like other states in its confinement of a disproportionate number of minority youth. The U.S. Census reports that in 2002, about 13 percent of Ohio's twelve-to-eighteen-year-olds were black and 82 percent were white. Ohio's juvenile facilities, however, housed about 50 percent blacks and 47 percent whites (Ohio Department of Youth

Services, 2009). The racial composition of Ohio and its prisons makes it different from states like California and Texas, where Latinos constitute a large segment of the population. In this study, only Freddie identified himself as Latino, while sixteen youth self-identified as black (40 percent) and twenty-three (58 percent) as white. At first, I was concerned that the overrepresentation of whites in my study was an indication of sample bias, but further examination revealed two other likely reasons for the disparity. As described, I interviewed every eighteen-year-old admitted to the DYS for the first time during the study period. I also interviewed any younger males for whom I had parental permission. The race disparity occurred at the eighteen-year-old level (only nine of the twenty-four eighteen-year-olds were black), rather than at the younger ages. It is possible that the DYS happened to admit fewer eighteen-year-old black males than usual during the study period. It is also possible that eighteen-year-old first-time admissions are, in general, more likely to be white than those youth admitted for the first time at younger ages. Because the DYS does not provide analyses of first-time admissions separately from the general population, it is not possible to identify which of these explanations is correct. Importantly, however, neither explanation suggests that the overrepresentation of eighteen-year-old whites was a result of bias in the sample.

The majority of the youth in the study—as in the prison population more generally—were from lower-middle class or poor backgrounds. It is difficult to get accurate information from teenagers about their household income, so I asked the youth in this study about parental employment and receipt of public assistance. With five exceptions, every young man (not including the three who lived on their own) reported at least one employed adult in their home. The exceptions were two single mothers on welfare, two families in which both parents were disabled and receiving social security, and one retired grandmother whose primary means of support was her social security check. The most frequent kinds of jobs the youth reported for their parents were, for mothers, day-care workers and, for fathers, laborers (e.g., tree cutters or auto detailers). Other jobs included nursing-home workers and clerks. The jobs held by the parents were not high paying. In fact, workers in almost every job category held by the parents earned below the national average wage ($35,560 in 2002). For example, the national average wage for a full-time day-care job was $15,650 per year, and nursing-home workers made an average of $19,790. People working in auto detailing made $34,820, and tree trimmers made $25,860 (Department of Labor, 2002).

Because I did not ask the youth directly about the crimes they had committed, I do not have this information for everyone in the study. I do, however, have information from the twenty-two youth who volunteered it. The four most common crimes among this group were assault (six youth), burglary (five), drug trafficking (three), and robbery (three). As another measure of criminality, I asked all of the youth whether they had been arrested and held prior to their commitment to the DYS. Thirty-one (78 percent) reported that they had been arrested and detained in their county-level detention facility prior to their most recent arrest. In terms of their current incarceration, the average minimum sentence length was eight and a half months, with almost all having a minimum sentence of either six or twelve months. The length of these sentences is fairly typical for first-time admissions to the DYS, but it is shorter than the length of sentences given to youth who return to the DYS for a second or third time.

Education and Employment

PROFILE: JOSHUA

Joshua was sentenced to the DYS for a year for aggravated robbery. Prior to his incarceration, he was living with his father, stepmother, stepbrother, and stepsister and planning to start work at JC Penney. Joshua officially dropped out of school at sixteen, but he unofficially left much earlier. Although he enrolled in high school at age fourteen, he never actually showed up for a class. As he tells it, he was too busy smoking marijuana to attend school. He entered DYS hoping he would be able to kick his drug habit and complete a GED.

Many incarcerated youth, like Joshua, begin having trouble in school long before they become involved with the juvenile justice system. The link between academic problems and prison is so strong that some scholars refer to it as the "school-to-prison pipeline" or the "prison track" (Wald and Losen, 2003). One group of researchers (Balfanz et al., 2003) uncovered evidence of this prison track in a study of four hundred ninth graders in a mid-Atlantic city. They found that the youth who ended up in prison typically "attended school only 58 percent of the time in eighth grade, failed at least a quarter of their classes, and on average, read at a sixth-grade reading level by the end of eighth grade" (76).

Joshua's story indicates that some incarcerated youth start having academic trouble because of poor choices or drug addiction. At the same time, research suggests that there are a number of other important factors related to school failure. In an ethnographic study of two high schools and a prison,

Ronnie Casella (2003) found that black and Latino high school students were routinely labeled as dangerous and put in out-of-school placements, even when their offenses were fairly minor. Ann Ferguson (2001) also found that the staff in a California junior high school negatively labeled black male students, hindering their ability to succeed academically. Additionally, many incarcerated youth come from troubled schools in impoverished districts. Students in these schools often fall behind grade level because the education they receive is simply not adequate. Such schools also have high drop-out rates.

Research indicates that, on average, incarcerated youth function three years below grade level (Rider-Hankins, 1992, 2). We have less reliable information about the percentage of those who have dropped out of school. Some youth bounce in and out, so their school status at any particular moment may not be correct a month or a year later. Freddie, for example, dropped out of school but later prepared for and received his GED. Other youth drop out, seemingly permanently, but later find a program that interests them and return. Incarcerated youth are particularly difficult to track because so many have a history of stays in detention centers and treatment facilities, all of which confuse the calculation of their educational level. Some are kicked out of one school and experience a delay while they try to enroll in another. It should also be noted that enrollment in school is not the same as actually attending school. As Joshua's case illustrates, some youth have not officially dropped out but do not attend enough to be considered enrolled.

Although there are difficulties with calculating drop-out rates, I did ask the youth in the study to tell me whether they were enrolled in school at the time of their arrest. Three young men had completed degrees or GEDs and did not plan to continue their education. Sixteen of the forty (40 percent) reported that they had dropped out (or were kicked out) of school and did not have any intention of returning. This figure is almost four times higher than the drop-out rate of 10.9 percent in the general population. It is also considerably higher than the percentage of poor youth who drop out nationally (Snyder and Sickmund, 2006, 15). The remaining twenty-one young men in this study were enrolled in school, although two commented that they attended so rarely that they belonged in the dropout category.

Among the youth in this study who were in school, most did not hold jobs. Two, however, reported that they combined part-time work with school. Several others who were enrolled in school indicated that, while they did not hold conventional jobs, they made some money by drug dealing. Of the nineteen youth who were not enrolled in school, only eight were working full-time prior to their arrest and one was working part-time. While the youth held various types of jobs, almost all were low skill and paid minimum wage. These jobs included grass cutting, telemarketing, paint mixing, and working the grill at fast food restaurants. The ten youth (25 percent of the sample) who were neither working nor in school reported that they spent their days hanging out or dealing drugs.

Family Relationships

PROFILE: MARCUS

Marcus came to the DYS from a poor neighborhood in one of Ohio's larger cities. At the time of his arrest, he was bouncing between his mother's and father's homes. His father, disabled by diabetes, did not work, and his mother was just starting a new job. Because Marcus's father was married to another woman when he was conceived, his parents never lived together. His father continued to live with his wife and their eight children, and his mother lived alone. Marcus had a good relationship with both of them but was extremely worried about his father's health.

Marcus's family situation was complicated and, at times, quite painful for him. His mother struggled to stay out of poverty and received little financial help from Marcus's father. Marcus clearly felt bitter over this situation but remained close to his father. Like Marcus, many of the youth in this study came from families dealing with divorce, sickness, and separation. Only 25 percent lived in a two-parent family prior to their arrest (seven of these families contained two biological parents, and the other three were parent-stepparent homes). Among the general population, 64 percent of fifteen-to-seventeen-year-olds live in two-parent families (U.S. Census Bureau, 2004). Thus, it is clear that prisons draw disproportionately from single-parent families. In fact, a full 63 percent (twenty-five) of the youth in this study spent the majority of their childhoods in single-mother homes. Research suggests that this living arrangement increases the risk of incarceration because of its association with poverty, low-parental education, and racial inequalities. The absence of a father also appears to be directly linked to a youth's risk of incarceration (Harper and McClanahan, 2004).

Kenneth and Tim came to the DYS from the foster care system. Kenneth lived with his father after his parents divorced and his mother relinquished custody ("she didn't want me" is how Kenneth explains it). When Kenneth was fifteen, his father was accused of abuse and Child Protective Services placed Kenneth in foster care. Kenneth continued to have irregular contact with both his biological mother and father. Tim, as described earlier, was sent to live with a foster family at age seven when his biological father went to prison and his mother disappeared. He went through several placements until, at age sixteen, his foster family asked that he be removed from their home. They told his social worker that they feared his violent tendencies. Because of his age and his history of anger and mental instability, he was placed in a group home. At the time of the first interview, he was no longer in regular touch with any of his foster families.

In the United States, foster children like Tim and Kenneth represent less than 1 percent of all children (Kreider, 2007), but research suggests that they are dramatically overrepresented in prisons (Kerman, Wildfire, and Barth, 2002). Especially vulnerable to incarceration are foster children who are placed in care between the ages of twelve and fifteen and those who live with more than one family (Jonson-Reid and Barth, 2000). It appears that foster children are at an increased risk for incarceration because of the unique stresses they experience in the foster care system (Alltucker et al., 2006). Pre-existing problems, like neglect and abuse in their families of origin, are also important explanations for high rates of criminality and incarceration (DePanfilis and Zuravin, 2002).

Tim and Kenneth were unique in this study because their histories of abuse and foster care meant that they arrived at prison with few family connections. The rest of the youth had at least one (and usually many more) family members actively involved in their lives. Even though their families had gone through challenging times, most of the youth felt very attached to them and expected to remain in close contact during their incarceration. Many told me that they were hopeful that incarceration might even improve their relationships. David said,

> Coming here I'm locked up and away from my family. Right now I know what I had. I mean, we will always be really close compared to the other families. We've been really close and stuff, but my relationship now when I get out will be even closer. I mean, because now, I will always have my mom around and my sister, but now being away so long I miss 'em. I don't know. I know it could be better than it was.

Dion also thought that being in prison might make him closer to his father:

> Now I can like really sit down and really have a conversation face to face with my dad where I just talk about my problems and ask him to forgive

me for what I did to him in the past. Hurting them and stuff. It [the relationship] is going to change a whole lot.

David and Dion were like many other youth in the study who expressed hopefulness about their incarceration. These young men thought that incarceration had the potential to help them improve family relationships, reduce drug addiction, and finish their educations. Interestingly, many of their families expressed similar feelings of hope. Hope is not a feeling we normally associate with prison, but many families with juvenile offenders have exhausted the options for helping their children outside prison. These parents have dealt with years of drug use, violence, and arrests. Many are at their wit's end and desperately want to believe that the prison system might finally be the wake-up call their children need to turn their lives around. In *Doing Time Together*, Megan Comfort (2008) discusses a similar desperation among the wives and girlfriends of adult prisoners. Like parents, these women have weathered the consequences of risky behaviors and hope that prison can help their partners.

One of the reasons parents are hopeful about prison is that it holds out the promise of treatment services. There are few community resources for poor people with drug addiction or mental disorders, and prison is sometimes the only place that offers affordable services. Drug rehabilitation programs outside prison, for example, have long waiting lists and are not always covered by insurance. In my study, Dan and his mother were in exactly this situation. Dan was addicted to drugs, but their insurance would not cover treatment services. Dan's mother was forced to go into debt to pay for a program that she hoped would help him. Dan came back and remained sober for several days. He then resumed his life of crime and drugs, plunging his mother into despair. She finally reported Dan's behavior to his probation officer, hoping that state prison could help him. She told me,

When this first went on with Dan, he was getting into a lot of trouble, and he had been living with his father for eighteen months and he came back home in September. By December I knew things were getting really, really bad. So I had made arrangements and I sent him to a ranch out in Utah. It was this sixty-day program. Dan ended up staying ninety days. He came home and within two days broke into the house of a kid that used to be his friend. That's how he got into all this trouble. . . . So anyhow, he was put on probation and stuff. Well, you know, if he was supposed to be home at a certain time or he didn't do what he was supposed to, I was on the phone calling his probation officer. You know,

"This is [Dan's mother]. It's eleven o'clock at night. I just wanted to let you know that Dan is not home yet."

Like Dan's mother, Alex's mother was frantic as her son descended into drug addiction and became violent at home. There were no reasonably priced community rehabilitation programs available so she finally called the police, knowing that it would result in Alex's incarceration. She told me that she was sad he was in prison but that she also felt hopeful he would finally receive the drug rehabilitation he needed. Charles's mother was also desperate to find help for her son. Unlike Alex's mother, she was not terribly hopeful about prison programs, but she thought that being away from his family and friends might jolt her son into change. She said,

I kinda want to stay away from Charles for a little while and give him time to think about what he has done. Because I don't want him thinking this is a game. I want him to learn from all this. You know? Maybe if he would miss the family a little bit more, maybe, just maybe, he'll come out and do a little better than he has been doing. That's why I haven't went up there yet.

While hope was a frequent theme in the family interviews, it would be misleading to suggest that it was the only emotion parents experienced at the incarceration of their sons. Themes of sadness and grief also appeared frequently in the parental interviews. Frank's mother, for example, was devastated when he was arrested and convicted. She said, "I made it to work every day but I didn't answer the phone. I didn't answer the door. . . . It was bad. It was really bad. And then I started going to the counselor that me and Frank had been seeing." Other parents talked about crying for days or falling into a depression. These responses made it clear that the incarceration of a child is both a devastating and a hopeful experience for parents.

Children

PROFILE: GABE

Before Gabe came to the DYS, he lived with his mother, father, and two younger brothers in a rural area of the state. He attended a career center with plans to become a carpenter, and he worked part-time in his uncle's tree-cutting business. Both of his parents were employed, his mother as a nurse, his father as a laborer. Gabe came to the DYS on grand theft charges, his first crime. He was sentenced to twelve months. Soon after his arrival at the DYS, Gabe's seventeen-year-old girlfriend gave birth to their daughter. At the time of my first interview with him, he had not yet met her. Gabe told me he plans to go back to work for his uncle and live with his girlfriend and their child after he is released.

PROFILE: JOSEPH

Joseph is from a big city in southern Ohio. Prior to being locked up, he lived with his girlfriend. Joseph has a baby by a previous girlfriend, and his current girlfriend is pregnant. In the tenth grade, Joseph dropped out of school to support his daughter. He had little family to help him since his father had disappeared years before and his mother suffered from alcoholism. Joseph himself was raised by an elderly grandmother. He is hoping he will be released from prison in time to attend the birth of his child.

Most people do not associate juvenile prison and fatherhood, but research suggests that the two are closely linked. In studies of state prisons in Ohio and California, about 25 percent of juvenile inmates reported that they were fathers (Abeyratne, Sowards, and Brewer, 1995; California Youth Authority, 1995). This study mirrors the others, with six of the forty youth (15 percent) reporting that they were already fathers and an additional four youth (10 percent) reporting a pregnant girlfriend. In the general population, only 5 percent of youth father a child before their twentieth birthday (Darroch, Landry, and Oslak, 1999).

There are several reasons that fathers are overrepresented in juvenile prison. First, it appears that young fathers are more likely than their non-father counterparts to engage in delinquent behaviors and to go on to prison (Christmon and Lucky, 1994; Elster, Lamb, and Tavare, 1987; Lerman and Ooms, 1993; Thornberry et al., 2000). For example, one study found that fathers are more than twice as likely as nonfathers to engage in delinquent behaviors (Stouthamer-Loeber and Wei, 1998). A second reason that young fatherhood and incarceration are linked is that minority youth are overrepresented in both categories. For example, black youth between the ages of fifteen and nineteen father children at over twice the rate of whites, with 41.5 births annually per one thousand black men as compared to 17.5 for whites (Ventura et al., 2001, 48). Young Latino males have a birthrate that is comparable to the rate for blacks (Ventura et al., 2001, 10). The overrepresentation of black and Latino youth in our nation's prisons is one of the factors resulting in the disproportionate incarceration of young fathers.

The fathers in this study were, in general, fairly involved with their children prior to incarceration. As described, Joseph saw his daughter regularly and provided money to help with her expenses. Dion cared for his daughter at least four times a week—in large part because she lived with Dion's father. Prior to his arrest, Ethan was living with his girlfriend and their daughter and he provided some amount of care for the baby. Steven had four children with a young woman who was not his current girlfriend. He did not provide a lot of support for the children, but he did go see them at least once a week. At the other end of the spectrum, Andrew had never met his one-year-old son (the product of a one-night stand) and had little contact with the child's mother, and Gabe was still waiting to meet his six-month-old daughter. In the chapters that follow, I describe what happened to these fathers' relationships with their children over the course of their incarceration.

Friendships

PROFILE: ERIC

>Of all the youth in the study, Eric lived in the most rural area. I remember driving to see him and thinking that it was simply not possible that a town could be located in such a remote location. Until his arrest, Eric lived with his mother, father, and brother, but just days after his arrival at the DYS his father moved out. Eric was confused and upset by this turn of events. I asked him whether he was receiving support from his friends, and he told me that he had a lot of people in his life but that most of them were just people he "hung around with." He did value the support of four people he considered true friends outside prison.

One of the advantages of interviewing the youth soon after their arrival in the DYS was that they were able to give detailed accounts of their friendships prior to incarceration. Most of the youth told me that they had one or two close friends outside prison, but four of the youth said that they had no close friends. When I pushed the youth to tell me about the criteria for "close friendship," they said that a friend is someone they have known for a long time and who has proven his or her loyalty ("someone I can trust to be there for me"). I asked Alex to describe a close friend. He said, "Me and my friends, we talk about stuff like if they're having problems, I talk to them about their problems. Just like if I'm having problems. My friends John and Matt, they'll sit there and talk to me about my problems and try to solve the stuff with me." It is clear that the youth reserve the term "friend" for long-standing relationships with a high level of trust and proven loyalty. Given this definition, it is probably not surprising that many of the youth reported that the people they spent time with on the outside were not friends, but merely acquaintances. As Eric remarked, there is a difference between people you hang around with and those you consider to be friends.

The fact that the youth in the study reported few close friends made me wonder whether incarcerated youth are different from young men in the general population. Research suggests, however, that delinquents and nondelinquents have the same size friendship networks (Claes and Simard, 1992). Studies also suggest that friendships of delinquent youth are as close as those of nondelinquent youth. A series of interviews conducted in 2001 with nonincarcerated African American, Asian, and Latino adolescents from low-income families provides further evidence that newly incarcerated youth are similar to their counterparts outside prison (Ways et al., 2001). The researchers found that about 20 percent of the nonincarcerated youth reported having no close friends at all. They described another 30 percent as experiencing "ambivalence" about their friends. These ambivalent youth told the researchers that they had acquaintances rather than friends. Overall, the nonincarcerated sample and my study's newly incarcerated sample gave very similar responses to questions about friendship.

When youth enter prison, they are removed from the daily lives of their friends. I talked at length with each of the young men about what they expected would happen to their friendships during their incarceration. Their responses fell into three categories. The first category, and by far the most common, included youth who expected to maintain their relationships through letters and phone calls. Kirk, for example, had a best friend he was expecting to hear from soon:

> KIRK: I haven't heard from him yet. My mom gave him the address, but she said she may have given the address to Scioto [the intake facility], so she said she was gonna call him on Sunday. But he's like, he's like my closest friend. I'll do anything for the kid. . . . When I got kicked out of the house or when I left the house, he let me stay with him for a couple of months.
> ANNE: So you assume he'll write to you once the address works out?
> KIRK: Yeah. I can't call him 'cause all he's got is his cell phone and it won't accept collect calls. . . . When I talked to my mom, he bought a calling card and he was gonna send it to me, but I can't use a calling card.

Kirk was confident and excited that his friend would write soon. Other youth echoed his thoughts, telling me that they expected regular letters from their friends.

While most youth wanted and expected contact, there was a second group of youth who said that they would like contact but did not expect it. Looking at the differences between the first and second groups of youth, it became clear that friendship expectations were largely based on prior experiences at county-level detention homes. If a youth's friends kept in touch with him at county, he generally expected this pattern to continue. At the same time, however, there were a few young men who had heard from friends at county but still said that they did not expect contact at the DYS. These young men told me that their friends had busy lives and might not have the time or energy to sustain contact with an incarcerated person. While this response indicated a realistic assessment of teenagers' lives, it might also have been driven by the youth's desire to protect their image (and feelings) if their friends failed to remain in touch ("no, I'm not hurt, I knew he wasn't going to write . . .").

The final category of responses about friendship was strikingly different from the previous two. The four youth in this group told me that they did not want to hear from their friends and did not plan to contact them. They explained that, for them, hearing about their friends' lives outside prison made time go slower inside. Here is Freddie explaining why he did not want his friends to write: "You sit there waiting for a letter, you know, and you're sitting there telling things that are going on outside and they're saying they miss you and all this and all of a sudden it just hits you right there like, *man, I gotta get out of here.* It's always on your mind." Freddie wanted to cut himself off from life outside prison so that he could concentrate on getting through life inside prison. In *Fatherhood Arrested* (2002), I used the term "hard timing" for this phenomenon. I did not hear this term in Ohio, but California youth used it to describe cutting oneself off from the outside world to make time inside easier. It is not the most common response to incarceration, but a significant minority of youth choose to adopt it.

There was clear variation in youth's expectations about contact with their friends, but most were hopeful that they would maintain relationships from prison. The fact that the youth had just arrived at their permanent placement institutions, however, meant that their expectations were not based on a realistic understanding of how a lengthy term in a tightly regulated prison might affect their friends' desire and ability to stay in touch. We return to this issue in Chapter 5 when I describe how much contact the youth ended up maintaining with their friends over the course of their incarceration.

Girlfriends

PROFILE: COLBY

I first interviewed Colby just a few days after his eighteenth birthday—a day he had spent sleeping to make it pass as quickly as possible. Colby grew up in Mississippi, coming to Ohio with his mother at sixteen to be closer to some relatives. Prior to his arrest, he lived with his mother and his brother. His brother had been attending a local college while Colby went to high school. Colby had met his girlfriend about a year before I came to the prison to interview him. He reported that they had had a close relationship on the outside but that she was furious about his arrest because she had repeatedly asked him to quit dealing drugs before "something bad happened." Colby was fairly confident that, even though she was angry, she would wait for him.

PROFILE: JAKE

Jake came to the DYS with a conviction for breaking and entering. At the time of his arrest, he was living with his mother, father, and brother. He had dropped out of school two years earlier—when he was in the ninth grade—because he hated school and wanted to spend more time "partying." Partying quickly devolved into alcoholism, and he began to spiral downward. Amazingly, he continued to work full-time at a pizza place. Jake started dating his girlfriend a year and a half before he was arrested. He was very doubtful that she would wait for him.

Most of the youth in this study (thirty-one of forty) reported that they had been dating someone before they were committed to the DYS. There was a great deal of variation in how long they had been involved in their relationships. The median was about four months, but the relationships ranged from a couple of weeks to six years. Colby and Jake had two of the longest relationships. I asked all of the youth whether they thought their girlfriends would wait for them and not date anyone else during their incarceration. The answers were strikingly similar and tended to convey a small amount of hope and a large amount of doubt. Tom, for example, replied, "She says she will." Dan said, "That's what she says," and Freddie, even more pessimistic, commented, "Girls these days, you know, some of them you can't trust." They told me over and over again that girlfriends might say that they would wait, but that their words could not be trusted.

Part of the reason the young men put little trust in their girlfriends was that they realized their sentences were going to hold them in prison for a long time. In fact, most of their minimum sentences (six or twelve months) were longer than the period they had been dating their girlfriends. The youth seemed unable to imagine that their girlfriends could wait that long—especially because they doubted their own ability to wait if the situation were reversed. This realization caused the youth considerable anxiety and led a few to tell their girlfriends to go ahead and date other people. Jason, for example, told me he wouldn't want his girlfriend to wait, because she "has a life of her own." He continued,

> If a person waits too long, they mind and stuff like that, they stuck on one thing and they start getting socially invalid. You know, they can't, they can't trust anybody else or nothing like that. And I wouldn't want to hurt her like that. You know, have her wait for me and then she regret it for the rest of her life for the past, you know. . . . I didn't break up with her. I just told her, you know, that we can be friends and stuff like that and write. But, you know, I'd rather you see another person while I'm in here, you know, or see other people.

Jason encouraged his girlfriend to date others because he would feel guilty if she waited and later regretted it. He also thought that being single for too long would make his girlfriend isolated. Three other youth also told me that they had encouraged their girlfriends to date while they were away. They explained that if they set their girlfriends free, they did not have to sit around wondering whether they were cheating. This is a form of hard-timing, as illustrated by Kyle's comments in response to my question about whether his girlfriend was waiting for him:

> KYLE: Most likely. I believe in her that she is. I wrote her a letter saying "You can go on and get something like another boyfriend until I get out,"'cause I don't want her sitting there and waiting for me. Try to move on . . . [If] you were in here for a year, would you wait for a person?
>
> ANNE: Maybe. But I'm old now. I don't know if I would've when I was fifteen years old.
>
> KYLE: I don't know. I just, I just wouldn't be able to wait and just hear from her by letter and letter. I don't know.
>
> ANNE: So are you telling her to date other people to be nice to her or because it makes you feel better?
>
> KYLE: It makes me feel better. I think in both ways. Make her feel better and me feel better. So she don't have to just sit there and wait for me.

Kyle had a very realistic view of his relationship, understanding that a year is a long time in the life of a teenager, and he did not want to sit around wondering what his girlfriend was doing on the outside. Like low expectations for friends, the youth's doubts about their girlfriends may serve as a defense mechanism to protect them from getting hurt in a relationship over which they have little control. Incarcerated youth can write letters or call their girlfriends, but they cannot monitor their girlfriends' behavior or force them to respond to letters. Because this is a significant change from life outside prison, youth have difficulty adjusting to the new power balance. In Chapters 5 and 6, I return to this topic and explore how the youth's relationships fare under these new circumstances.

Conclusion

In this chapter I introduced some of the forty young men whose journey I will trace through the prison system and back out into the community. In Ohio, the starting point for this journey is Scioto, the DYS intake facility. The purpose of this facility is to provide short-term housing while DYS staff members make decisions about which institution would be the most suitable placement for each youth. During the few weeks the youth spend at Scioto, the staff assess their mental health and substance abuse issues, their risk level, and their educational needs. Based on these assessments and on the youth's criminal histories, the staff decide where the youth will serve their sentences.

Youth spend a great deal of time at Scioto worrying and talking about which facility they will be assigned to. Rumors about each institution are spread by both youth and staff and usually assert spectacularly high levels of violence or chaos in the institutions. These rumors significantly increase youth's level of anxiety about their new institution. Steven, for example, told me, "I thought for myself it was gonna be worse, and everyone in Scioto, even the staff there, were saying, 'Oh, when you get there, you're gonna have hell in the next institution.'" Nelson's experiences at Scioto were similar to Steven's. In response to a question about his new institution, he said, "It's all right. I ain't gonna say I like it, but when I first heard about it, they said, 'Oh, Oak Hill. You going to Oak Hill? Oak Hill is rowdy.' This place ain't nothing. I was worried. It's stupid. . . . At Scioto, . . . people who already came here said this place was bad and all that."

Like Nelson and Steven, most first-time admissions arrive at their new facilities with fears and preconceived notions about what it will be like.

While most of these ideas come from youth (especially those reentering the system) and staff, the youth also draw on stories they have heard from others in their home communities who have been through the DYS system. These stories frighten the youth and cause their first few days at the new facility to be especially tense. It does not take long, however, for the young men to realize that the horror stories they have heard—while having many elements of truth—are somewhat exaggerated. They are then able to adjust to the routines of their new lives.

Chapter 3

Institutional Order

When youth enter prison, their days take on a whole new rhythm structured by the established routines, rules, programs, and practices of the institution. These elements of formal organization are important because they provide the context within which incarcerated youth live, associate with each other, and create a culture. This chapter examines those key elements by identifying the goals of the juvenile prison and exploring some concrete ways staff and administration attempt to meet those goals. I also use the perspective of the youth in this study to look at the formal structure of the prison.

While mission statements do not necessarily reflect what happens on the ground, they do set a tone for an organization and provide insight into its primary goals. I looked at a wide range of juvenile justice mission statements, and while there was some variation, three main goals—punishment, order, and rehabilitation—emerged as particularly important. Utah's mission statement clearly states these goals:

> Provide comprehensive services for at risk youth within the framework of the Balanced and Restorative Justice Model. The Balanced and Restorative Justice Model is a philosophy of correctional care that emphasizes three equally important principles.
> - Accountability: When a crime occurs, a debt is incurred. Youth must be held accountable for their actions and to restore the victim's losses. JJS [Juvenile Justice Services] will be held accountable for the efficacy of services provided to youth.
> - Competency development: Offenders should leave the system more capable of productive participation in conventional society than when they entered.
> - Community protection: The public has a right to a safe and secure community. Youth also have the right to be safe while in the custody of the Division of Juvenile Justice Services.

Like those in other states, Utah's juvenile justice mission statement reveals the agency's major focus on rehabilitation, accomplished through training, treatment, and education. This heavy emphasis on rehabilitation is hardly a surprise since the creation of the juvenile justice system was motivated by a desire to reform youth. At the same time, rehabilitation is clearly not the only goal. Language about "holding youth accountable" reveals punishment as another central objective. Finally, Utah's mission statement indicates that the maintenance of safe, secure, and orderly facilities is seen as vitally important.

Once organizations set goals, they try to translate them into day-to-day activities and procedures. Many factors go into the decisions prisons make about how to achieve rehabilitation, punishment, and order. These factors range from the history of the institution to its level of funding. Numerous stakeholders are involved, including prison administration and staff, the governor, advocacy groups, state legislators, and the public. The views of these stakeholders about youth and the causes of crime are a decisive factor influencing prison policy. For example, if delinquency is understood as a product of a youth's own deficiencies, stakeholders are likely to push for a more punitive and hierarchical system than if delinquency is seen as a product of social causes. These assumptions about delinquency help administrators at both the state and institutional level determine the methods used to attain order, how punitive the prison's policies are, and the types of therapeutic and educational programs offered. The process of setting prison policy, however, is never straightforward; assumptions about delinquency can be contradictory, and officials have to respond to fiscal and efficiency considerations. The policies that result from this process are, not surprisingly, often inconsistent and fragmented.

In this chapter, I explore some of the ways that juvenile prisons try to achieve their goals of rehabilitation, punishment, and order. While I choose to discuss the three goals separately, it should be noted that they are not always mutually exclusive. For example, having a well-structured treatment program can create a well-ordered environment, and in turn, a well-ordered environment can enhance rehabilitation services (DiIulio, 1987).

Goal One: Rehabilitation

If you ask a prison administrator about rehabilitation efforts in their facilities, they will tell you about the educational and therapeutic programs available to inmates. Of course, rehabilitation can take place in less formal ways, but programs are the standard institutional method used to achieve the goal of rehabilitation. Here I discuss only the most common programs available in juvenile prisons, starting with the two that have been in operation the longest and are the most deeply ingrained in institutions: education and job training. I then describe the two most common treatment programs: substance abuse and mental health. Finally, I look at some new programs that have become popular across the nation. These include anger management, victim awareness, and fatherhood programs.

Education

Education has been part of the juvenile correctional system since the mid-1800s when the first reform schools were established. Steven L. Schlossman (1995) points out, however, that this early "education" generally did not go beyond basic skills and was frequently focused on training youth to help maintain the institution. At the same time, education was seen as an important way to shape youth into good workers and responsible citizens. This aim was reinforced by the National Prison Congress held in Cincinnati in 1871, where education and religion were declared to be the two most important factors in deciding whether a prisoner had been reformed (American Correctional Association, 1983). In the early 1900s, Ohio was at the forefront of providing education to institutionalized youth. At the Ohio Boys' Industrial School, both vocational and academic instruction were emphasized (Schlossman, 1995).

Today, juvenile facilities generally require that youth in custody attend school or prepare for a GED. However, some states, like Florida, provide education but do not require youth to attend (Cutting et al., 2004). States vary in how they determine which youth receive a high school education and which prepare for a GED. At the Ohio DYS, for example, all residents under the age of seventeen must take classes toward a diploma, but those seventeen and older can choose between GED preparation and high school classes (until 2008, the cutoff age was sixteen). Georgia has a slightly different policy: only youth who are two or more years off track, are sixteen or older, and have parental permission can opt into the GED program.

There has been no research conducted on the factors that determine whether a youth chooses to pursue a GED or high school diploma while in prison. My study suggests that, when given a choice, youth generally choose a GED because it is potentially faster to complete. Caleb, for example, wanted to finish school before he was released from the institution: "I chose to get a GED 'cause I figured if I don't, when I get back home I wasn't going to go to school. I was gonna drop out before I got locked up. But I got locked up before I could do that. So I decided to get my GED so I don't have to worry about it when I get out. I'll have my education done." In Ohio, Caleb and other youth seeking a GED spend their days in a classroom working individually in their GED preparation book. If they encounter something they do not understand, there is a teacher available to help them. This system seems to work reasonably well for youth who are very self-motivated and bright. Those with a weak academic background, however, have a less positive experience. Darius was one such student:

DARIUS: I wanted to get my GED and stuff but they didn't want to help me. They weren't giving me the help that I needed. I needed them to talk to me. But they wouldn't talk. You have to do all the work on your own.

ANNE: There was no teacher?

DARIUS: Yeah, there was a teacher. But he don't, like, sit in front of the classroom and you all do it together. You just all do it by yourself and if you have any questions, go up there and ask him.

As it turned out, Darius was not able to get himself through the book. He was released from prison, tried to take GED classes on the outside, got discouraged, and gave up. Darius might have done better in prison high school classes, but this is difficult to know—and impossible to generalize to all incarcerated youth. In Chapter 7, I return to this issue and explore the policy issues raised by the GED/diploma decision.

Because of age and other restrictions, most youth do not have to decide between a GED and a diploma—they are simply assigned to high school classes. There is not a lot known about high school classes in prison, but it appears that they are of widely varying quality. This is, in part, a result of lax or confused oversight. Only 65 percent of states require that juvenile facilities follow the statewide curriculum or educational standards. In addition, only 59 percent of states have clear teacher certification requirements in place (Mulcahy and Leone, 2006). Reflecting confusion about oversight and responsibility, states assign jurisdiction for prison schools to a variety of state agencies. In 37 percent of states, the juvenile justice agency itself is responsible for the school. Another 27 percent of states assign multiple agencies responsibility. Education in 16 percent is provided by the state education agency and in 6 percent by the local school district (Mulcahy and Leone, 2006).

Unfortunately, regardless of which agency is in charge of education, the school systems in most juvenile correctional facilities are mired in problems. This is partly because incarcerated juveniles are a very challenging group to teach. As described in the second chapter, many juvenile prisoners have dropped out of school and function, on average, three years below grade level (Rider-Hankins, 1992, 2). This strikingly high educational lag is linked to the fact that the prison system tends to draw from impoverished neighborhoods, where schools have limited resources and are frequently deficient academically. Further complicating matters, a large proportion of the prison population has been diagnosed with learning, conduct, and cognitive disabilities. Some estimates place this figure as high as 70 percent (Leone, Meisel, and Drakeford, 2002, 46). While this number is disturbing, it may not be completely accurate, as critics point out that "disabilities" labels are sometimes a convenient way for the school system to write off children they perceive to be difficult or troublesome. Research suggests that such labels are all too often applied to black males—a group that is stereotyped as being particularly criminal (Ferguson, 2001). At the same time, it is clear that many juvenile offenders come to prison with very real and significant learning challenges.

Correctional institutions today are ill equipped to handle the complex needs of the juvenile prison population. Most state prison systems are extremely overcrowded and are working with tight budgets. As a result, their schools are understaffed and their teachers underpaid. In a review of the literature, Peg Rider-Hankins (1992) found that while teachers are concerned about preparing youth for life after release, they lack the ability and training to control their classrooms. Because of this, the classroom can be an unsafe and unpleasant place. As an example, I present a short excerpt from my own field notes:

Walking down the hallway toward the interview room, I pass by a room where all the youth are wearing bright orange jumpsuits. At first, there appears to be some sort of social event going on because there is a lot of talking and some laughter. I quickly realize, however, that this is actually a classroom. A few of the youth are sitting down and working in workbooks, but most are talking to each other or staring off into space. I ask somebody what the room is for, and they tell me that it is for youth whose behavior is so problematic they cannot be in the facility's regular school.

The "orange jumpsuit" room is a particularly chaotic space, but the regular classrooms are often not much better. One youth I spoke with, Ben, told me that he was excited about having an opportunity to work toward a degree but that the environment was not conducive to learning.

> They're teaching me, but it's kind of hard to learn when, I don't know, you've got a lot of clowns in the classroom and stuff. Got a lot of clowns in there, just the teachers can't, well some of them can, but some of them can't control the kids, so they're all jumping around, going out of their seat, turning off the lights, hiding the books, just doing whatever they want to do, and the teachers can't control them.

One reason for the chaos in prison classes is that the juvenile prison population is transient and new youth are constantly joining the class while other youth are being released. On any given day, there are many interruptions as youth are pulled out of school for court dates, meetings with lawyers, or counseling (Rider-Hankins, 1992). Other youth leave class for a time when they are put into isolation for behavior problems. Teachers are in an extremely difficult situation as they are given few resources to educate a diverse, large, and ever-shifting group of youth—some of whom are actively hostile toward being in a classroom.

Ohio is an example of a state that, at the time of this study, was struggling to provide even a minimal level of education to the youth in its juvenile correctional facilities. As part of a fact-finding report, one researcher found that on a randomly selected day, only 43 percent of youth in DYS institutions received a full day of classes (Cohen, 2008, iv). To explain this low number, he cited factors including a teacher shortage and a lack of appropriate space. Those students who were in school received generalized instruction aimed at the third or fourth grade level. Like many states, Ohio places incarcerated youth of various ages and skill levels into classes together, making it hard for the teacher to choose a target audience. As a result, youth spend most of their time working on a workbook for their grade level. The youth's reactions to this type of schooling are generally negative. Here are excerpts from interviews with Sam and Eric:

> SAM: I thought it just went easier and quicker [than schools outside prison]. Didn't get much out of it 'cause teachers just sit at their desks and you have something to do. It's not like they talk to us. It's like you can never get a break. You always just gotta like sit there. Reading something. Writing something.

ERIC: The science was pretty boring. Everything was pretty dumb. You never learned anything. . . . I mean it's not like the teachers taught you to do anything. Just went in there and did it yourself.

Ohio is well aware of the educational problems that Sam and Eric report. In 2008, as part of the resolution of a class-action suit, the state was required to upgrade its educational system. They decided to purchase computers and programs so that youth could work independently on interactive software. Further research is needed to ascertain whether these upgrades turn out to be an improvement over the old system.

Special Education

In 1973, the Rehabilitation Act mandated that special education be provided to youth who are classified as "disabled" and whose disabilities make it difficult for them to receive an education in the mainstream classroom. The law's application to youth in custody was affirmed in 1975 (Keeley, 2004). In 2004, the Individuals with Disabilities Education Improvement Act mandated improvements in the way that special education was implemented and tracked. One important part of this law required that students who qualify for special education must have an individualized education program (IEP) prepared for them. An IEP, in theory, spells out the needs of the child and a plan to meet those needs. Both parents and educators are supposed to be involved in its creation.

As described in the preceding section, a large percentage of students in juvenile correctional custody are eligible for special education. National estimates range from 30 to 70 percent (Leone, Meisel, and Drakeford, 2002, 46). The true number is probably somewhere in the middle—in Ohio, for example, half of incarcerated students qualify (Cohen, 2008, 109). Although improvements have been made in special education services over the years, deep problems still remain. Some of the problems, like unqualified and underpaid teachers, a high student-teacher ratio, and a lack of space, are not unique to the special education classes (Leone, Meisel, and Drakeford, 2002). Other problems, however, affect only special education students. These include a lack of screening for youth when they arrive at the institution, a failure of public schools to forward a youth's records to the correctional institution, and a failure to involve parents in the creation of the IEP. Some institutions undermine the idea of the IEPs by writing plans based on what services are available in the institution rather than on the youth's needs. Others simply use a standardized IEP for all youth (Meisel et al., 1998).

Employment and Job Training

Employment and job training have a long and controversial history in prisons. The most controversial programs are those that allow (or force) inmates to work for private companies, thereby raising revenue for the prison. After the Civil War, black inmates were leased as labor to farmers and other employers. Until the Great Depression, adult inmates of all races (and any juveniles housed with them) frequently provided factory or farm labor. Then the economic crisis of the Depression sparked protests about inmates taking jobs away from those in the free labor force, and laws were put into place mandating that inmate labor be used only to provide limited goods and services to the government. This meant that inmates could make things like license plates or war goods. Prison labor could also be used to provide food or services for their own consumption or for that of inmates at other institutions.

In 1979, important changes were made to prison labor laws, allowing some private industries to operate using inmate labor and relaxing the caps on federal government purchase of inmate-made goods. These legal changes resulted in the creation of the Prison Industry Enhancement (PIE) program. This program, run by the Bureau of Justice Assistance through the Department of Justice, has fifty waivers available to jurisdictions (states or local governments) allowing them to contract with private industries. Waivers for these programs can be granted to either juvenile or adult facilities. Approved programs must show that they are not taking away jobs from free labor and that they are operating in industries that do not have a glut of unemployed workers.

One of the important stipulations of PIE is that participating employers must pay inmates "prevailing wages." This does not mean, however, that an inmate receives his or her full wage. The prison system can use up to 80 percent of a worker's gross wages to pay taxes, make a worker's child-support payments, contribute toward victim restitution funds, and, notably, reimburse the state for the cost of room and board. The PIE program is attractive to private companies because they receive discounted rent and utilities (since the work space is owned by the prison) and tax breaks, and they do not need to provide health care benefits. Employers also potentially save money because they can lay off workers knowing that they will be available to be rehired. California and Texas both have PIE programs at the juvenile level. California's program began in the 1990s through a partnership with Trans World Airlines. The airline trained incarcerated youth as customer service representatives and then hired them to book reservations. Today the PIE program still exists in several California facilities with new industrial partners. Texas has a similar program, enabling youth in the Gainesville State

School to work in a metal fabrication shop, a venture of the Gulf Coast Trades Company.

The PIE program is one way that prisons can provide youth with job training. Critics have pointed out, however, that the programs exist on shaky ethical ground since inmates are not supposed to be forced to work for a private industry. Since PIE is the only source of real wages in the institution, an inmate who wants or needs money has no choice but to work for the one available industry. The idea that the inmate is there "voluntarily" is questionable. Workers in prison industries are not able to unionize or organize to demand better conditions or pay. Additionally, it is not clear that the PIE program necessarily trains youth with skills that will help them once they are released from prison.

A less controversial option for employment training is programs that simply teach job skills. In Ohio, for example, youth are trained in computer literacy, a potentially useful skill in the free market. Wisconsin trains youth at some of its facilities in small-engine repair and welding. Massachusetts partners with community groups to provide vocational training. There are also several other states with innovative programs. Virginia is particularly notable, with a work-release program that allows some youth to work or attend college classes off site. They also have a fairly extensive apprentice program with job-training opportunities in areas such as sign making, embroidery, and barber skills.

In the summer of 2009, I visited a maximum-security juvenile facility in Washington State that operates an extensive vocational training program. The local school district pays for youth housed there to take classes in welding, auto maintenance, computer design, woodworking, and fiber optics. The welding program even offers an opportunity for certification. I was impressed to find that the teachers all have extensive real-world experience in their fields and each of them works to combine academic training and job-readiness skills in their classes. The facility also houses a graphics program that trains youth to make banners, posters, and T-shirts. The program pays for itself through sales of products to local government and nonprofit organizations. Any profits are used to purchase up-to-date computer and printing equipment.

While such programs appear to be potentially beneficial to youth, many others operate under serious constraints. First, it is hard for prison administrators to project the future needs of the market, and once money is invested in one kind of training program, it is difficult to adjust it quickly to changing market needs. Limited budgets also mean that prisons must sometimes train inmates using outdated machines or technologies. For example, at the time of this study, Ohio trained youth on older-model computers. Additionally, the types of job-training programs available may not be matched to the interests, talents, or future plans of the youth. An example of this is a facility in New Jersey that runs a fully operational dairy farm. Dairy farming is certainly an important occupation, but it may not be useful to a youth from Trenton who plans to return to his urban neighborhood. Washington State's vocational program avoids many of these pitfalls because the local school district invests considerable resources, many different courses are taught, and the staff are committed to providing youth with marketable skills. The fiber-optics program, for example, was recently added to the curriculum because a staff member realized that there were jobs available in that sector of the economy.

Substance Abuse Treatment

One of the most widespread types of rehabilitative programming in juvenile prisons is substance abuse treatment. About 66 percent of facilities report that they provide these services on site to youth. Because prisons with substance abuse programs tend to be larger than those without, about 83 percent of all incarcerated youth theoretically have access to these services (Snyder and Sickmund, 2006, 225). There is a high demand for substance abuse services because a significant percentage of the youth in juvenile prisons experience problems with drugs and alcohol. While it is hard to get a reliable figure for users, records show that about 8 percent of all incarcerated youth are in prison for a drug offense (Snyder and Sickmund, 2006, 198). This number, however, only includes youth who were arrested with a drug violation as their most serious crime. In other words, the number does not include a youth who held up a liquor store while on drugs. Additionally, it does not include youth with substance abuse issues that have not come to the attention of officials. Because of these omissions, it is estimated that the percentage of users in the prison population is considerably higher than 8 percent. For example, a study conducted with a random sample of youth in secure detention in Cook County, Illinois, found that fully half met the criteria to be diagnosed with a substance abuse disorder (Teplin et al., 2002).

Research suggests that high-quality substance abuse treatment can reduce drug and alcohol dependency in prison inmates (Federal Bureau of Prisons, 2000). There are many different types of treatment, however, ranging from therapeutic communities to group or individual counseling. Therapeutic communities are the most intensive option, placing addicted youth together in a highly structured environment built around counseling, self-help, and community building. In Ohio, at the time of this study, one entire facility was devoted to a therapeutic community for substance-addicted youth. The other Ohio facilities had drug and alcohol treatment as well, but it was conducted through group and individual counseling sessions. Sometimes educational classes were offered, with youth learning about dependency issues by reading on their own in a workbook. The most common types of substance abuse programming provided in juvenile correctional facilities nationally include, in order of frequency, drug education, the development of treatment plans, individual counseling, and group counseling (Snyder and Sickmund, 2006, 225–26).

The drug- and alcohol-addicted youth in this study uniformly expressed gratitude for the opportunity to become involved in treatment. At the same time, they clearly felt that some types of treatment were preferable to others. Specifically, they felt they gained the most from the therapeutic community experience and the least from writing in workbooks. Their views are consistent with the findings of research studies on the efficacy of various types of treatment (CASA/Columbia University, 1998). In fact, in a meta-analysis of studies conducted prior to 1996, researchers found that only therapeutic communities had a statistically significant effect on recidivism (Pearson and Lipton, 1999). Studies of other methods of substance abuse treatment showed either a very small positive effect (group counseling) or a negative effect (boot camps). It is a great loss for incarcerated youth when their state does not have therapeutic community programs, or has canceled them. In 2010, Ohio joined the ranks of these states with the closure of their therapeutic community facility.

Delivering addiction services in juvenile prison is potentially beneficial, but its efficacy is significantly decreased when communities are unable to provide follow-up services to youth who return home. Research suggests that such follow-up is essential to long-term success (CASA/Columbia University, 1998; Hiller, Knight, and Simpson, 1999). It appears to be fairly easy to remain sober while in juvenile prison (although a range of drugs and homemade alcohol are sometimes available on the prison black market). Once youth return home, however, their resolve to remain sober is tested as they reunite with drug-using friends and connections.

Psychological and Social Work Services

Since the 1990s, there has been an upsurge in concern about the availability of mental health services in juvenile facilities. This concern grew out of the discovery that many incarcerated youth had diagnosable mental health conditions but few received services. One study conducted in secure detention facilities in Cook County, Illinois, found that newly admitted male youth exhibited high rates of psychiatric disorders, particularly depression (13 percent), anxiety disorders (21 percent), and attention deficit disorders (16 percent) (Teplin et al., 2002, 1136). These figures are considerably higher than estimates for these disorders in the general population of youth. Overall, estimates suggest that one incarcerated youth in five has a serious mental health disorder (Cocozza and Skowyra, 2000).

According to 2003 figures, 63 percent of juvenile correctional facilities in the country offer mental health services (Snyder and Sickmund, 2006, 232). Given the high rates of mental illness in the population, however, the available services still fall far short of the needs. This services gap has been documented in investigative reports on state juvenile correctional systems. For example, the U.S. Department of Justice (2008) found that Texas was providing inadequate psychiatric help to its residents. And in California, a researcher found that mentally ill youth were inappropriately placed in restrictive housing rather than receiving the help they needed (Krisberg, 2003).

The first step toward providing appropriate psychiatric services to youth involves screening them for mental health issues. About 40 percent of public juvenile prisons and 62 percent of private facilities screen all youth. At the other end of the spectrum, 10 percent of public and 16 percent of private facilities conduct no mental health screening whatsoever (Snyder and Sickmund, 2006, 227). Most of the time, screening occurs as part of the intake process, allowing the correctional system to take a youth's mental health status into account when making decisions about institutional placement or treatment plans. Some states concentrate their psychiatric services in particular institutions and make an effort to send youth with mental health issues there. In some Ohio facilities, youth with serious psychiatric problems live together in a separate wing or dorm. Two of the forty youth in this study were housed in such a dorm.

In addition to pre-existing mental health issues, youth in prison may need psychiatric help to get through crises that occur while they are incarcerated. During the course of this study, for example, a number of the incarcerated youth experienced family tragedies. Most notably, Dion's brother was murdered and Casey's mother died of cancer. These youth needed help and counseling to work through these tragedies, particularly since they were not able to be with their grieving families except for a few brief moments at the funerals. Psychiatric services may also be useful for youth dealing with the crisis of their own incarceration. As described in subsequent chapters, life in prison is extremely stressful and requires youth to constantly maintain a front. Some of the young men in this study told me that they felt overwhelmed by incarceration and feared that they were going to break down. In the absence of systemic prison reform, psychiatric services are one potential resource for youth feeling high levels of stress.

Talking with the youth in this study, it became clear that psychologists were an important resource but were not the only source of mental health help. Social workers were, in some ways, even more valuable to the youth. Social workers are clearly different from guards—in Ohio they wear street clothes and have an office. They are also different from psychologists because they are much more involved in the youth's day-to-day lives and are able to intercede for them in some very practical ways. A number of youth talked gratefully about times that social workers had helped them, listened to them, or interceded on their behalf. For example, I asked Sam whom he talked with when he was upset:

> SAM: Oh, the social worker. I went in the office and he could just see I was mad 'cause everything. . . . He's like, "You need to cry?" I just started crying and stuff. Just 'cause everything.
> ANNE: Yeah. That's a lot of stuff you were dealing with.
> SAM: And he just did it too. He just shut the door and gave me napkins and like, he could just see. I didn't even show it. I was just like dissing. All of a sudden he could just tell or something. He ain't my social worker, but my social worker's out sick for the next three weeks so he like deals with her caseload until she'll come back or whatever.

As Sam discovered, a social worker's office can be a rare refuge from the constant stress of prison life. Social workers cannot substitute for psychiatric staff, but their presence in the institutions can help youth deal with difficult emotional issues.

Anger Management

> I've taken so many anger management classes though, but, like, I still have anger. But who doesn't?
> —Kenneth

"Anger management" is a general term that refers to programs that train people to better manage their angry emotions. It is based on research showing that anger is often a precursor to aggression. The number of anger management classes, both in prison and out, have skyrocketed in the past twenty years. Today, they are found in schools, in psychiatric facilities, and as a court-ordered alternative to jail time. An article in the *New York Times* in 2001 reported that three thousand people a year were attending court-ordered anger management classes in New York City (Lewin, 2001).

Anger management courses are offered in most juvenile and adult prisons in the United States. Psychologists have identified particularly high levels of anger in offender populations, which provides the rationale for the programs (Mann and Mann, 2007; Novaco, Ramm, and Black, 2001). Proponents of prison anger management claim that classes help offenders to be less aggressive both while they are in the institution and when they return to their communities, thereby lessening recidivism. Typical program elements include problem-solving skills, teaching students to understand the perspective of others, and relaxation techniques. Anger management treatment is often based on the principles of cognitive behavioral therapy, in which therapists work to change the way participants think and then help them to change their behavior to match their new thinking. In other words, participants figure out what situations trigger anger for them and then learn to change the way they think about those situations. When thinking changes, behavior should change accordingly. People in these types of anger management classes practice their new techniques through role playing.

To date, studies of the efficacy of anger management training are scarce and are generally of very low quality. A meta-analysis conducted in 2000 concluded that there were simply not enough studies to draw any conclusions about anger management's efficacy (MacKenzie, 2000). In an earlier meta-analysis with less stringent inclusion rules, researchers found that anger management programs were associated with a moderate reduction in self-reported anger (Beck and Fernandez, 1998). They did not explore, however, whether anger management has an effect on actual behavior or whether any behavior change holds over the long term. Russell Skiba and Janet McKelvey (2000) report that research looking at behavior between one and three years after the conclusion of treatment shows mixed results. A three-year follow-up with aggressive boys, for example, found that the youth decreased their drug and alcohol use but not their delinquent behavior (Lochman, 1992). A one-year follow-up with pre-adolescents in psychiatric care found that the youth maintained their ability to desist from problem behaviors (Kazdin et al., 1987).

The youth in this study tended to be critical of anger management classes, commenting that the curriculum was mostly common sense. For example, Colby said "They just give you a way to control your anger. Basically, they say leave it to God." When asked further about what the class taught, he responded, "They teach … how to prevent fights … how to walk away from it. But it isn't nothing that you shouldn't already know." Colby's reaction to his anger management class was fairly muted compared to other youth. Ethan, for example, thought it unfair that youth were encouraged to express their emotions but were forced into anger management courses if they actually did so:

> 'Cause every time you talk to somebody . . . you're angry. You need anger management. Blah, blah, blah, blah. Motherfucker, you never been mad before? . . . People have problems and issues. They will even tell you that theirself. Well, yeah. Problems and issues. You need to express 'em. . . . No wonder nobody expresses 'em. You always talking about giving 'em six months and shit. . . . Somebody died. Whew, man. Somebody died in my family. Oh, oh, oh, oh. You know what? You have emotional stress problems. You got real issues. You need to go to this treatment. What the fuck kinda shit's that?

When I remember this discussion with Ethan, I always laugh because he delivered his opinion in a loud and angry voice—making me think he might be a perfect candidate for the very anger management courses he does not believe he needs. At the same time, his comments point to some of the contradictions involved in implementing these courses in prisons. Researchers raise similar issues. Anger can be a healthy emotional outlet, especially if it does not turn into aggression. Also, not all offenders have excessive anger, and not all offending behavior is related to anger (Novaco, Ramm, and Black, 2001).

In their work, Kevin Howells and Andrew Day (2003) point out that readiness for treatment is an important predictor of eventual success. There are several reasons that readiness for anger management might be particularly low in offender populations. First, offenders are generally forced to attend treatment (rather than volunteering), which may make them less receptive to the program. Second, offender populations contain disproportionate numbers of people with personality and other mental disorders, groups who may be less amenable to anger management training. Finally, and perhaps most important, the institutional environment itself may contradict the lessons taught in anger management. In other words, anger management techniques may be disadvantageous in the violent atmosphere of the prison. If anger and aggression are effective ways to survive in the institution, it may be difficult to convince offenders that they should change. Reports from juvenile correctional facilities also suggest that staff often become angry and engage in verbal abuse, providing a very poor role model for anger management (Krisberg, 2003).

Victim Awareness

Victim awareness is a fairly recent innovation in correctional programming, introduced by the California Youth Authority in 1984 (Monahan et al., 2004). The program has spread rapidly into both adult and juvenile prisons across the nation. In 1996, 36 percent of adult facilities offered victim awareness courses, but in 2004 a full 73 percent offered them (National Center for Victims of Crime, 1996; U.S. National Institute of Corrections, 2004, 10). In terms of juvenile facilities, 37 percent had programs in 1996 (National Center for Victims of Crime, 1996). The exact number of programs today is unknown, but it appears to be at least as high as in adult facilities. Both California and Ohio provide victim awareness in all their juvenile facilities. Texas has a "victim empathy" component in their treatment program, and they also host victim impact presentations in their facilities. North Dakota has a "Victim Impact Group" that puts on presentations in their facilities. South Carolina provides victim awareness and empathy in its sex-offender program.

Most of the victim awareness programs in the country are based on the California Youth Authority curriculum—a forty-hour program that is taught over a ten-to-twelve-week period (Gaboury et al., 2008). In 2005, the Department of Justice awarded the California Youth Authority and MADD (Mothers Against Drunk Driving) a grant to develop a more standardized curriculum. Today there is a national initiative, also funded by the Department of Justice and led by the California Youth Authority (now named the Division of Juvenile Justice), to evaluate and enhance this curriculum.

Victim awareness programs assume that offenders commit crimes because they have a reduced ability to empathize and because they fail to take into account the perspectives of others. Offenders are also seen as relying on neutralization strategies to justify their participation in crimes. For example, an offender might minimize the harm experienced by the victim or blame others for their part in the crime. Victim awareness was developed to help offenders understand how crime affects victims and to encourage them to take responsibility for the harm they have inflicted on others. The long-term goals of the program are to reduce recidivism, improve institutional behavior, and give victims a way to be involved in the effort to rehabilitate offenders (Gaboury et al., 2008).

Almost all of the youth in this study took a victim awareness course during their stay in prison or while they were on parole. When I asked them about these classes, most said that they were fun because they involved storytelling about real crimes. It became clear that victim awareness was popular because it was less boring than their other activities. However, only three youth told me that the classes helped them. Here is Gary discussing his experiences:

> GARY: I'm going to victim awareness. Victim awareness class lets you know about, like, how you feel about who you hurt and stuff like that.
> ANNE: What do you think of that class? Is it good? Is it bad?
> GARY: I think, I think it helps you a lot. 'Cause we learn about charges. Like different charges and how the ripple effect . . . like when you hurt one person, it could hurt more people than just that one.

Gary indicates that he thought victim awareness made him more knowledgeable. Sam also thought that victim awareness helped him—but not in the way the prison system intended:

> SAM: I had victim awareness and I did pretty good. Even though I got minimal participation. I don't even know how I got it. I just, like, did. . . . I guess I was being kept to myself too much. That's why I got the minimal participation, but I passed it. They brought in victims and real live murderers and stuff.
> ANNE: So did you find that helpful?
> SAM: Yeah. It worked in court when I talked about it.

Sam did not think that victim awareness made him less likely to commit crimes, but he was pleased that his completion of the course appeared to help him earn an early release. But Gary and Sam were unusual; most youth told me that they did not think victim awareness helped them in any way. At the same time, it is difficult for youth to assess the efficacy of programs—especially when they are still in the prison environment. For a more reliable picture of the effects of victim awareness, we must turn to the research literature.

There are relatively few studies assessing the efficacy of victim awareness programs. Those that have been conducted fall into two categories: studies that look at behavioral measures (like recidivism) and those that look at attitudinal variables (like empathy). In terms of behavioral research, Doris Layton MacKenzie (2000) conducted a meta-analysis of studies looking at the link between victim awareness programs and recidivism. She found that there were simply not enough high-quality studies to draw any solid conclusions. The one study deemed to be of high enough quality for inclusion found no difference in recidivism between inmates who were in the program and those who were not. A more recent study looked at the effect of victim awareness on the behavior of adult offenders in an institution (Gaboury et al., 2008). It found that the classes were not associated with a decrease in serious institutional infractions, except among African American men. The authors did not know why the curriculum appeared to be effective for this group but not for others.

Turning to studies that do not focus on behavioral outcomes, Aldis Putnins (1997) conducted a study with incarcerated juveniles in Australia looking at the effect of a victim awareness program on "sociomoral reasoning." Low sociomoral reasoning is defined as "a narrow worldview that fails to adequately encompass the perspectives and experiences of, and relationships with, others" (709). Putnins reported that low sociomoral reasoning is correlated with reoffending and that participants in the victim awareness program had significantly greater improvement in sociomoral reasoning than did their counterparts in a control group. In 2004, another study found that victim awareness classes provided to adult incarcerated males "increased knowledge of victim rights, facts of victimization, and sensitivity to victim's plight" (Monahan et al., 21). Notably, younger offenders (ages twenty-one to twenty-five) had less knowledge of victim legal rights and less understanding of victim suffering at the time of the pretest. Younger offenders also experienced larger gains in all areas than older offenders. One of the few studies conducted entirely with juveniles (Winoker et al., 2003) found that Florida's victim awareness program was associated with statistically significant gains in knowledge about crime's impact on the victims and their communities and a decrease in antisocial thinking. The program, however, did not appear to have an effect on empathy. Further research on the effects of victim awareness programs is needed.

Fatherhood Programs

The first parenthood programs began in women's prisons during the nineteenth century. Fatherhood programs did not make an appearance until the 1970s but became increasingly common through the 1980s. At first, these programs were limited to adult facilities, but that began to change in the 1990s as policy makers realized that a disproportionately high percentage of male juvenile inmates were fathers—about 25 percent, according to 1995 estimates (Abeyratne, Sowards, and Brewer, 1995; California Youth Authority, 1995). Fatherhood programs are not as prevalent as anger management or victim awareness classes, but a considerable number of states (and individual prisons) now offer fatherhood programs to incarcerated and paroled juveniles.

Advocates of parent education argue that there are at least two compelling reasons for offering classes to fathers in prison. First, there is evidence to suggest that parents who maintain close contact with their families during incarceration are less prone to recidivism (Hairston, 1991). Second, research shows that there may be improved outcomes for children of participating parents. We know that children of prisoners experience higher rates of behavior problems in school, depression, and academic problems than children whose parents are not incarcerated (see Parke and Clarke-Stewart, 2002, for a review of the literature). What is less clear is whether these problems are linked to parental incarceration or to pre-existing problems. Regardless, classes in prison are intended to help parents guide their children away from negative behaviors.

There is no standardized curriculum for parent education classes, and there is tremendous variation in focus, content, and duration of classes. Some classes concentrate on changing parenting attitudes, with the idea that behaviors cannot change unless the underlying attitudes change first. Others focus on self-identity issues and on improving participants' self-esteem. Also popular are courses that cover parenting skills and child development. An important component of many courses is the discussion of issues pertaining to parenting from prison. These classes may cover such topics as how incarcerated parents can actively participate in children's lives, how to explain incarceration to children, what happens to children who are placed in foster care, and what legal rights incarcerated parents have. Courses for incarcerated fathers also commonly focus on co-parenting issues (Palm, 2003).

Ohio does not systematically provide fatherhood education in its juvenile facilities, although there is a program run by an enterprising social worker in one institution. By contrast, California has one of the largest programs in the nation. Community members are hired to provide classes both in prison and to parolees. Texas also has a large program, contracting with a private company to provide institutional and parole-side fatherhood classes.

As with other types of prison programming, fatherhood programs have received somewhat mixed evaluations, in part because of problematic research methodologies. Glen Palm (2003) reviewed the available evaluation studies of parenting classes in prison, and he concluded that they appear to have at least a short-term impact on prisoners' attitudes and self-esteem. He also reported that some studies looking at the effectiveness of classes found improved parenting skills, more appropriate use of discipline, and enhanced knowledge of child development. Because the majority of the studies followed participants only during the class term, or for a few months following, we do not know whether any of these effects persisted over time. Furthermore, since most research on the effectiveness of parenting classes has been conducted with adults, we know very little about juveniles. One large-scale evaluation research project in California, however, found that there were a number of positive effects on juveniles' knowledge and attitudes (Cohen et al., 1997). These changes were similar to those reported in the studies conducted with adult fathers.

Goal Two: Punishment

The goal of punishment, unlike that of rehabilitation, is not accomplished through organized programs in prison. Instead, the prison experience itself is set up to achieve punishment. I concentrate here on the ways that incarceration punishes all prisoners, even those who maintain a perfect behavioral record. In the following section on order maintenance, I discuss punishment as an important way for prisons to maintain control when individuals or groups are disruptive.

Many years ago, Gresham Sykes (1958) identified the "pains of imprisonment" experienced by inmates. He argued that prison structure inevitably takes away inmates' liberty, autonomy, and security. Additionally, prison residents are deprived of goods and services as well as any opportunity for heterosexual sex. These deprivations are not taken lightly since they represent freedoms and rights taken for granted in the outside world. Sykes's list of pains, although dated, accurately reflects the experience of juvenile inmates today. Incarcerated youth are unable to make decisions for themselves and fear for their safety in prison. Their loss of autonomy is so great that youth have to ask permission for anything outside their routine—including such mundane activities as using a restroom during an activity period. The bodies of young inmates are also monitored closely, further depriving them of autonomy. For example, incarcerated youth in Ohio move within the institution in single-file lines with their hands "checked" behind their backs. Allowable personal goods in the Ohio juvenile prisons are limited and highly regulated. There is even a specific limit placed on the number of photos a youth can have in his possession. Sykes saw these types of deprivations as important, not only in terms of the psychological health of the individual inmate but also as a major factor driving the shape of the inmate culture and social system.

Erving Goffman's work on total institutions (1961) adds depth to our understanding of punishment in prison. He describes a process of the "mortification of the self" in which inmates are stripped of their identities from the moment they walk through the door of the institution. Prisons accomplish this when they force inmates to give up any sign of individuality, requiring them to wear uniforms and cut their hair in one style. Policies that limit the amount of contact prisoners can have with their families and friends outside prison further remove them from their old selves. The experience of institutionalization, Goffman believes, causes inmates to experience a radical dismantling of their sense of self-worth. While many develop coping techniques, it is clear that the mortification of the self is experienced as a significant form of punishment.

As I describe in subsequent chapters, virtually all of the youth in this study hated prison and desperately wanted to get out. There is no doubt that they experienced their incarceration as a form of punishment. While I did not directly ask them what they found to be most difficult about life in prison, my impression was that they were most upset by their separation from their families. Joel Harvey's interviews with newly admitted youth in English prisons (2005) suggest that this impression is probably accurate. The youth in his study overwhelmingly told him that their major concern about prison was the separation from loved ones. As Sykes might predict, the youth's other concerns involved the loss of control, freedom, and security that a prison term entails.

Goal Three: Containment and Order

All prisons strive to maintain order and control in their facilities. Prior to the 1980s, one of the primary ways that adult prisons maintained control was through a tight hierarchical social system. Inmates trusted by the administration and staff were given a great deal of responsibility as well as special privileges. They became invested in controlling other inmates in order to maintain their privileged position. Ben Crouch and James Marquart's (1989) detailed description of the Texas prison system in the 1970s and 1980s makes it clear that this model can be fairly effective in maintaining control—although the Texas system was also violent and riddled with abuse. Juvenile prisons, probably because of the transient and immature population, have relied less on social hierarchy to maintain order. At the same time, elements of the system are in place in some juvenile prisons. In Ohio, for example, high-ranking youth are sometimes enlisted as "mentors" to younger residents. Mentors receive some very limited privileges when they help to guide other youth toward sanctioned behavior in the institution.

While I do not focus in this chapter on facilities and technology, both have a bearing on a prison's ability to maintain control. A report about conditions at the California Youth Authority, for example, pointed out that the architecture of the state's prisons served as a barrier to order (Krisberg, 2003).

The author commented that the facilities were antiquated and not designed with security in mind. This resulted in blind spots that made it impossible for staff to monitor all of the youth. The architecture of housing units is also important, as it appears to have a direct effect on levels of violence. Specifically, open dorms with a large number of beds are the most dangerous. The least violence occurs in facilities with single rooms, followed by those with double bunking (McCain, Cox, and Paulus, 1980; Krisberg, 2003). Finally, there is some evidence to suggest that less tangible elements of the prison environment are related to levels of violence and vandalism. Some of these elements include the institutional and sterile feel of the housing unit, and the level of control inmates have over their environment (Flynn, 1976; Suedfeld, 1980; Wener and Olsen, 1980).

While there is no question that architecture and technology can have an effect on the level of control in prison, some argue that too much attention is placed on these factors, especially in the immediate aftermath of a crisis like a race riot (DiIulio, 1987). Blaming architecture or technology for a crisis deflects attention from the more complicated issues of prison conditions, policies, or interpersonal management. It is also likely that other methods of control are equally (or more) important than architecture in maintaining day-to-day order. In the sections that follow, I explore these other methods, specifically the use of punishment and incentives, policies that discourage solidarity, staff-youth relationships, and legitimate authority.

Punishment and Incentives

Prisons rely heavily on systems of punishment and incentives to gain compliance from inmates. The two systems are related—punishment, however, focuses on bad behavior and usually involves inflicting pain or taking away something that brings pleasure, while incentives focus on good behavior and promise a reward when it occurs. Of course, the threat of punishment can serve as an incentive, just as a failure to achieve an incentive can feel like a punishment. Often the two are used together (the "carrot-and-stick" approach). Prisons are quite good at devising methods of punishment but are sometimes constrained in their use of incentives. For example, when political pressure takes away potential incentives—like weight rooms or cable television—the prison staff is forced to rely more heavily on punishment.

The most obvious and well-documented method of punishment in prison is violence. As reports from California and Texas indicate, violence remains a primary means of control in juvenile prison. These reports document cases of hitting, painful leg and arm restraints, and the use of chemical agents

(Krisberg, 2003; U.S. Department of Justice, 2008). I did not directly ask the youth in the Ohio study about guard violence because it was not my focus and because it could have jeopardized my access to the institutions. Including this type of question was also quite unnecessary given the amount we know about the topic. Although I steered away from directly asking youth these questions, they frequently talked about staff violence when they answered completely unrelated questions. All of the youth understood that violence is a real possibility and that even when actual violence is not employed, it hovers in the background as the social control mechanism of last resort.

Violence is not always necessary to maintain control, since prison staff have other methods of punishment at their disposal. A common method of control is isolating youth from the general population—either in a special dorm or in solitary confinement. These areas have many different official names, including "temporary detention" and "special management unit." Prison staff place youth who cause serious disciplinary problems into these units for a specified period of time. I visited one of these units in Washington State. It was a small windowless building with individual cell-like rooms and a small common area where youth eat. I was happy to get out of the building after only a few minutes, but youth can be held inside for up to thirty days.

Withholding objects—such as hygiene items, media, or types of food—can also be a powerful tool for order maintenance (Krisberg, 2003). For example, Ben Crewe (2006) discusses the behavioral effects of the introduction of in-cell television in Britain. Once the prisoners had television, the costs of misbehavior increased as the administration threatened to punish prisoners by taking it away. A different type of punishment involves embarrassment—in Ohio, youth who cause disciplinary problems are required to wear an orange jumpsuit. This makes them more visible to staff and also causes embarrassment, especially if the youth are forced to wear the jumpsuits during visiting hours.

Incentives, like punishments, are a common way to control behavior in juvenile institutions. Sometimes incentives are used on a small scale, when guards bribe individuals to maintain control—for example, they might bring fast food to work for lunch and, in violation of the rules, offer to share it with a select (often high-status) youth. The youth, in turn, might help them to maintain order (Cloward, 1960). Incentives can also be a larger-scale method of control when they are instituted systematically. The "level system" represents such use of incentives. In a level system, youth score points for good behavior. These points allow them to move up through a series of levels, with each higher level having more privileges associated with it. In Ohio, for example, youth can earn more phone calls as they move up levels. Once a youth has attained a new level, he does not want to be demoted. John Irwin (1980) points out that these level systems are effective in maintaining social control because they act as an incentive for youth to follow the rules while, at the same time, dividing inmates from each other and reducing the possibility of group resistance.

Juvenile systems also have a particularly potent "privilege" with which to modify youth behavior or attitudes. Because young people can be committed to the system until they reach a maximum age set by the state (twenty-one in Ohio), they are under constant threat of having extra time added to their minimum sentences if they engage in fighting or serious misbehavior. In other words, if a youth is fifteen years old and has a one-year minimum sentence, he could conceivably be held until his twenty-first birthday if he behaves badly. While behavior is the most important reason for holding youth past their minimum release dates, attitude is also factored in. Attitude is most directly examined during interactions in either group or private sessions with psychologists or social workers—designated experts who have substantial say in when youth are released. An extreme example of this is an intensive program in Texas that works with both male and female delinquents deemed at high risk of recidivism. In order to "pass" the program, the youth must engage in detailed and emotional self-revelation in front of social workers, psychologists, and other youth in the program. The ultimate goal is to have the group and the social worker or psychologist help the youth accept a new version of him- or herself—one that takes responsibility for past actions and has agency in shaping the future (Hubner, 2008). The program reports high levels of success (as measured by recidivism), but it employs extreme power over youth as they must retell their story until it is "properly" told and until they define themselves in the terms the program requires.

One of the problems with indeterminate sentences is that, as in Texas, youth can continue to accrue time because they do not exhibit what officials consider to be the proper attitude or because they do not seem to be rehabilitated or remorseful. Michel Foucault (1980) argues that this is exactly what makes modern-day power so insidious—it has the capability to reach into the very core of who people are. Prisoners are no longer required simply to refrain from violence and keep out of the guards' way; they must engage in self-revelation and actively work to define themselves in very specific ways. Sam and I talked about this when I expressed amazement at how much personal information he seemed to know about other youth. He told me that he learned all about his fellow prisoners in group therapy. It surprised me that the youth would reveal so much, but Sam said, "The kids that just sat there wouldn't get no points. Like kids during group, they just sit there, they get

no proof of participation, so it would be hard for them to go up [a level]."
Like Sam, all of the youth know that they must participate in group therapy
sessions in order to move up levels or to prove to a judge or the DYS that
they are ready to be released.

It is tempting to be critical of programs that demand youth to engage in
intense impression management (like the one in Texas described above). At
the same time, staff in those programs are deeply involved with the youth,
and there is good evidence to suggest that intensive behavioral programs can
reduce recidivism (see, for example, Inciardi, Martin, and Butzin, 2004). Because incarcerated youth face significant challenges in their lives outside the
prison walls, it makes sense that, for some, intensive intervention might be
necessary to overcome abusive pasts and destructive patterns. In the prison
world that has, for so long, been controlled through violence and an absence
of individualized attention, perhaps these programs represent forward movement. It is important to ask, however, whether there are cultural biases in the
behavioral and attitudinal standards. While not a lot of research has been
conducted on this question, it appears that different racial/ethnic groups may
express remorse in different ways or, for historical reasons, be less willing to
express remorse at all. For example, black adults are less likely than white
adults to plea bargain or "accept responsibility" for crimes (Everett and Nienstedt, 1999). It is likely that this is driven by a quite rational distrust of the
criminal justice system. Another important study (Bridges and Steen, 1998)
suggests that even when black juveniles do express remorse, it is less likely to
be read by officials as "real" because the officials see black crime as caused by
internal factors (such as a bad attitude). Officials are more likely to see white
crime as caused by external factors (such as a broken home). Therefore, they
tend to see blacks as being at high risk for committing future offenses.

There are other reasons for concern about using attitude as a measure of
rehabilitation. Prison is a controlled environment where it is fairly easy to
"fake" the proper attitudes because there are few true behavioral tests. For
example, incarcerated youth do not have their rehabilitative attitude tested
while they are out drunk at a party or when they need money to support a
drug habit. Most of the youth are smart enough to quickly figure out what
the proper attitude looks like. At the same time, youth who really have
changed their attitudes may not be willing to put on the "proper" act. As I
describe in the next chapter, the prison youth culture demands a tough and
masculine act that is opposite to the one the administration requires. Young
men who are genuinely committed to a new life on the outside may engage
in impression management that contradicts their new attitude, simply to
survive the institution.

Control through Division

One of the most frightening situations a prison guard can face is when a group of inmates refuse to cooperate or when they coordinate an attack on staff. This fear gives guards a vested interest in maintaining control by discouraging inmate solidarity. Of course, staff's fear of groups has a basis in reality—race riots and gang warfare have cost both staff and inmates their lives. Yet at the same time, in trying to prevent these extreme problems caused by groups of youth, staff discourage any kind of solidarity. One way they do this is by encouraging youth to "do their own time" and frequently reminding them that friendships with other youth can be risky. Other youth are portrayed as dangerous—as trouble just waiting to happen. Juvenile prisons are not alone in their attempts to convince inmates to stay away from others; this practice has been documented in adult prisons as well (Cloward, 1977). As I discuss in the next chapter, youth seem to agree with this message. Although they might not always abide by it, they talk frequently about the wisdom of doing time alone.

Another way staff discourage solidarity is to collectivize punishments for individual infractions. For example, youth in this study told me that if one person talked in line, the staff would force the whole line to stand up for a set period of time. The young men told me they hated this method of punishment—it is one of the things they saw as most unfair about the institution. This kind of group punishment is an effective social control method, however, as it encourages youth to police each other to avoid standing up. Anthony told me that he hated standing so much that he spent a good deal of time in line trying to convince other youth to be quiet. This type of group punishment is also effective because it prevents solidarity—the youth end up so angry at each other that they are unwilling to see others as potential allies. I asked Kyle whether he thought that group punishment was effective:

> KYLE: Uh-uh. . . . That's how come fights start up in here.
> ANNE: How come? Like what happens?
> KYLE: Just one kid will be talking and the other kids gotta tell him to shut up and then "I'm not gonna listen to you" and then another kid's yelling, "Yeah, you better shut the fuck up," and then there goes a fight.
> ANNE: So you don't think it helps discipline?
> KYLE: It just causes fights.

Freddie, like Kyle, told me that group punishment seemed to incite the very violence it attempted to stem. He thought, however, that this was a smart strategy for staff because it resulted in inmate-on-inmate rather than inmate-on-staff violence. Freddie and Kyle seemed to believe that group punishment allowed the staff to sanction the perpetrator of the original disturbance harshly (for fighting rather than talking) while decreasing solidarity that might lead to group violence against staff. Indeed, the desire to limit violence against staff may even be the cause in documented cases in California and other states of staff encouraging inmate-on-inmate violence (Krisberg, 2003).

Physical separation is another way that prison staff attempt to stem the possibility of group violence. The separation of rival gang members in California prisons is the most obvious example of this. Another example is when prisons separate inmates by race, ostensibly as a way to decrease institutional violence. Prior to the 1950s and 1960s, blacks and whites were often housed in entirely different facilities, particularly in the South. After that, facilities were integrated but housing was not. Sometimes blacks and whites lived in separate wings or dorms, while other times only room or cell assignments were segregated. A Supreme Court case in 1968 challenged these arrangements. *Lee v. Washington* specified that racial segregation in prison, like in society more generally, was not legal. An exception was made, however, for cases in which segregation was deemed necessary for "security, discipline, and good order" (*Lee v. Washington*, 334). It was this loophole that allowed prisons, until recently, to continue to racially segregate. In a 1997 survey of prison wardens at adult facilities, only half reported the existence of a state-level policy mandating racially integrated cells. Another 4 percent operated under a policy mandating racial segregation, and the remainder operated under a policy that allowed wardens to make their own decisions (Henderson et al., 2000, 302). Unfortunately, there is not comparable data for juvenile institutions, but it is unlikely that they are considerably different from adult institutions in their housing policies.

Whether racial segregation is actually effective in controlling the prison population and stemming race riots is a matter of some debate, but a good deal of research concludes that segregated housing does not decrease violence levels. In fact, some researchers believe that it may have exactly the opposite effect. James Robertson (2006), for example, argues that racial segregation sends the message to inmates that the races are hostile toward each other and that at least one group will do the other harm. A 2005 Supreme Court case echoed this argument. *Johnson v. California* was filed by an inmate objecting to California's policy of racially segregating cells during an inmate's intake process. The rationale for the policy, given by the state, was that gangs in California were race-based, and that the prison administration needed to keep potential rivals separated until they could determine which inmates were involved with gangs. In this case, California claimed to be using race as a proxy for gang affiliation. They failed, however, to prove that segregation prevented violence, and the Court ruled against them. *Johnson* is a particularly important case because it makes it much harder for prisons to claim that segregation is necessary—states must meet a strict test showing that violence is reduced through segregation. Otherwise, all prisons—juvenile and adult—must be desegregated. The Court's decision was based in part on the argument that desegregation might actually reduce racial violence since housing by race reinforces racial divisions.

Control through Relationships with Staff

An important element in the maintenance of order in prisons involves the relationships that develop between staff and the youth. As early as 1958, Sykes pointed out that inmates' numerical advantage makes it necessary for staff to engage in relationships of compromise and negotiation in order to maintain control. Anthony Bottoms (1999) comments, "The incidence of acts of interpersonal violence in prisons is influenced by the characteristics of inmates but also by aspects of the prison environment and by the continual dynamic interaction between prisoners, prison staff, and the physical and social context within which they are placed" (205). In this study, I was not able to ask youth directly about their relationships with staff because the DYS had not approved the topic. The subject came up frequently, however, in responses made to other questions.

The youth told me that in general they were wary of staff but felt close to at least one staff member (usually a social worker but sometimes a guard). The attitudes that the youth expressed toward the staff mirror those found in other recent studies of inmate-staff relationships. One study, for example, found that adult inmates in Britain liked some staff members and not others (Crewe, 2006). Another study found this to be true among youth incarcerated in Canadian correctional facilities (Peterson-Badali and Koegl, 2002). Similarly, the young men I spoke with refused to make generalizations about staff, preferring to speak of them as individuals. For example, Dion said, "Some staff, they treat you good. Some staff, they don't care nothing about you." Similarly, Tom commented, "Some of 'em cool, some of 'em just ignorant." Andrew talked at greater length about his feelings toward staff:

> Depends on how you are to them. Like if you want respect you better give
> them respect. They look at each other left and right so you can make sure
> you get extra time. Staff want you to get extra time, and some don't care

and there are some staff that do. There's one staff . . . he helps us out. He tries to understand, but he has his boundaries, like he could help you to a certain point. Like if one of us ask for early release he'll type that out and print it so you could have it in a respectful way. There's a couple nice staff, and there are some that just push you.

Andrew and the other youth clearly resisted the idea that guards were all alike. Interestingly, Crewe (2006) argues that this is a change from the past, when inmate solidarity led prisoners to see guards as an undifferentiated other.

Youth identified a number of factors that led them to dislike and distrust certain guards. Most common were complaints about staff members who engaged in favoritism by giving certain young men special privileges or turning a blind eye when they broke the rules. Similarly, youth did not like guards who were inconsistent in their application of the rules. When I asked Tom what "ignorant guards" did, he said,

> They let half the people use the phones and the rest gotta wait till tomorrow, know what I'm saying, but everybody suppose to use the phone on the same day. They just make half of 'em use it and then the rest of 'em use it tomorrow, and then when I ask to use it he'll say no, but then let some of them use it. He'll say no to the majority of us, and then like when the other people ask to use it, he'll let them get on.

The kind of favoritism and inconsistency Tom reported makes youth angry and resentful, and it causes them to become unwilling to obey a guard's orders. For example, Kirk (and several other young men in the same facility) told me about the increased level of fear in the institution when there was a particular staff member on duty. This guard had been working at the prison for several months but was inconsistent with discipline and had failed to develop positive relationships with any of the youth. Kirk said,

> He's reasonably new. He's been here a couple of months. But, I mean, he's not a rookie. He knows what's going on. But they won't listen to him at all. We've had fights. We've had code whites where people get like knocked unconscious in fights, their heads bashed in. We had a kid . . . he got punched and he just, he just went flat on the ground and had to call a code white. He started having seizures and throwing up. That's because nobody listened to the staff at all. . . . They won't do that when some staff's here. They just . . . they won't do it. You so see the difference

on the weekends [when that guard is working]. People will act up. People,
I mean, people just act stupid.

Kirk and other incarcerated youth understood the importance of good staff-
youth relationships in the maintenance of institutional order. When they respected and liked the guards, they were much more willing to comply with
orders. This made the institution a less unpredictable and more secure place
for everyone.

Control through Legitimacy

Ohio's juvenile prisons, at the time of this study, controlled youth primarily
through coercion and the manipulation of the reward system. A number of
researchers point out there are other possible routes to compliance in the
prison (Liebling, 2004; Sparks, Bottoms, and Hay, 1996). They argue that
people tend to comply with rules that they see as legitimate. Legitimacy is
based on the perceived fairness of the rules—when people think that the
rules are based on shared values, they are more likely to see them as legitimate. One of the reasons that the youth I talked to got so angry about group
punishment was that it violated the core American values of individual
choice and action. In order to control through legitimacy, a prison would
need to draw on shared values and convince inmates that the rules are just
and in their interest. The rules would also need to be applied in a consistent
way. As described in the previous section, the youth hated that prison rule
enforcement seemed arbitrary. For example, they reported that they were
sometimes allowed to keep more than the officially sanctioned number of
photos in their rooms and then suddenly, seemingly out of the blue, staff
would sweep through and remove them as "contraband." Enforcing these
kinds of policies erratically makes it impossible to achieve control through
legitimacy.

Creating legitimate control structures is a very difficult (some would say
impossible) task in a prison, where the power balance between youth and
staff is inherently skewed. At the same time, there are some examples where
it has been at least partially achieved. One such example is a unique program
that existed in the early 1990s in Arizona. In response to a lawsuit, Arizona
had to make dramatic changes in their juvenile correctional system. They began a special cottage that ran with relatively little violence and coercion. The
cottage inhabitants met together for group sessions several times a day and
worked with each other to develop their own goals—goals that were created
with an eye toward a successful transition to the outside world. Groups com-

posed of both staff and youth made decisions regarding what to do about disruptive behavior, and everyone was required to treat others with respect. The program was tremendously successful at first as the youth saw the rules as legitimate and were generally willing to follow them. Over time, however, funding and support for the program were reduced. The philosophy (and expense) of the program met with resistance from an administration concerned with efficiency, punitive public sentiments, and cost containment. It also became clear that some longtime staff could not accept the new philosophy. While the program was eventually dismantled, it stands as an example of the use of legitimacy to maintain order in a juvenile prison (Bortner and Williams, 1997).

Work from a series of studies in Massachusetts also suggests that legitimacy can be achieved, at least in limited ways. These studies were conducted in the late 1960s and early 1970s, when the state's juvenile corrections branch hired a new director who shut down the large training schools and moved to a system of small, therapeutic cottages. Craig McEwen (1978) studied these new cottages. He found a number of important organizational factors that seemed to influence perceptions of legitimacy. These included levels of equality (meaning the level of social distance between inmates and staff) and participation (how much influence youth had over organizational decision making). High levels of equality and participation were associated with youth showing more respect and less violence toward staff, and higher levels of self-esteem. Youth in high-participation and high-equality cottages were much more likely to feel empowered and to recognize the rules and policies set forth by staff as legitimate.

Conclusion

A number of prison researchers (Cressey, 1959; Sykes, 1958) have argued that the goals of prison are inevitably contradictory. In particular, they believe that the goals of order and rehabilitation lead prison staff in different directions. Efforts to control inmates result in repressive structures that work against treatment goals. Other researchers, however, have argued that it is quite possible—even necessary—for the two to go hand in hand. For example, John DiIulio (1987) argues that a secure and structured environment is a necessary prerequisite for effective treatment, noting that it is impossible to provide real education or therapy in an unsafe and chaotic environment.

Because the Massachusetts cottages of the 1970s were fairly free of central control, there was ample opportunity to study how rehabilitation, punishment, and order could be related in a prison setting. Barry Feld (1981) compared ten cottages across four different institutions. He found that whether a cottage was oriented more toward rehabilitation or punishment determined the kind of control exerted by staff. In custody-based cottages (in which youth were simply held with little access to programs) staff tended to rely on physical coercion, while in treatment-based cottages (which provided education and treatment) staff were more likely to negotiate with youth or to revoke privileges. This was partly because the staff in treatment cottages tended to see delinquency as a result of social forces rather than inherent deficiencies, allowing them to treat youth in a way that emphasized respect and the potential for change. Not incidentally, youth violence was also less prevalent in the treatment cottages.

What the Massachusetts experiment suggests is that rehabilitation and order are not inherently in conflict. In fact, rehabilitation appears to lead to order. It may be the case, however, that certain kinds of punishment (extreme levels of deprivation or lack of respect) may be in conflict with both order and rehabilitation. This does not mean that youth should be put in charge of running the institution; it simply suggests that, in small settings, it may be possible to set up environments of respect where inmates have a limited but real voice. This shift may lead to order and also to rehabilitation as making decisions, getting along with others, and treating others with respect are skills that will help youth in their lives outside prison.

Unfortunately, there is considerable evidence to suggest that today's prisons are not engaged sufficiently in rehabilitation and that treatment goals often take second place to the maintenance of order. Additionally, prisons are not strategically planning how to accomplish rehabilitation. Part of the reason may be the lack of conclusive research on the effectiveness of programs such as anger management and victim awareness. It is quite possible that these programs are having little—or no—effect on recidivism or on youth's quality of life. Prisons have limited budgets and need to choose the programs they fund carefully. What we do know is that high school education and substance abuse treatments help youth when effectively administered (Wilson, Gallagher, and MacKenzie, 2000; Petersilia, 2003). High school education is dramatically underfunded, however, and its quality is low. In addition, substance abuse programs do not reach all the youth who need them, and aftercare services need to be increased to maximize the benefits of the program.

In this chapter, I described a number of key aspects of the formal organization of juvenile prisons. This was a necessary prelude to the material that follows. In the next chapter, I turn to the informal organization of the prison—the social structure, status systems, and friendships of incarcerated youth. As researchers point out, the informal structure is driven, at least in part, by the formal organization of the institution (Berk, 1977; Feld, 1981; McEwen, 1978; DiIulio, 1987). The ways in which prisons attempt to achieve their goals of rehabilitation, order, and punishment provide the context in which the youth organize themselves inside the walls of the prison.

Chapter 4

Youth Culture on the Inside

The formal organization of a prison is important, but it provides only a limited picture of the daily lives of its residents. This chapter fills out that picture through an examination of the informal organization or "culture" of the institution. Culture is a major determinant of inmate behavior. It is influenced by prison structure and history, and by outside sources. It is also actively created by the youth living inside the walls. In the 1960s and 1970s an academic debate raged between those who thought that the prison culture reflected a reaction to the deprivations of the prison and those who thought it was imported from lower-class culture outside the prison (Cloward, 1977; Irwin and Cressey, 1977; Sykes and Messinger, 1960). Today, researchers recognize the importance of multiple influences in the creation and maintenance of a prison's culture. This complexity makes it impossible to discuss all aspects in one chapter. I focus, therefore, on the elements that the youth in this study identified as most important to their daily lives: social groups, social status, and friendship.

Solidarity and Social Groups

Donald Clemmer's book *The Prison Community* (1940) launched academic interest in social solidarity among prisoners. The resulting research, spanning some twenty years, suggested that there was considerable solidarity in adult prison, as inmates shared a code of conduct and an "us versus them" mentality against prison guards (Clemmer, 1940/1958; Sykes, 1958; Sykes and Messinger, 1960). While it is possible that the researchers who conducted these studies overlooked some signs of division (particularly racial division), their data revealed that inmates shared a certain degree of loyalty and camaraderie (Bosworth, 2009). More recent research suggests that there is significantly less solidarity in adult prisons today. This may be a result of an increase in the number of younger inmates and gang members, or it may be that there is more racial hostility in prison, serving as a barrier to group solidarity (Hunt et al., 1998; Owen, 1988). Other researchers think that decreased levels of deprivation in the prison may have reduced the need for inmate solidarity (Carroll, 1974; Jewkes, 2002). It is also possible that prison staff have developed new incentive systems that encourage inmates to do their time alone (Crewe, 2006).

While there is compelling evidence to suggest that solidarity has de-creased in adult prisons, it is unclear whether a similar trend has occurred in juvenile facilities. Few studies have examined social solidarity among juvenile inmates. From the research available, however, it appears that there has never been a high level of social solidarity in juvenile facilities, probably because the conditions are less conducive to the formation of a group identity than those in adult prisons. This may be due to a more transitory population (Gender and Players, 1989), but it may also have to do with the fact that juveniles are more likely to receive indeterminate sentences, encouraging them to limit contact with other incarcerated youth that might lead to trouble. My study, like others before it, found little evidence of a "prison community" in juvenile facilities. Instead, youth report that there are loose social groups with limited degrees of solidarity. These groups, described below, generally do not compel strict loyalty but do have a strong effect on institutional life.

Region

In Ohio juvenile prisons, the most important social groups are based on area codes. When a young man arrives at the DYS intake center, other youth im-mediately ask where he is from, and once this is ascertained, someone from his area usually approaches him to find out more about his neighborhood. In the prisons I visited, the largest area code groupings are Cleveland, Co-lumbus, Akron, and Dayton. Youth from smaller cities sometimes manage to establish and maintain their own groups, but because of low numbers they are usually forced to combine with the larger urban groups. Virtually every young man in this study emphasized the importance of the area code system in the prison culture. For example, Freddie said,

> This is how it is in here though—all Cleveland people hang out with each other. I mean they all clique up, like if you're cool with a certain person or something, then you're going to be cool with 'em. Like if this man's cool

with that kid and he's from Toledo, then all his Toledo boys is cool with him. He's from Cleveland and I'm from Cleveland, then I'm going to be cool with him and I'm going to be cool with his boys over there. If they got problems with those boys over there from Akron and . . . I don't know anybody from Akron and he don't know anyone from Akron, we're going to be messing around with them. We are going to have problems with them. That's how it is.

The area code groupings Freddie describes are fairly rigid, and a newly admitted youth is not usually able to lie about where he is from. He is questioned intensely about his school and friendship history, and if he refuses to divulge any personal information, other young men can ask a guard who has access to his files or they can steal his prison identification papers. I asked Charles what happens when a new youth from his area arrives. He said, "[We] just sit down and talk about stuff. I just start talking about people in my neighborhood and the other person will know the person in my neighborhood and then we start being cool." On a rare occasion, it is possible for a youth to switch code affiliations if he knows a lot of people from another area code or if he has cousins or other family members in the same prison who claim another affiliation. Kenneth, for example, managed to switch his affiliation from a small rural code to a large urban code because he knew a lot of people in the urban code.

Area codes are a useful group marker because they are obvious and can be quickly assessed. They are similar to "crowds" in social situations outside prison, such as high schools. In a review of the literature about crowds, Margaret Stone and Bradford Brown (1999) find that they serve a dual purpose: they provide a way for youth to quickly identify potential friends while also providing an identifier for themselves. Crowds allow for a safe group identity that does not ask people to reveal too much personal information. Finally, and perhaps most relevant for the prison situation, crowds give people a temporary identity while they figure out the more personal identity they would like to project. Coretta Phillips (2008) points out that regional affiliation is particularly meaningful to youth in prison because it gives them an outside identity (rather than an institutional identity) with which to define themselves. Area codes are also a rich form of group solidarity because they are based on shared spatial knowledge as well as common connections. Regional affiliation is not a peculiarity of the Ohio prison system—these types of alliances have been found in other U.S. prisons as well as in British prisons (Irwin, 2005; Phillips, 2008).

Gangs

Area code groups share some features with gangs and are sometimes identified as such by Ohio prison staff. Gangs and area codes are certainly linked—gangs outside prison are often regional, and consequently, area codes and gang territory overlap. In fact, the prison literature suggests that gangs sometimes emerge from area codes (the 415s in California's adult prisons are an example of this). The youth in this study, however, saw the two as distinct entities. They reported that what they regarded as true gangs were present but not prominent in the Ohio system. Freddie and I talked about gangs during an interview shortly after his release. He confirmed the presence of gang members but said that it was safer to claim an area code instead:

ANNE: Are there gangs in there?

FREDDIE: There's not gangs there. It's not gangs. It just people cling Cleveland to Cleveland, Columbus to Columbus.

ANNE: So there are no Bloods and Crips?

FREDDIE: Oh, you can find those. There is people that are in there that are Bloods and Crips but they don't say it 'cause you never know who is and who is not. So you might as well run with your city. And just keep it clean, you know?

Freddie's assessment of the weak presence of gangs in Ohio juvenile prisons was supported by the fact that only one incarcerated youth in the study reported serious gang involvement. The gangs that do exist in Ohio prisons appear to be street gangs that establish a presence in prison, not prison-specific gangs.

The reports of low levels of gang involvement in Ohio juvenile facilities contrasts with what is happening in other states—particularly in California, with its long history of gang activity inside juvenile prisons. For example, the rival gangs the Nortenos and Surenos originated in California Youth Authority facilities and continue to cause significant problems for staff as well as for other youth (Hunt et al., 1998). In a national survey of administrators at juvenile correctional facilities, nine out of ten reported that their centers were home to gang members (Curry, Howell, and Roush, 2000). About 45 percent of these facilities said that at least one-third of the incarcerated youth were gang members, while the other 55 percent reported lower membership rates (8). The authors of the survey discuss some of the problems caused by a strong gang presence in prison: gang members tend to be more dangerous and violent than other inmates, they more often attempt to "run" the facility, and they recruit others into their gangs. Strong-arm recruitment tactics result in nonaffiliated youth feeling threatened if they do not join.

While it is clear that gangs are very much present in juvenile prisons and can cause significant problems, some care should be taken when trying to quantify the issue. There is no agreed-upon definition of gangs, and authorities may have incentives (more funding or more staffing) to identify serious gang issues in prison. Additionally, the small amount of research on this issue may be inaccurate. In the survey of administrators mentioned above, for example, a significant proportion (about 20 percent) of gang-identified youth were classified as such based solely on observation by staff (Curry, Howell, and Roush, 2000, 11). This introduces a strongly subjective component to the definition of gang member. An additional 20 percent were identified based on self-report—a method that might lead to overreporting (because it's "cool" to be in a gang) or underreporting (because of fears of institutional sanction).

Race-Based Groups

The prison literature from the 1960s and 1970s identifies strong solidarity groups among black adults in prison (Carroll, 1974). These groups, prompted by the civil rights movement, began to make demands for equality within the prison walls. While racial solidarity still exists among imprisoned black adult prisoners today, it is weaker and less focused on achieving equality in prison policy (Irwin, 2005). Juvenile prisons have a somewhat different history. Research from the 1960s and 1970s indicates that solidarity was less common among incarcerated black juveniles than adults, and that juvenile groups were less focused on civil rights issues. At the same time, black youth exhibited somewhat more solidarity than whites (Bartollas, Miller, and Dinitz, 1976).

My study indicates that, in terms of racial solidarity, the situation in juvenile prisons today is much as it was in the 1960s and 1970s. Black youth do feel some amount of solidarity with each other, but it tends to be weak and become visible only when a white person does something that is perceived to be racist. When this happens, the blacks unite, using words or physical violence to punish the white youth. In less conflictual situations, black youth generally hang out together but do not feel a strong loyalty to the group. Chad even told me that he thought much of what passed for solidarity was simply talk: "Niggas always talking about we stick together and this and this, but they be the first ones trying to knock you. You know what I'm saying? Or bring you down when they on another level to get you on their level.

You know what I'm saying? 'Cause it's all about the mind thing. They want to bring you down to their level 'cause they feel bad about theirself." Chad's views are somewhat more extreme than those expressed by other black youth. A more common response was that racial solidarity does exist in prison but that it is very limited. At the same time, Chad's comments reflect the general level of distrust in the institution—a distrust that tends to override potential racial allegiances.

Unlike blacks, whites do not generally unite on the basis of race. In fact, some whites actively avoid solidarity as they try to curry favor with blacks and "act black" as a method of gaining status. Conclusions about racial solidarity should be drawn carefully, however, since race overlaps with other characteristics. For example, while gangs and area code groupings are theoretically interracial, in practice they tend to be fairly homogeneous due to residential segregation outside the prison (Massey and Denton, 1993). Ethan, who is white, told me that when he arrived in prison and told people where he was from, everyone laughed because all of the other youth from that area code were black. At the same time, racial solidarity is not the main point of area codes and gangs. The Aryan Brotherhood and other white supremacist gangs are an exception to this rule, but the young men in this study reported that these groups were not a significant force in their specific prisons. This is consistent with findings from other researchers who have identified strong black groups in prisons, but not white (Carroll, 1974; Pfefferbaum and Dishotsky, 1981; Irwin, 1980).

It is somewhat puzzling that incarcerated whites fail to form solidarity groups since many feel that they are an oppressed minority. Both juvenile and adult prisons in the United States house disproportionately large populations of African Americans and Latinos. In Ohio, this translates to prison populations that are about half white and half black. The perception of the youth, however, is that blacks hold a strong majority. Similarly, the youth believe that many more guards are black than white, although in actuality it is about half and half. The perception of a black majority causes both black and white youth to believe that blacks are at an advantage. For example, Ben, a white youth who was housed at the maximum-security prison, told me that it is easier to be black than white in the institution. When asked why, he responded, "'Cause most of the staff are black, and I believe that they, they favor 'em, not all the time but sometimes." Richard, a white youth, echoed Ben's sentiment when he said it was easier to be black "because most of the staff are colored people, and they let [black] people get by with a little bit more than what other people do."

It is beyond the scope of this study to explain why whites do not organize themselves against perceived discrimination. It is likely, however, that because whites are dominant in society, they are not used to the idea of race-based solidarity for themselves. As described, there is also little precedent for white solidarity groups in the transient juvenile prison population. Whites' predominant response to their unaccustomed minority position appears to be confusion rather than organization. Interestingly, a 1970s study of a black-majority juvenile prison found that whites responded in the same way—the authors commented that whites were "bewildered" and did not pursue group solidarity (Bartollas, Miller, and Dinitz, 1976).

Status

One of the best entrees into prison culture is through the status system. Status drives relationships, conversational topics, and behavior. The term "status" is difficult to define, however, and researchers have used it to refer to two distinctly different concepts. The first, status as sociometric popularity, refers to youth who are well liked by their peers. To measure it, researchers generally ask youth for a list of the peers they most like and dislike (Coie, Dodge, and Coppotelli, 1982; Cillessen and Mayeux, 2004; Parkhurst and Hopmeyer, 1998). A related but quite different concept is status as perceived popularity or social power. This term refers to youth who are well known, respected, and emulated. Youth in prison, unlike researchers, have no need to define status—they have a keen sense of what it is and a complex understanding of how it works. The youth in this study were quite clear that it is the social-power component of status, not likeability, that really matters in prison.

Status is a significant preoccupation in juvenile prisons, at least in part because adolescence is a developmental stage during which youth seek to define themselves. As they move through this important stage, they are granted little power or autonomy in society and, as a result, the opinions of others become paramount to their self-concept (Milner, 2004). The search for status among adolescents is intensified when they are in prison because there is so little of it to go around. Correctional institutions are set up to create a degrading experience with few chances to earn respect. In addition, prison draws disproportionately from groups of youth who have received little respect in their lives outside prison—those who are poor, who have had trouble in school, and who are not involved in mainstream activities. Prison becomes a status hotbed where the youth who most need opportunities for respect are trapped together in a place where respect is at a premium. As a result, these youth spend endless hours examining every nuance of how they are being treated in order to assess whether they are being given the proper respect. In a discussion about how he felt about the other youth in prison, Gabe talked about the quest for respect in prison: "I don't know. I just don't like 'em. You get on their bad side. You know. I've been in a lot of fights since I last seen you. Just, you know, just saying the wrong things and stuff. You disrespect somebody and he disrespects you. It's all about respect when you're locked up." Young men, like Gabe, who want respect while they are incarcerated have few officially sanctioned avenues through which to achieve it. Thus, the informal prison culture with its multiple routes to respect becomes the place where youth focus their energy.

The social group affiliations discussed above (area codes and gangs, specifically) provide one route to respect in prison. For example, some area codes have more status than others, and that status translates to the individuals who can claim an affiliation. The high-status codes tend to be those that have the largest representation in the institution, but certain area codes have also developed reputations that give them status. For example, youth from the 330 area code, which includes Akron and portions of Cleveland, are feared and respected because they have a reputation for being violent. In general, the urban area codes have the most violent reputations and therefore the most status. These group affiliations, however, are only one source of respect. In the pages that follow, I describe a number of individual-level criteria that the youth also see as important status markers.

Hegemonic Masculinity

Violence, misogyny, and homophobia are three key status markers in the prison environment. While they are seemingly separate, they are all linked through their connection to the construction of masculinity. As Robert Connell (1987) points out, there are many ways to demonstrate masculinity, but violence, misogyny, and homophobia are all part of what he calls "hegemonic masculinity." Hegemonic masculinity is the overriding cultural prescription for a successful gender display. In the United States, it includes violence, sports proficiency, homophobia, and sexual conquests of women. As ethnographies of elementary and high schools demonstrate, hegemonic masculinity is a pivotal concern for nonincarcerated males (Ferguson, 2001; Adler and Adler, 1998; Eder, 1995). Incarcerated young men, however, appear to cling to it even more tenaciously, probably because there is little room in prison for alternative masculinities to be expressed. All youth are forced to participate in the same extremely limited set of activities. Also, the residents in a juvenile facility are from diverse backgrounds and do not know each other well. It is easiest for them to use standards of hegemonic masculinity, which are known to all, to come to a common understanding of what masculinity means.

All the youth in this study concurred that violence (or a violent reputation) is the primary way to gain status in the prison. This finding is hardly a surprise—virtually all prison researchers find that violence is central to the prison society (see, for example, Santos, 2004; Hunt et al., 1998). Youth in prison have an opportunity to establish their violent reputation early on because almost all of them are tested within days of their arrival. This test usually comes in the form of one youth or a group of youth demanding a new arrival's meal (a practice known in Ohio as "taxing"). How the new person reacts to this challenge determines how he is viewed from then on. To be considered tough, a young man must take a stand and refuse to give up his food. This standoff frequently ends in a physical fight. If the new youth wins this fight decisively, he gains respect and status.

Violence may appear to be an "inside" status marker because it is often assessed by youth's behavior within the walls of the institution. Interestingly, however, violence is also measured by "outside" standards. The prison walls are highly permeable, and because prison draws many young men from the same neighborhoods, a youth's street reputation can be quickly evaluated. Often, there is someone in prison who knows what a new youth was like on the outside. If not, outside social networks can easily be accessed to determine a youth's street reputation ("my cousin lives in that neighborhood, I can ask him"). A criminal record can also serve as a proxy for violence. Youth who have been incarcerated before—particularly in the DYS system—are accorded high status. Some types of crimes are also considered higher status than others. Specifically, violent crimes such as assault and murder are seen as more prestigious than crimes such as low-level drug use or burglary. When asked who was popular in prison, Ben commented, "People with murder, felonious assault, gun charges, drug charges that they got caught with a bunch of crack or whatever." Sometimes youth with convictions for a relatively minor crime like burglary try to convince others that they are actually imprisoned for something else.

In part because of its association with status, violence is endemic in our nation's correctional facilities. For example, an investigation conducted at six California Youth Authority facilities found that there were an average of ten serious documented assaults per day (Krisberg, 2003). The report went on to say that while all youth were at risk of violence, certain categories of youth—including those perceived to be gay, sexual offenders, and those trying to exit gangs—were most often the target. Immature youth who insulted other youth, either accidentally or in order to provoke them, were also frequent victims.

The youth in Ohio prisons, like those in California, often engage in violence against immature youth who "run their mouths" (insult others and brag about themselves). These youth are easy targets because they are frequently young and small. Youth who are perceived to be gay, however, are the victims of even more intense harassment and violence. Striking out against these youth is a way to score "double" masculinity points for being both violent and (seemingly) heterosexual. Even in my Inside Outside criminology course, where the inside students were invested in putting their best selves forward, homophobic insults and references were common. I had a policy of pointing out racism, sexism, and homophobia in the class. Students became used to this and were willing to think about and discuss racism and sexism. The rejection of homosexuality was so absolute, however, that the inside students simply refused to engage in conversation about homophobia. Students who were normally serious and involved in class would go so far as to make faces at each other to show that they were not participating in the conversation. Even the appearance of tolerance for homosexuality was too dangerous a move in an environment where one's safety and status depends on a rigid show of masculinity.

Research suggests that the levels of homophobia in Ohio prisons are not unique. Youth who are gay (or perceived to be so) are frequently the targets of violence, rape, and verbal harassment (Krisberg, 2006; Peek, 2003). One reason that homophobia is so rampant in prisons is that staff implicitly encourage it when they refuse to intercede or when they "protect" the victim by segregating him or her in disciplinary units or in a unit designated for sex offenders (Feinstein et al., 2001). This "blame the victim" approach sends a message to the other youth that it is acceptable to abuse others on the basis of sexual orientation. Some guards even go so far as to actively participate in the harassment. In his second interview with me, Alex told me that while the guards were generally fair to him, they were quite different with youth who were perceived to be gay:

> Staff will just make fun of them, like, "you little faggot" or "you little faggot, you want to get beat up?" and all this other stuff. And . . . staff will be like, "I'll go and pay him six candy bars to beat you up. I'll betcha he'll do it." And all the staff will go, like, "I'll give somebody a candy bar that beat them up." Everybody be jumping up to do it. I mean, he won't, they won't give them a candy bar in front of nobody, but I'm sure it's being

done in there. Actually, I know for a fact it's being done in there pretty much.

Alex's description of homophobia is disturbing, particularly because gay, lesbian, bisexual, and transgender (GLBT) youth are overrepresented in juvenile prisons (Feinstein et al., 2001). This overrepresentation is primarily a result of the discrimination and prejudice GLBT youth experience in their homes, schools, and communities. For example, families sometimes reject these youth, putting them at high risk for homelessness. Homelessness is linked to incarceration through drug use and involvement in "survival" crimes like prostitution or theft. GLBT youth who do not have family support have difficulty hiring a lawyer when they are arrested, thereby increasing their odds of being sentenced to prison. Juvenile prisons also house a disproportionate number of GLBT youth because the peer harassment and societal disapproval they experience can lead to increased rates of mental health problems (like depression) and to drug use (Feinstein et al., 2001).

Misogyny, like violence and homophobia, is an aspect of hegemonic masculinity that is deeply rooted in the status system of the juvenile prison. This misogyny plays itself out in boastful tales about sexual escapades and in negative talk about women. Because the youth cannot engage in actual heterosexual conquests, they rely on stories of their past prowess to prove their masculinity. Tom told me that the number of conquests a youth can convincingly claim is an important element in status. He said, "There are always guys talking about sleeping with so many girls and stuff like that. They can get any girls. Just stuff. Half the stuff is not true, probably. But you'll never know." Sheer numbers of conquests are important, but youth seeking status also try to emphasize that the women they had sex with were sexual objects that they "did" or "fucked." David's comments highlight this:

> There'll be arguments over people saying, "Well, yeah, I know your girl on the outs." And then, you know, "Yeah, I fucked her. . . . I know your sister. She gave me head." And I mean, all kinds of stuff, and they'd be calling, or there would be people in there writing girls saying, hey, write me this nasty letter of things we're going to do and things we did. And they'd write back with these letters. And now he'll get to walk around with his letter bragging, like, "Hey, check this out. These are the kind of girls I got."

Caleb concurred that youth try to emphasize power over women in their stories. He said,

Call 'em bitches and stuff like that. Call 'em ho and all that. They'll say, "Yeah, I went over to my bitch's house." Put 'em down and call 'em names and stuff. Talk about 'em all the time. Tease each other. Like, "I've got this girl at home, she does everything I want." The other one will go like, "yeah," and start talking about it.

Caleb and David both recognized that dominance over women serves as a status marker—one that youth are so desperate to attain that sometimes they invent whole scenarios in order to show their control over women. Like the expression of homophobia, stories about past sexual involvement with females serve as a way for youth to demonstrate masculinity in two ways—dominance and heterosexuality.

Social Connections

The centrality of area codes in the prison social organization indicates how connected the youth's lives outside prison are to their lives inside. Social connections are another way that the outside world enters through the prison door. Youth examine each other's social connections to determine the number of people they know in common. Being acquainted with a lot of people on the outside is considered to be prestigious, so inmates try to claim as many friends, girlfriends, and family members as possible. These claims are verified by the amount of mail the youth gets. Mail is distributed by calling out the name of the recipient, so it becomes obvious over time who is more connected on the outside. I was talking with Kenneth about people who have low status in prison, and he said that these people would write to their connections outside and ask them to send mail. He continued, "It makes 'em look like they actually have people they associate with when they're out. That actually care about 'em. I mean, 'cause I did the same thing when I was at rehab. I'd write letters every day to people and beg 'em to write me back." Steven echoed Kenneth's remarks:

They have no support, basically. . . . Somebody's not even willing to write them a letter. You know. Take ten minutes out of their day to write them a letter. You know. To ask them how they are doing or something. . . . They write letters and they write letters and they write letters but nobody sends letters back. Nobody accepts their phone calls and stuff. This kind of tells you something.

Caleb was also very clear about why letters can give a youth more status: "When you don't get none, . . . nobody cares about you. When you get more, they think, 'Well, this dude . . . he's awesome. He gets all kinds of people writing him. People must like him.'"

These quotes indicate that simply having a lot of social connections can grant a youth status, but other young men pointed out that some connections bestow more status than others. Since prisons tend to draw from the same impoverished areas, there is a lot of overlap in the connections the youth have. For example, one young man's best friend might hang out with another's cousin. Incarcerated youth spend hours figuring out these common ties. While this game is fun, it is also somewhat dangerous, for it can lead to unwelcome discoveries. Joseph told me that while seeking common connections, his roommate and another youth had discovered that, unbeknownst to each other, they had simultaneously dated the same woman. Typically, however, connections serve to strengthen a youth's status in the institution, especially if he shares ties with high-status youth.

Not surprisingly, youth who are connected to a lot of young women—as measured by the amount of mail they receive from them—are granted particularly high status, especially if the girls are good-looking and include photos with their letters. This status marker intersects with masculinity because it is one way to prove heterosexuality and dominance over women. If a young woman is willing to take the time to write, it is assumed that the youth receiving the letter must have some control over her. Some youth are so desperate to receive letters from girls that they try to convince others to give or sell them girls' names and addresses. I asked Nelson if he had ever heard of this practice. He said it was common and that he had engaged in it himself:

> Dude be writing his own girl. This other dude be like, "She got a sister or something?" And then, "Let me write her." I'm supposed to be getting, probably tomorrow, [a letter] from this one girl. But basically you wanna just ask the dude, "Dude, you got a sister that I can write?" But mostly dudes don't be naming their sisters. They let you write one of his sister's friends probably.

By trying to get more women to write to him, Nelson was attempting to gain status. Of course, this is not the only—or even necessarily the most important—motive youth have for seeking outside contact. The strong link between social connections and status, however, is one factor that encourages youth to claim as many friends, girlfriends, and acquaintances as possible.

Possessions and Class

Like outside social connections, outside possessions can bestow status on an incarcerated young man. The youth spend a great deal of time discussing the clothes, stereo equipment, or cars they own. Ownership is obviously hard to verify from prison, so some youth have a family member send pictures of their possessions. For example, I was conducting an interview with Darius in a restaurant in his hometown. It was a fairly casual interview, and at some point we started chatting about his new girlfriend—a young woman he described as extremely good looking. To show me, he took out a brand new cell phone that had the ability to take photographs. I watched over his shoulder as he scanned through the photos stored in the phone's memory. To my surprise, I saw several photos of his shoes. I immediately asked him why he would keep photographs of tennis shoes. He laughed and told me that it was in case he got locked up again—he wanted proof that he owned them. He planned to ask his mother to print the pictures and send them in the mail.

One might think that given the emphasis on material possessions, those youth of middle- or upper-class origins would be accorded high positions in the prison hierarchy. Ethnographies conducted in some middle and high schools certainly suggest that upper-class youth do better in terms of status (Eder, 1995), but this is not the case in prison. Because a primary goal is to appear to be "street" or to be a "gangsta," youth do not want people to think they are from middle- or upper-class families. These classes are not seen as tough or masculine; instead, they are associated with weakness and femininity. What a young man wants instead is to appear to be from poor origins but to own a lot of expensive things. This implies that he has a large stream of income, from either legal or illegal sources (the latter usually related to the drug trade).

Youth spend endless hours talking about their outside possessions, but they are also interested in what they have in prison. As Gresham Sykes (1958) points out, one of the pains of imprisonment is the lack of personal property in prison. He and others have noted that this opens the door for a black market to develop. This is certainly true at the juvenile level; there is an active market for both goods and services. Youth who have access to desired goods (identified as "merchants" or "peddlers" in Sykes and Messinger's 1960 work) are admired and given protection. Hot commodities include Irish Spring soap, chewing tobacco, pornography, drugs, and extra food. Peddlers, however, can get quite creative with what they sell. Kenneth, for example, had a talent for artwork and was particularly good at drawing a woman's face from a photograph and attaching a naked body to it. He quickly rose to the top of the status hierarchy.

Having money in a prison account allows youth to buy some desirable goods such as brand-name soap from the institution's store. Another way to obtain goods and privileges is through the guards. Youth who are particularly adept at getting what they want from guards are said to have "clout." These youth are ranked high on the prison status hierarchy, and people want to have a good relationship with them. Guards will sometimes share outside food with favored youth or allow them special privileges. In response to my question about popularity, Ben told me,

> I don't know, some youth will get popular because of staff. Like, they can tell the staff to do anything. "Let me out [of my room]," "Let me use your whatever." All right, then the kid down the hallway wants to come out. "No, you ain't coming out." They call it clout, like, some kids have more clout than others. Like, staff will bring in dip or whatever, staff will bring in something for those youth or whatever.

As described in the previous chapter, guards engage in this informal privilege system to help maintain order. Most of the youth, however, do not seem to perceive it as a system of control. They tend to admire youth who have clout for having manipulative skills. At the same time, not every type of clout is equally admired. Joseph explained, "It depends on how you use it though, 'cause some people in here got clout and they be snitching on everybody. You know what I'm saying? . . . And you got some with clout that are real cool with everybody." Youth who get their clout through snitching may get food or privileges from guards, but they do not gain status. By contrast, youth who charm their way into the guards' good graces gain respect. What might be perceived as "kissing up" on the outside is seen in prison as a clever way to get scarce goods.

Race

> It is more socially acceptable to be [black]. . . . everybody wants to be dominant, everyone wants to be urban, urban has to be black. Basically, everyone just wants to have that kind of attitude. It is attitude.
>   —Freddie

> If you can be cool with the blacks, it means you're cool irregardless.
>   —Jake

Race is important in prison because of its potential to lead to both group solidarity and hostility. It is also important because it is deeply ingrained in the status system of the prison, at least indirectly. The most admired incarcerated young men are those who appear to uphold the ethos and lifestyle of the violent "gangsta." This image is not raceless—it is decidedly black. Black males are seen as violent, tough, and masculine, while white males are portrayed as being weak. The image of the black male is further enhanced by its association with urbanity (Ramos-Zayas, 2007). Indeed, it is the inner-city young black male who provides the template for the high-status youth in prison.

Patricia Hill Collins (2006) points out that the popular image of the black urban gangster is highly problematic because it sells products for a few (usually white) businesspeople while the lives of real black men are limited by the cultural notions of them as violent and hypermasculine. In the prison context, the gangster stereotype is similarly problematic. At first, it appears to be advantageous to blacks because it gives them an edge in convincing other youth that their tough act is true—allowing them a greater measure of safety. In the long run, however, it results in a circular situation in which black youth act out the stereotypes, thus reinforcing them. Ironically, the white youth act essentially the same way as the blacks, but their act is less likely to be believed since whites are generally characterized as the opposite of blacks—weak and passive. Below is part of a discussion I had with Ben, a white youth, about his interactions with black inmates: "They'd just pick on white people 'cause, like, they think we're soft or whatever. That's where most of my fights come from. That's about where ten of my fights came from, was black people running their mouth thinking I'm soft. 'Oh you white boy, you ain't gonna do nothing.'" Ben and other white youth told me that being characterized as "soft" caused them to fight more and to work especially hard to appear tough. It also increased their perception that they were being discriminated against in prison.

Youth reported engaging in two different strategies to get around the stigma of being white. One strategy simply involved denying that they were fully white. Here is an excerpt from an interview with Caleb, a white youth:

CALEB: There's a lot of racist stuff down at this place. And people, like, they're white and they say, "Oh, I'm not white." 'Cause they're afraid of the other black people down here for them to criticize 'em so they'll say they're something else.

ANNE: Like what?

CALEB: Like Indian and stuff like that. And Italian and stuff like that. And it kinda makes me mad, too, because they need to be who they are instead of trying to be somebody else.

Twice during his interviews with me, Kenneth mentioned that he had "black family." When I finally pushed him on the point, he admitted that the black relative was related to him by marriage, not blood. It was clear, however, that he normally omitted this detail from his story, hoping that the other youth would assume he had some amount of "black blood." Another youth, Frank, did not exactly claim to be black in his interview with me, but he implied it: "I grew up around a whole bunch of black people. I was raised by a black family for real so it's in my blood. That's the way I look at it." Although Frank technically grew up with his white single mother, he used a close family friend as a way to claim a black family.

The attempt to gain status by denying one's whiteness is a risky strategy because it is fairly easy to disprove. Prison identification papers list a youth's race, and the permeable prison walls allow other youth to access community networks to find out whether somebody really has "black family." For this reason, few white youth attempt to deny their race—a much more common strategy to gain status involves "acting black." When asked to define what this term means, the youth told me that it has mostly to do with slang. There are certain terms associated with African Americans, and if a white person uses them, he is considered to be acting black. Some youth also said that acting black involves claims about having grown up around blacks or being "down with" blacks. Caleb, the white youth quoted above, told me that many whites in the prison try this strategy: "They try to do slang words like black people do. They'll say they got all kinds of stuff like black people do. Like they got all these different outfits and everything. And they just say that 'cause they want to fit in with everybody." Interestingly, Phillips's research (2008) indicates that acting black is also a way to gain status in British youth facilities.

When I first talked with the youth about acting black, I assumed it would be a problematic strategy as blacks and other whites would see these youth as fakes. Frequently, this did turn out to be the case, but it seemed only to bother the whites. Most of the blacks I spoke with shrugged it off or seemed to think that it was a compliment that whites would try to fit in with them. They recognized that the whites were acting, but because they felt powerful in the prison culture, it was easier to find the phenomenon funny. The whites, who were struggling for power, were much more critical of the practice. Here is Ben (a white youth) talking about his opinion of acting black:

I ain't racist, it's just, white people try to, well, most of the white kids in here try to be black. And it's funny because you're just looking at them and you just know that they're not that type, it's not them, you know. It's just not them, for them to sit there and act like that. "Oh, I carried guns on the outs." I'm not saying this just because, oh, most black people do that, it's just, I don't know.

Ben's quote is interesting for several reasons. First, he reinforces the stereotype of blacks as "real" gangsters when he suggests that black people really do carry guns but whites just claim to do so. The quote also illustrates his contempt for people who lie about who they really are. Although I do not have clear evidence for this, I suspect that acting black is particularly upsetting to Ben and other white youth because it seems to suggest that being white is inferior to being black.

Acting black as a way to get status is not unique to juvenile prisons—it has also been reported in high schools. For example, in a 1999 study of a midwestern middle and high school, researchers found that one of the seven identifiable crowds was the "wanna-be blacks." These youth were from a variety of ethnicities and adopted black mannerisms, slang, and dress. As in prison, this strategy had only mixed success: while the authors report that the youth met with "varying degrees of acceptance from the black crowd," their crowd tended to be looked down on by whites (Stone and Bradford, 1999, 9). Similarly, my study and Phillips's work in Britain (2008) suggest that acting black in prison can gain youth a limited degree of status among blacks but that it sometimes results in a status loss among other whites. Because blacks are perceived to be the most socially powerful, however, some whites find the status gain to be worth the cost.

Friendship in Juvenile Prison

Even a cursory reading of the prison literature suggests that friendship in prison is rare and tends to be weak. Erving Goffman, in his work on institutional life (1961), found that friendships were possible but were usually limited by the institutional structure and by the staff's fear that friendships might be the basis for disruptive activities. Research conducted since then has provided some significant support for his conclusions. For example, a 1976 study with juvenile inmates indicated that while there was a clear social structure in the prison, there was little room for friendship (Bartollas, Miller, and Dinitz, 1976). Instead, the prison was structured as a network of roles that served to exploit the weakest in the prison for the benefit of the few at the top of the power structure. While another study did find evidence of adult friendships in prisons in Canada, these friendships were usually transitory and superficial (Zamble and Porporino, 1988).

At the beginning of my research, the interviews appeared to confirm that few youth in prison form deep friendships. The youth were quite adamant that they planned to avoid others as much as possible and do their time alone. When I asked why, the most common response was that the other youth in the institution were not suitable friends, primarily because they could not be trusted. Doug told me, "You can't really have friends in here 'cause the people you think you're friends with, they will go stealing your stuff, so I don't really have any friends. I've got certain people that I talk to and certain people that I don't. I got like one friend but I know him from the outs and I know he wouldn't do anything like that." Marcus made a similar comment about the other youth in the institution: "I see a couple that's headed for the good but most of 'em they still gotta a long way to go. A long way to go." Other youth described their fellow residents as being liars, stupid, and violent. These sentiments echo those expressed by prisoners in other studies. For example, respondents in one study of a maximum security prison said that other prisoners were "superficial" and "unhelpful" (Toch, 1992, 79). Similarly, the adults in another study repeatedly insisted that they were "not like those other guys" (Zamble and Porporino, 1988).

While distrust of others was the primary reason given for avoiding friendship, youth also felt that there was little point in investing time in a friendship that would not last past their stay in prison. Richard, for example, said, "The way I look at it, if you're not gonna see this person again why try to make friends with them? Just while you're there at your stay? But there is no point of making friends while you're there because you won't see them when you get out." Nick also thought that it was not worth his time to make friends. He, like a number of others, felt that his time in prison should be focused exclusively on finding ways to get out and that friendship would only serve as a distraction. Nick said, "Well, I don't really got no friends here. I mean, I don't got no friends here. I'm just here to do whatever I need to do. I ain't here to make friends or anything."

Ben Crewe (2006) points out that indeterminate sentences—like those being served by the youth I interviewed—serve as a disincentive for friendship formation. His study of British adult prisons concluded that the implementation of programs reducing sentences for good behavior made it rational to limit emotional ties that might require rule breaking. The youth in my study were aware of this potential liability of friendship. They told me that friends might be able to pull them into fights or other illegal activities, resulting in extra time being added to their sentences. As described in the previous chapter, the institution reinforces this idea. From the time the young men walk through the door at orientation, prison staff stress the idea that the best way to get out of prison is to get involved with as few people as possible.

It is clear, from the research cited and from this study, that most youth do not enter prison with the intention of making friends. Getting to know this study's participants over time, however, gave me the opportunity to see whether they followed through on their plans. Early in the second round of interviewing, indications began to emerge that doing time alone was not easy. Alex, for example, spoke at length about how he tried and failed to refrain from friendships:

> It's just hard, because, I mean, when I went in there I tried to keep to myself, but you just get so lonely that, oh my God, I just want someone to talk to. You just, you get so lonely, that's why I had just one friend in there and that was that kid, Mick. I talked to him every day. Every day at lunch, I talked to him every day. That's the only person I really communicated with besides staff. I don't know. It just, it got me through my time faster.

As it turned out, Alex was not alone—many youth in this study ended up making friends with one or two carefully selected prison residents. The most common pattern was for a young man to pursue a friendship with a person he knew before he was locked up, like a friend from the neighborhood, or someone known through connections or by reputation. This method of selecting friends is a wise choice given the strength of the area code social system. Under this system, youth from the same area code encourage (or sometimes force) each other to confine associations to within the group. Jake commented, "You ain't really got no friends really, but like if they are friends, they're friends from when they were on the outs. But we only chill with people that's from like Cincinnati, Columbus, wherever you're from. That's about the only way."

The area code system is one important reason youth prefer friends with whom they have previous connections. A second reason is that prior associations allow youth to assess whether potential friends are acting out their "true selves." Because everyone in prison understands the rigorous impression management requirements imposed by the informal culture, it becomes hard to trust that anyone's act is real. In other words, if a youth knows that he is being forced to put on an act himself, he has good reason to believe that everyone else is too. Having known someone prior to prison provides some protection from duplicity as it enables a comparison of the potential friend's prison self to his outside-world self.

Given the youth's distrust of others they meet in prison, it is somewhat surprising that a few of the youth in this study told me that the friendships they forged with "prior connections" were actually made with people they had met in the DYS intake center. Jeremy said,

> When I was in Scioto, I met these kids, Trevor and Adam. We were real good. We got to be real good friends and always hung around in Scioto. I came here and they both in my unit. So yeah, I was happy about that. And there is this other kid I know, kinda know, from the outside. I've only seen him like once or twice. So now I talk to him too. Besides that, I kinda stay to myself.

Like Jeremy, Gabe also made friends with someone he knew from the intake center. He said, "I talk to some kids, but I don't make friends here. . . . But I have one friend that I was in Scioto with. He was in my unit. . . . He left though." As described in Chapter 2, the intake center differs from a permanent placement institution because its population is extremely transitory. This transience may result in fewer pre-set social groupings and somewhat less pressure to put on an act. The youth seem to trust others who entered intake with them more than they trust youth they meet in their permanent placements. If nothing else, a youth from intake is an appealing friend because he represents a familiar face in a new and frightening environment.

While friendships are most common among youth with prior connections, there are certain circumstances that appear to foster friendship among strangers. Several of the youth told me that Bible study was a safe space because it brought together others who shared their interests and values. When I asked Kevin whether he had made friends in the institution he said, "There was one youth there that . . . actually there were a couple of them . . . one of them I talked to almost every day while I was there. And the other one I met at Bible study one time and me and him was walking around one day talking about the Bible and religious stuff. He said he needed some spiritual support." Other youth told me that Bible study was one of the few places where they felt free to "really talk" and that friendships formed there had the potential to be genuine.

In addition to Bible study, housing arrangements provided another possible avenue for friendship. The two prisons in this study had different sleeping arrangements. In the maximum-security facility, residents slept two to a room. In the medium-security facility, fifty residents slept in one large room filled with bunk beds. There were clear differences in the two groups' propensity to make friends. Specifically, youth in the facility with semi-private rooms were more likely than those in the communal bunkroom to report making friends. Being together in a separate room provided the opportunity for a youth to come to know his roommate well enough to consider him a friend. For example, Nick talked about his roommate with great enthusiasm. I asked him what they talked about and he said, "As far as just talking we, you know what I'm saying, down in our rooms, sharing conversations. Talking about what he gonna do when he go home. I talk about what I'm gonna do when I go home. Mutual." During the third round of interviewing, I asked Frank whether he had made any friends in the institution. He said, "Well just one—my bunk mate. . . . We just talking every day. . . . He reminds me so much like my cousin or something." The tendency to make friends with a roommate obviously has something to do with proximity (see Slosar, 1978, on effects of proximity on friendships in prison), but it also has to do with the relative privacy a shared room affords.

Friendship does take place in juvenile prison, but it happens around the edges—between roommates, in Bible study class, or between youth with outside connections. Because impression management requirements force youth to maintain the image of heterosexuality, friendships are often kept private or made to appear to be very casual. When friendships cross regional or gang lines, youth have a double incentive to keep them quiet. Even with all these restrictions, however, many youth do forge friendships. These friends are important because they can provide some amount of support and companionship in a lonely place.

Conclusion

This chapter examined three aspects of the informal culture of the juvenile prison: social groups, status hierarchies, and friendships. Although I discussed them separately, it is clear that these areas are closely linked. For example, youth make friendship choices based partly on status concerns and partly on social group considerations. In addition, a young man's level of status is related to his social groups and friends. Navigating the complexity of this informal culture requires constant vigilance and is, as a result, emotionally exhausting for incarcerated youth. Those young men who want to achieve status or personal safety are required to act out negative stereotypes, reinforcing the idea that they are hardened gangsters, not youth who might be amenable to rehabilitation. Often, following the dictates of the informal culture results in write-ups, staff animosity, and extra time added to their sentence. This is particularly problematic for black youth, who, because of racist stereotypes, put on the most convincing tough-guy act. The requirements of the informal culture also contribute to a low level of trust between youth, as the youth have a hard time believing that anyone's presentation of self is real. Friendships become rare and private in an environment where trust is low and homophobia fierce.

In the next chapter, I turn away from an exclusive focus on life inside prison and investigate the relationships incarcerated youth maintain with family and friends. Such connections potentially offer a respite from the demands of the prison culture, but they also impose a different set of pressures on the youth.

Chapter 5

Contact with the Outside

Prison walls are a highly visible symbol marking the physical boundaries of inmates' worlds. These seemingly solid walls, however, turn out to be extremely permeable as incarcerated youth watch television, communicate with friends and family, and interrogate new arrivals for information about what is happening in their neighborhoods. This permeability enables youth to devote a great deal of their energy and attention to life outside the walls. This outside focus is tempting because, as many told me, "real life" is with their families and friends. At the same time, life inside the prison demands their attention as youth are forced to negotiate requirements of the formal and informal systems. The incarcerated youth have to decide how much of their energy will go into matters of the outside world and how much will be saved for life inside. A few choose to cut off any contact because they see the world outside as out of their control. Other youth, however, are not as concerned about their lack of direct control. These young men spend most of their free time writing letters, calling family and friends, and thinking about their "real" life outside.

The decision about whether to focus inside or outside the walls has important consequences for incarcerated young men. Focusing exclusively inward, for example, can lead to what the youth call "institutionalization." In our second interview, Colby announced proudly that he had not become institutionalized. I asked him what he meant by the term and he said,

> I don't know. It's like, say, like the way we move around—like when you going to dinner or we going to the gym or whatever and staff be like "about face" and sometime I be like forgetting the way to turn 'cause, you know what I'm saying, I'm not used to it. Some people they go right to it. Boy, they act like an inmate. [They say,] "What time are we eating?" . . . asks the staff . . . and the youth would be going all over the schedule. It be like a jail battalion unit—like an incarcerated world.

Colby saw institutionalization as getting comfortable with the prison routine and becoming totally invested in the "incarcerated world." Other youth commented that institutionalized youth have no focus on the future and are willing to risk extra prison time to climb to the top of the status system. This phenomenon of institutionalization is not unique to the juvenile prison—Donald Clemmer most famously identified it in adult prisons in the 1930s. In his words, inmates become "prisonized" as they adopt "the folkways, mores, customs, and general culture of the penitentiary" (1940/1958, 299).

Clemmer believed that too much focus inside prison had negative consequences, especially when inmates try to transition back into their communities. At the same time, placing too much concentration outside can also be problematic. Those youth whose primary reality is outside prison desperately seek attention and information from their families, friends, and old neighborhoods. When outside people disappear or give them little attention, it can be devastating. This chapter looks at the issue of outside contact through an examination of the amount and kind of contact youth have with their families, friends, and girlfriends. Because their contact is largely determined by institutional policies, I include a discussion of the rules regarding visitation, mail, and phone calls. The second part of the chapter looks at how youth's outside contact changes over the course of their prison sentence. Finally, I draw from the interviews I conducted with the families of incarcerated youth to describe their experience of contact and incarceration.

Visitation

Visitation is important to incarcerated youth because it is the most intimate way for them to connect with their families. Most would love to have visitors come every week and are disappointed when their families miss opportunities to visit. Prison policies can facilitate a family's ability to visit, or they can present serious challenges. While all juvenile correctional institutions in the United States allow some type of visitation, specific policies vary by state, institution, and sometimes by the behavioral level of the youth. These policies have an impact on both the ability and the desire of families to come to the prison.

All visits to juvenile correctional facilities in Ohio start off at a security checkpoint in the front lobby of the building. Visitors are required to show identification and pass through a metal detector. To speed up this security process, visitors are not allowed to wear coats or bring in bags. Guards stationed at the front desk check everyone's clothing to make sure that it meets the institution's dress code. This dress code prohibits items of clothing like shorts and sheer blouses; it also bans clothing that might be gang related. Visitors who fail to meet these requirements are asked to leave unless they can obtain a change of clothing. At the maximum-security facility in Ohio, the nearby Wal-Mart is an inexpensive source for replacement clothes. Such a convenient outlet, however, is unusual. Many prisons are located in rural or isolated areas and lack options for purchasing appropriate clothing.

Once visitors clear security, they are allowed to go to the visiting room in the main part of the facility. The visiting areas at DYS institutions are a lot like high school cafeterias. They have the same tables, vending machines, and even the same institutional (fried) food smell. Visitors can sit with the youth in this room or, during the warmer months, go outside to a patio area. During visiting hours, people talk and eat food from the vending machines. Although there is nothing particularly remarkable in the vending machines, they take on a special importance to youth and parents. Visitors cannot bring in outside food, and parents who want to do something for their sons bring lots of coins for the machines. I talked with one mother about visiting hours. She started to cry as she told me that the last time she had been to see her son, the vending machines had been broken and she was not able to purchase food. Because buying food was one of the few things she felt able to do for her son, it came as a terrible disappointment.

The conditions of visitation are in some ways extremely conducive to connecting with family members and rebuilding relationships. Families are forced to sit together for an extended period of time (up to three hours), during which the intense interaction can lead to better and closer bonds. Yet visiting hours also have the potential to be awkward and difficult. One reason is that the visiting room is noisy and crowded, and youth are sometimes distracted by other conversations in the room. Their distraction is understandable, as personal information about other youth can be valuable for improving one's position in the status system. Additionally, although the length of the visit can be beneficial in some cases, in others it leads to awkwardness as people run out of conversational topics. Caleb described how visits with his mother started off well but then became strained. He said, "You talk like for the first hour and a half, two hours, and then you run out of stuff to say."

All juvenile prisons have specific rules regarding who is allowed into visiting hours. Every facility in the DYS system, for example, admits parents and legal guardians, and most also allow adult siblings, grandparents, or other members of a youth's "immediate family." Scioto (the intake center) has a different policy, allowing parents and legal guardians visitation by appointment only. Because children are not allowed at visiting hours, incarcerated youth are not able to see their own children or their younger brothers and sisters. This rule is problematic for parents with young children because it requires them to find a babysitter while they are visiting the prison. Incarcerated youth also dislike the policy because it causes them to miss long periods of their children's and siblings' lives. Matthew, for example, was extremely close to his thirteen-year-old brother. When I asked him how his brother was doing, he said,

> Well, me and my brother are like . . . he's like my best friend. We've done almost everything together, and I can tell when I talk to him and he's just ready to start crying and stuff 'cause I'm not there to see what's going on. I'm not seeing him grow up . . . and not seeing him go through high school 'cause I'm in this facility. And . . . it's just hard to talk to him on the phone. . . . He probably got a whole bunch of questions and stuff. And I don't know how to help him.

The DYS recognizes that the rule banning children from visiting hours is difficult for youth like Matthew. For this reason, they do allow social workers to arrange special visiting privileges for well-behaved youth. Other states have approached the problem more directly and permit children to attend regularly scheduled visitation hours. In Alaska, for example, incarcerated youth can receive visits from their younger siblings (Alaska Division of Juvenile Justice, 2009). Residents of Arizona juvenile facilities are allowed, with staff approval, to see parents, guardians, grandparents, aunts, uncles, siblings, and "other people who are significant" to the youth (Arizona Department of Juvenile Corrections, 2009). California has a particularly open policy allowing both a youth's own children and his younger siblings to come to the prison. As I described in *Fatherhood Arrested* (2002), these visits are important to fathers who are trying to establish or maintain a bond with their children. At the same time, visiting with children can be difficult because all visitors, including children, must remain seated at tables for the duration of the visit. Any parent who has struggled to make a two-year-old sit still understands the difficulties involved in this policy. Incarcerated youth, who often do not know their children well, become particularly frustrated and angry when their children refuse to remain still.

The kind of flexible visiting policy in California's juvenile prisons is helpful for youth trying to maintain contact with their children and with other members of their families. This policy, however, can also lead to problems when unfortunate combinations of people come to visit a youth on the same day. For example, an incarcerated youth in California can put one "girlfriend or wife" on his visiting list. It can be awkward when the girlfriend arrives at prison to find the youth's mother is already there. This is particularly problematic when the two women do not get along or the mother disapproves of the girlfriend. An even more unpredictable situation occurs when there is a potentially difficult or dangerous conflict between guests. For example, an uncle of one youth and the father of another might be in rival gangs. If they both come to visiting hours it can be socially awkward or possibly dangerous. Even under Ohio's rigid visitation policies, this type of problem can occur. Eric's father had left his mother just days after Eric went to the DYS. Needless to say, there was a great deal of animosity between them, and Eric arranged for his parents to visit on alternating weekends. This worked out well until one of his parents came on the wrong weekend: "There was one time that all of us were together, and there was another time when they . . . since it was like three hours and they screwed it up and one would leave and then Mom would go out and my dad would come in for an hour or an hour and a half." Like Eric, Frank had some difficulty ensuring that his estranged parents did not run into each other. At first, they both kept arriving on the same day, causing many uncomfortable interactions. Frank finally figured out that he needed to intervene and set a schedule for them.

Prisons try to minimize visitation problems by limiting the number of visitors allowed on any given day and by restricting who is allowed to visit. Sometimes, however, the policies that most severely limit the ability of families to visit are not visitation policies at all. Ohio, like many other states, decides the institutional placement of each youth based on his treatment needs and risk level. As a result, some youth are placed far from their homes, making it difficult for family members to visit. This is not just a problem in Ohio; juveniles nationally are placed an average of fifty-eight miles from their homes (Parent et al., 1994). Because this figure includes youth in county-level detention, it actually underestimates the distance for youth in state-level facilities. The long distance between home communities and prisons is made worse by the fact that many correctional institutions are located off public transit routes. In Ohio, for example, a car is a virtual necessity for visiting many of the facilities. Parents without a car are unlikely to be able to make the trip unless they can find a ride with a friend or borrow a car. Marcus's mother, for example, had no access to a car and was never able to make the three-hour journey to see her son. Chad's mother had a car but did not have enough money to pay for gas.

The distance and expense involved in prison visits means that some parents, like Marcus's and Chad's, are unable to see their sons. Parents who have weekend jobs also face significant barriers to visitation since all of Ohio's visiting hours are held on Saturdays and Sundays. I talked at some length with youth whose parents were unable to visit due to these types of logistical issues. Most told me that they felt sad, but they were also fairly philosophical about it, recognizing the difficulties involved in a visit. Dion's family tried to come but could not always make it. He told me, "I know it's too far away for them to drive in the snow. . . . My mom, she got to take care of her kids, and my dad, he got to run his business. It's just like, it don't matter if I don't see them or not. As long as I talk to them, or I'm in touch with them, I'm cool." Although Dion understood the difficulties his family faced, he continued to encourage them to come to visiting hours. Other youth, however, felt so guilty about the hardships that visitation imposed that they discouraged their parents from coming. Nick was one of five youth in this study who asked his family not to come see him. He said, "I don't think I should put that burden on 'em for them to come see me. You know what I'm saying. As far as me doing, you know what I'm saying, committing a crime and come down here. I'll feel bad if they was coming to see me and they had an accident or something."

Youth who do not receive many visits—either by their own choice or because of circumstances outside their control—try to focus on other things to avoid feeling sad or lonely. This can be difficult, however, when other youth make fun of them for their lack of outside contact. It is also hard when weekend visiting times arrive and only a few young men are left behind to watch television while everyone else goes to the visitation hall.

Phone Calls

Phone calls are the most regular form of contact between incarcerated youth and the outside world. Phone call policies vary widely across states and institutions, so it is difficult to make generalizations about how often youth are allowed to make calls. Ohio appears to be fairly typical, however, with youth allowed to make at least one call per week to their friends or family members. Youth place their calls from a large room with phones arranged in a row along one wall. The fact that the phones are placed near each other can be upsetting because youth know that their conversations are being overheard by others. Additionally, the noise level in the room can get quite high as several youth talk on the phone and others chat while they wait their turn. Frank's mother told me her calls with Frank were always filled with background noise. One call was particularly upsetting:

> I was talking to him on the phone, and there was someone screaming in the background. I mean, I mean just the gutter mouth. She cussed. And I

was just, I was freaking out on the phone. I'm saying, "Who is this? Who is that?" And Frank is kinda laughing. And that made me even more mad. And he said that it was the guard. And I said that there was absolutely no way that that woman was talking like that. And he's going, "Mom, they do that all the time."

Noise and chaos in the prison phone area make it hard for people to hear and concentrate on each other. Furthermore, similar to visitations, calls tend to start out well as the youth ask their friends and family members to tell them all the news from home. Next, however, the person on the outside asks what is happening in the youth's life. Prison life is both so routine and so complicated that the incarcerated youth find it difficult to answer this question. Tom complained about this problem, so I asked him what he and his friends talked about. He said, "Too much of nothing. You know what I'm saying? You just get on the phone and you just—'How you doing?' Ask me how I'm doing and I be like, 'I'm all right.' He be like, 'You need anything?' Probably tell him what you need as far as money order for some commissary. Something like that. . . . They be like, 'Take care, you take care.'" Even though Tom sometimes found phone calls to be awkward, he, like most of the other youth, continued to call family and friends. The desire for outside news and contact is so strong that youth are willing to endure the chaotic conditions and lack of conversational topics.

Because phone calls are so important and opportunities to make them so limited, youth think carefully about whom they are going to call. Most choose to call their mothers or their girlfriends. This is probably a wise choice because mothers are the most frequent visitors and provide the most consistent support for the youth. Girlfriends are a source of comfort, and, as described in the last chapter, contact with them can increase a young man's social status in the institution. Here is Will talking about his prison phone calls:

> I always pick my mom first, I mean, because I always gotta find out if she's gonna come visit me and whatnot. What's going on at the house? Is my brother doing good and everything? So I always try to call my mom, and if I can't get a hold of my mom I try to call my friend. If I can't get a hold of him, I try to call my other friend, Jay. Like, yesterday I got a phone call, I think it was yesterday, no, it was the day before yesterday, I got a phone call. I tried calling my friend Mark, but he wasn't home and his mom accepted his call and I talked to her. So, I talked to her with my phone call. 'Cause I couldn't get a hold of my mom.

Jason also called his mother as much as possible: "I would talk to her like every time I got a chance to get on the phone. I would talk to my mom until like . . . if they were trying to take the phone off my ear then I had to hang up. You know, I would talk to my mom all the time. I write her all the time. I write her every day for like a daily log and stuff like that. I talk to my mom like every day or so."

Will and Jason, like most of the youth, had a particular person they generally tried to call first. Phone policies, however, sometimes make it difficult to reach these first-choice people. Because phone call hours are not held at the same time every day, families do not know when to expect calls and their sons often find no one at home. Youth quickly learn to keep a mental list of people who are willing to accept their calls. During phone hours they frantically dial numbers until they reach someone or their call time runs out.

An irregular schedule for phone calls makes calling from prison difficult, but not impossible. A policy with a much greater impact involves the type of calls prisoners are allowed to place. All calls placed from DYS institutions (and from many other juvenile institutions nationwide) must be made collect, which involves special restrictions. For instance, some phone companies do not allow collect calls to go to cell phones. Because many people rely solely on cell phone service, this is a significant problem for incarcerated youth trying to reach friends and family. Other phone companies refuse to connect collect calls that originate with another phone company. Finally, some people have a collect-call block on their phone, precluding them from accepting an incarcerated youth's call. Phone companies often install call blocks when they fear that customers will not be able to pay their bills. Hospitals also have call blocks—a situation that makes it impossible for incarcerated youth to call their sick relatives. During the course of this study, Marcus's father was hospitalized because of complications from diabetes. Marcus was very frightened about his father's fragile health and was frantic when he discovered that he was unable to speak with him.

Restrictions on collect calls are a significant barrier for incarcerated youth who would like to stay in touch with the outside world. In this study, three youth reported that they were not able to call at least one of their parents, and many others told me that they were unable to call friends or girlfriends. Andrew was one of the youth who could not reach his mother. When I talked with her, she told me,

> I'm not happy with the fact that he can't call home because I don't have a collect-call service on my line. He can't call me at all. I was told when he was down [at Scioto] that he could, you know, as soon as he got where he

was supposed to be situated at. Once he was transferred. That I could get him a call card that would be put in his file so that he could call home, you know, once in a while. Then he gets up here at Perry Point, and he's not allowed to have a call card. He's, he can't call home in any way, shape, or form, and I can't call him. The only contact I have with him is mail and the visitation.

Youth like Andrew have two options for getting around a call block. One is to ask a social worker to allow them to make a special call. Some young men, however, figure out that it is easier to call a third person and ask them to place a three-way call to the person with the block. Three-way calling is a feature on some phone plans that allows three phones to be connected at the same time. While effective, three-way calling requires finding a person willing to pay for the call. It also sacrifices privacy, as the third person is able to listen in on the call. Requesting a three-way call can be tricky because, if done improperly, one person can feel used. Charles's mother provided an example of this. She wanted to talk with him as much as possible, but he kept requesting that she three-way other people during their calls. She told me that this made her feel angry and hurt.

Collect-call blockages limit the number of people youth can call from prison. The expense of such calls results in further limitations. A collect call from prison generally costs much more than one placed from a residential phone. This is because the state contracts with just one phone company to provide prison service, effectively giving them a monopoly. States are complicit in driving up rates because they receive a portion of the profits. In fact, states choose phone companies partly based on which will give them the highest rate of return. At the time of this study, juvenile facilities in Ohio charged $1.75 to $2.50 per minute, with additional charges of up to 36 cents per minute (families who prepaid could receive a 20 percent discount on these rates). The state collected a 49.5 percent commission on each call made (Wilson, 2006). Parents in this study reported receiving monthly bills of between two and three hundred dollars.

In recent years, prison-rights advocates have drawn attention to high prison phone rates. Their efforts have produced results, although initially these were confined to solving the problems in adult prisons. Soon, however, states began to focus on phone policies in juvenile prisons, resulting in changes at this level. For example, Montana's website for families of incarcerated youth reports that the average call (twenty minutes) from a juvenile facility to anyone in the United States costs $8.75 (Montana Department of Corrections, 2008). Other states, like Minnesota, have at least partially abandoned collect calling for new systems. Youth in some facilities there can receive incoming calls from their parents during restricted hours (Minnesota Department of Corrections, 2009). Another option adopted by some states is a system that allows families to buy prepaid calling cards for their sons' or daughters' use.

Even with phone policy changes, families across the nation suffer from the high phone bills that result from their children's calls home. This study indicates, however, that most families continue to accept at least a limited number of calls. Chad's mother agonized over the bills and finally asked him to cut back his calls to once a week. She told me, "I would love to talk to my son every day but I just can't. I'm a single parent and I can't send him money when he needs money or runs out and maintain the house and pay two to three hundred dollar phone bills." Caleb's family did not directly ask him to limit his calls but they were clear about the effect the expense was having on them. He finally decided to limit his number of calls home:

> My mom, she's out of work right now 'cause she got her shoulder and everything messed up and has to have surgery on it. They don't know if they can do surgery. They think it's too late. She's out of work. My dad don't work. He's got a bad back. Having a hard time paying the bills and stuff. I don't want to run up the phone bills 'cause they don't have no way to pay it. I started slowing down on calling. Call 'em like once or twice a week.

Families with incarcerated children face a very difficult choice. Their sons clearly count on phone calls home, and families believe that regular contact is crucial to their sons' well-being. Phone calls are also useful because they are an immediate way to stay in touch and make sure that their sons are all right. At the same time, the crushing expense of collect calls can jeopardize families' ability to pay the rent or other bills. For example, Alex's mother accrued hundreds of dollars in bills and agonized over what to cut from her tight budget in order to pay them. Families end up being forced into a choice between two unacceptable alternatives—amassing huge bills or having to tell their sons not to call home.

Letters

In an era of e-mail and inexpensive phone plans, people sometimes say that letter writing is a lost art. While this is perhaps true outside prison, it does not apply within the walls. Incarcerated people avidly write letters, just as they make use of every other available means of outside contact. Juvenile inmates can, in theory, send as many letters as they would like. In Ohio, the prison provides each youth with two stamps a week, and youth who want to write more letters can either buy stamps in the commissary or ask their parents to send them. In addition to being able to send as much outgoing mail as they would like, youth can receive an unlimited number of incoming letters. All mail (both incoming and outgoing) is screened, but no youth ever complained to me about letters being censored. The screening process does, however, add time to mail delivery. For example, it can sometimes take several days (or even longer) for youth to receive a letter once it arrives at the institution. This can be frustrating when a letter contains time-sensitive information (for example, news that a relative is sick).

Most of the young men in this study—even those with low literacy levels—wrote letters throughout their incarceration. I did not ask them about their ability to write, but a few commented that letters were hard for them or that they were not "much of a letter writer." To get around this problem, these young men sometimes asked staff members or other residents to write while they dictated. Letters are an important part of life inside prison. As described in Chapter 4, youth who get lots of letters do well in the status hierarchy. Letters also provide an important way for the youth to find out about life outside the walls. Because of the time and effort required to send a letter, the youth see them as particularly strong signals that people still care about them. Phone calls, which the youth have to initiate themselves, do not carry this same value. The many emotional and practical functions letters fulfill give youth a strong incentive to write to people with the hope that they will respond.

Outside Contact over Time

As the months of a prison sentence go by, youth's contact with their family tends to remain stable, or in some cases to increase as families figure out ways to visit. In this study there was variation in how many visitors the youth received, but most (thirty-two youth, or 84 percent of the thirty-eight youth for whom I had visiting information) saw a family member at least once during their incarceration. Of these thirty-two youth, twelve told me that they saw their families regularly, at least once every two weeks. Four youth, however, only saw a family member once during their entire stay. The other sixteen received visits about once a month. Phone calls also remained stable, with most of the youth calling home at least once a week. While youth sometimes saw or called their fathers and grandparents, the vast majority of contact with family members was with mothers.

Contact with friends, unlike contact with families, began a precipitous decline soon after the youth arrived at their permanent institutions. By the end of their incarceration, some were in touch with one or two long-term friends, but many had lost contact with all of their friends. The youth who counted their cousins as friends, however, appeared to have more success in maintaining contact because the cousins could go to the incarcerated youth's home and talk on the phone from there. The parents of cousins were also fairly willing to accept collect calls from their incarcerated nephews.

Because I confined my interviewing to the incarcerated youth and their families, I cannot make any definitive statements about why friends cut off contact. The youth in the study, however, had a number of different explanations for their friends' behavior. Some attributed the decline to the expense of collect calls. Most of their friends lived with their parents; consequently, it was the parents who received the phone bills. Once the first large bill arrived, some parents forbade their children to accept another call. Other reasons youth gave for declining contact included busy schedules and their friends "forgetting them" over time. Out of all the explanations the youth offered, however, the most frequent was that their friends faded away because they had never been real friends. Tony, for example, said,

> All the people I thought were friends, they just, people I got in trouble with, they weren't friends, they were just, we was just making money together, that's all it was. They don't even, they don't write. They wrote a couple times when first I got locked up . . . just saying, "Oh, it's going to be messed up that you're getting two years" or whatever, and they didn't write after that. For the first couple months they just tell me how, like, I'll write you, and all this other stuff, but they never wrote.

Tony was clearly hurt when people he had considered to be friends did not write to him. One way he dealt with the pain was to reconsider the meaning of true friendship, defining "real" friends as those who stay in touch. In this way, contact became a type of litmus test for differentiating friends from acquaintances. We see this same idea expressed in Jason and Casey's interviews. Jason said: "They really not even friends. I thought they was friends just 'cause we was going out and having fun and everything, hanging out. But you find out who are your friends when you come to jail, or the ones that will help you out, and they ain't friends when you're saying, 'Let's go get high and let's go do this,' but none of them is really friends at all." Casey was similarly direct about his feelings:

CASEY: I don't mess with a lot of them people that I used to.
ANNE: How come?
CASEY: 'Cause like on the outs like they, they be around you all the time and stuff and like they your friends and shit. I mean, I ain't allowed cussing.
ANNE: It doesn't matter. Talk however you want.
CASEY: They act like they're your friends and shit and when you get locked up, you see who your friends and who ain't and shit.
ANNE: And how can you tell?
CASEY: They write you and shit.

Casey and Jason represent the majority of the youth, who felt angry and betrayed when their friends failed to remain in contact with them. There was, however, a small group of youth who reported that they felt disappointment rather than hurt or anger. These youth told me that it would be hypocritical for them to be angry at their friends because of their own past failure to write to an incarcerated friend. This experience gave them insight into how hard it is to maintain contact with an incarcerated person. Here is Nick commenting on his feelings about not receiving many letters from his friends:

I mean it make you think like, you know what I'm saying, a person can't take five, ten minutes' time to send you a letter back. . . . If you were outside, you'd all be together. While you in here they can't, you know what I'm saying, take time. See how you doing. But at the same time I look at it as, well, she working, going to school, and he doing whatever it is he's doing outside and it's summertime. Some people enjoying, you know what I'm saying, their life. You know what I'm saying. You can't really be too much of a burden on other people because you in here. That's just like my mom's father was locked up or people in my family, I ain't write back. I got the letter and I read it, you know. I thought about 'em. I still cared for 'em, it's just . . . you be so caught up in what you doing outside, a person don't never really think about how a person feel in here until you been in here.

Like Nick, Colby was sympathetic about his friends falling out of touch. I asked him whether there were people he had expected to write who had not. He said, "Not really. Not really. 'Cause I know how it is . . . like somebody locked up and you write him and he doesn't write you back. I know how it is. You want to get around to it but you never get around to it. You know, you want to write and you like, all right, I'm gonna write him tonight. Something will pop up and you'll forget about it." Nick and Colby's failure to write to their own incarcerated friends helped them to frame their friends' disappearances as the result of a busy life rather than as a betrayal. Youth who did not have this experience were far more likely to feel angry and resentful.

Contact between incarcerated youth and their friends showed a clear pattern of decline over the course of incarceration. Contact with girlfriends, however, generally took one of two different paths. As described in Chapter 2, thirty-one of the forty youth reported having a girlfriend when they entered prison. At first, these youth heard from their girlfriends regularly, but within a few weeks of their permanent placement, some began to receive "Dear John" letters. By the end of their incarceration, seventeen of the relationships were over. Few of the youth were particularly surprised when they got a break-up letter or heard about infidelity on the part of their girlfriends. Even in the first interviews the youth expressed doubts that their girlfriends would wait for them. Failed romances are extremely common among young prisoners, and the lack of privacy assures that the stories of these romances become part of a large communal archive of break-up stories. Youth who might have trusted their girlfriends at the beginning of their sentence are hard pressed to maintain that trust as other youth assure them that girlfriends never really wait.

The truth, of course, is that some girlfriends do wait for their boyfriends to come home from juvenile prison. In this study, there were at least ten relationships that survived incarceration. (I had insufficient information from four youth to know whether their relationships lasted throughout their sentences.) In Chapter 6, I discuss some of the common characteristics of these relationships. Suffice it to say here that the relationships that endured were, not surprisingly, marked by very regular contact. Girlfriends are not allowed to visit DYS facilities, so all contact occurred through phone calls and letters. The ten young women who stayed with their incarcerated boyfriends wrote at least once a week and accepted collect calls when they could. Several wrote to their boyfriends daily. These young women actively worked to maintain trust and connection over the course of the incarceration.

Family Reactions over Time

Chapter 2 examined parents' emotions at the beginning of their sons' prison terms. While sadness and disappointment were common, some parents also felt hopeful that prison could help their sons to change. Over time, parents continued to feel hopeful as their sons told them about the positive changes they were making in their lives. Dion, for example, described visiting with his mother: "She's surprised, like, she can't believe I'm talking about the Bible a lot. Like she just can't believe a whole lot of stuff about me, like I'm staying out of trouble, and all this. She just surprised. She like real happy." Many youth in this study were similar to Dion and maintained an upbeat attitude during visiting hours. This made their parents feel encouraged and helped to make visitation enjoyable. I asked Sam what he and his mother talked about during visiting hours. He said,

> What's happening at home. Then she complained about the drive here. Stuff like that, just, I don't know . . . I've been doing pretty good in here. So I might, probably, get out early since I got a certificate for completing a, like a Substance Abuse class, and when I get my report card it's gonna be straight A's 'cause that's all what I got in all my classes and stuff like that. And the Bible study thing, I told her that I'd be getting a Bible soon with my name engraved on it for completing the Bible study course, lessons. Stuff like that.

I was always a little surprised when youth like Dion and Sam told me about the positive tone they maintained during phone calls and visitation, since I knew they had many complaints about life in prison. When I asked them if they ever complained during visiting hours, many said that they did not want to upset their parents by talking about bad things. Several commented that there was no point in talking about mistreatment when nothing could be done to change it. Two also told me that they avoided discussing prison conditions because their mothers might call the institution and complain, potentially causing staff retribution. This is not to say, of course, that the youth never complained to their parents, but rather that most tried to avoid making it the focus of their time together. The positive interactions between youth and their parents helped to bolster the parents' hope for their sons. For example, Tom's father told me that his phone calls with his son convinced him that Tom was ready to change. He said, "As far as over the phone, he seems like he willing to do what he supposed to do . . . have the responsibility like he supposed to now . . . not like before. Like before he never was willing to do nothing but what he wanted to do."

At the outset of incarceration, parents were hopeful that prison would change their sons. Over time, many maintained hope but began to seriously question the ability of the prison system to effect that change. Hope was replaced by disillusionment and anger at the system. This sometimes happened when the institution did not provide promised programming, but it also happened when prison rules or policies made the system seem arbitrary, punitive, or impersonal. The Ohio prison system, like that in most other states, is large and confusing. My interviews with parents made it clear that they did not have a good understanding of how the system worked. For example, many parents were mystified by extra time and presumptive release dates and felt that their son's sentence was being changed without rhyme or reason.

Not understanding the prison system led parents to feel out of control and out of touch with their sons. Ironically, this feeling was enhanced by their children's attempts to shield them from unpleasant information. While the youth may have thought that their attempts at self-censorship were subtle, parents seemed to know exactly what their sons were doing. Here is Chad's mother answering a question about her son's experiences at the prison:

> CHAD'S MOTHER: As far as right now everybody's, you know, treating him pretty good from what he tells me. And I can only go by what he tells me.
>
> ANNE: Right. Well, it's interesting, you said earlier that there might be stuff that he isn't telling you. A number of people have told me that. Why do you suppose that might be?
>
> CHAD'S MOTHER: Some of it is he probably doesn't want to get me upset and get me worried. And then he knows how I am. If there are certain things that goes on, if I feel I need to call up there, then I would call up there. And then that could get him into more trouble so I don't know if he . . . is not telling me for me not worrying or not telling me because he knows how I am and then I will call up there and I would want to talk to somebody.

Chad's mother worried that her son was unwilling to tell her bad things that were happening in the institution. She feared, however, that an inquiring phone call might be perceived as making trouble. Here is Alex's mother describing similar concerns: "And just to find out, you know, what do I do? What does he do? And everything. But from things that I hear, it's better off not to bother them. Because the more you bother them, the more they pick on your kid. So it's better not to ask too many questions. I just find out what I have to know and that's it."

Alex's and Chad's mothers felt out of touch with their sons and were unable to find a way to reestablish a sense of control. They, like other parents I spoke with, had clearly expected that the prison system would be more active in facilitating contact and parental involvement. Parents believed this, in part, because the juvenile prison has an image of being more open and personal than an adult prison. As Kirk's mother commented in frustration, "You know, he's in juvenile. I mean, come on! I want to know how he's doing." The impersonality and closed nature of the prison also surprised some parents because of its contrast with their local detention centers. These centers tend to have much more liberal visitation policies, and because the centers are smaller, parents come to know staff there. This is not to say that local detention centers are necessarily better or safer, but they do feel more open.

Parents who expect that the juvenile prison will be personal and caring are further disillusioned by their experiences at visitation. As described, all visitors must meet the requirements of the dress code, and those who do not have appropriate clothing are not allowed to enter the facility. Although none of the parents in this study were ever turned away, several had problems getting in. Most notably, Frank's seventy-three-year-old grandmother was asked to remove a blouse she was wearing over her T-shirt because the rules stated that visitors were only allowed to wear one layer. She was embarrassed and never returned to the facility. Other parents felt that they were not treated with respect when they came to see their sons. While the dress code and other visitation regulations are set up to enhance prison security, they also have the potential to make visitors feel angry and alienated.

A final issue that turned parents against the prison system involved its relationship with the child-support system. When a child is removed from an Ohio home and placed in a welfare or correctional agency, the custodial parent can be asked to pay child support. Child support is primarily handled at the county level, however, and policies vary widely. This lack of consistency may be why child-support policies are not clearly spelled out in the DYS materials parents receive. The problem with the lack of information, of course, is that parents are completely surprised when a child-support order arrives in the mail. They quickly figure out that not all families with incarcerated children have to pay. In fact, the majority of parents do not have child-support orders issued against them. The unexpected and seemingly arbitrary nature of this situation leads the parents who receive these orders to become angry and feel that they are being unfairly targeted. There are other states, however, whose systems are better explained and more consistent. For example, the websites for Utah's and Oregon's juvenile correctional systems make it absolutely clear that all parents are required to make child-support payments.

The two cases of child-support orders in this study differ from each other, but both led the parents to feel disillusioned with the prison system. Chad's mother received a child-support order in the mail while she was at home fighting cancer. She was furious to discover that she and her husband would be required to pay child support for the length of their son's incarceration. When they did not immediately make payments, the child-support enforcement agency started garnishing both her husband's paycheck and her own disability payment. Dan's family's situation was a little different. He lived with his single mother, and she received child support from Dan's father. When Dan was incarcerated, the father's payment was not changed, but it was diverted to the DYS. Dan's mother was left to pay the high bills caused by his crime, including a set amount of money each month to the victim's insurance deductible. She was angry that she was not able to access any of the child-support payments for these costs.

Anecdotal evidence from DYS staff suggests that child-support orders cause strain between parents and the state and between parents and their children. If a youth is assigned extra time for bad behavior, the parents are forced to continue to pay child support. This either makes them angry at their sons for their misbehavior or, if the extra time is not explained to them, makes them angry at the state. The most upsetting situation, however, is when a youth is required to take a program that is not available prior to his release date. In this case, the DYS can hold the youth until he is able to complete the program. This means that families with child-support orders must continue to pay while they wait for the state to provide the required classes. For families who are already angry about their child-support order, this kind of unexpected extension simply confirms their view that the prison system is uncaring and impersonal.

Conclusion

A number of the youth featured in this chapter—including Colby, Chad, and Caleb—were extremely focused on their "real lives" outside prison. While this helped them avoid institutionalization, it also caused them to be hurt when friends fell out of touch. While almost all the incarcerated youth received visits, phone calls, and letters, the challenges associated with communication discouraged many of their friends and a few of their family members from contact. The collect-call phone system in the DYS—and in other state systems—presented a serious obstacle to outside contact. Visitation required families to travel many miles and endure the humiliations associated with the security protocols. Even with these challenges, many family members, mothers in particular, maintained high levels of contact during the youth's incarceration. They held out hope for their sons even as they became disillusioned with the prison system. Friends, however, did not hang on so tenaciously, causing anger and resentment among the incarcerated youth.

It is clear that incarceration has an impact on relationships. Whether that impact carries over into the youth's life after prison is one of the questions addressed in the next chapter. Incarceration, after all, has an unreal quality that may make events that happened in the institution irrelevant to youth after their release. At the same time, the emotions they felt in prison as they negotiated relationships with the outside world can have effects that extend well beyond their incarceration.

Chapter 6

Coming Home

If youth in custody have anything in common, it is their intense desire to get out of prison. Although one certainly expects the youth to have difficulties in serving time, I was still surprised by the depth of the youth's distress and by their unwavering focus on returning home. I spoke with Chad several weeks after he arrived in prison. He told me, "I hope I get [out] early so I can leave with my family 'cause . . . I'm really messed up inside. I'm just like, I'm tired of being here. I don't like, I don't like the place one bit, but I ain't like faking it to get out. . . . I'm doing what I have to do to get out. And this is changing me, too, 'cause . . . I can't be locked up like this. I just can't stand it."

Chad was far from alone in his misery and depression. As evidenced by the number of times release dates were mentioned in the interviews, Chad's focus on getting out was shared across the group of young men in the study. In this chapter, I explore the process of getting out of prison and discuss what happens to young men as they return to their communities. I consider their experiences with parole, education, and employment and then conclude with a discussion about the effects of prison on relationships with families, friends, and girlfriends.

Getting Out

Getting out of juvenile prison is not a simple or straightforward process. If you ask an incarcerated youth when he will be released, he will usually tell you a specific date, but he will also admit to some uncertainty about it. While there are some states, like Kansas, that use determinate sentences, most continue to use indeterminate sentences. This means that until a youth reaches the age of majority and the state is required to release him, a release date is just an estimate. Indeterminate sentencing fits with the original rehabilitative and paternalistic goal of the system since a youth can be held until he is judged to be reformed and ready to start a new life.

Ohio has a typical indeterminate sentencing structure with release decisions left up to the Release Authority, one of the bureaus of the Parole Services Branch of the DYS. The Release Authority is composed of the bureau chief plus four appointed members. They are charged with deciding each youth's presumptive release date based on intake assessments, criminal history records, and treatment requirements. Presumptive release dates are often considerably later than minimum release dates set by the judge. Not surprisingly, the disparity typically causes youth to become disappointed and upset. Joseph, for example, was horrified to find that his presumptive release was months later than his assigned minimum. He was so upset that he refused to tell his mother:

> JOSEPH: I ain't even tell her. I had my social worker tell her and I walked out the room, and I came back in the room and she was on the phone.
> ANNE: How come you had your social worker tell her?
> JOSEPH: 'Cause I ain't believe it, even when they were showing me the paper. I thought she put it down herself, so I walked out the door like well, so, whatever. Came back in the room, she was on the phone.
> ANNE: Did you really think the social worker would add time herself?
> JOSEPH: Oh, she told me. She explained it to me when I came back in the room that the police authority or something gave me the extra time.

It makes sense that Joseph was confused about the change in his release date. The presumptive date policy is not clearly explained to youth at their sentencing and, as a result, they are often angry when a social worker tells them the news. Further fueling their anger, the youth quickly learn that their new release date is not real either—it can be extended if they behave badly or if the institution cannot provide required programming in a timely manner. The rule allowing the DYS to hold youth until the age of majority does, of course, have a potential benefit to public safety and to the youth's own future. Tim, the youth with the serious mental illness and violence issues, had exhausted all the services that could be provided outside prison. The DYS chose to hold him until he aged out, knowing that he was a real threat to himself and others. Other youth were held until they finished their drug treatment, arguably preparing them to start a sober and more productive life on the outside.

Most sentence modifications lengthen the time that incarcerated youth are required to serve, but it is also possible for a youth to be released early. Judges have the power to grant these early releases (also known as judicial releases) up until the minimum sentence date. My first interviews with the youth in this study made it clear that early releases are a subject of much discussion and hope. When I told them that I would see them again in a few months, many told me that they would be back home by then because they were sure they would get their "early." In truth, however, early releases are relatively rare, and the majority of youth fail to get them. I was always a little surprised by the youth's insistence that they would get their early given that they saw lots of other young men try and fail. As it turns out, their optimism is not unique to incarcerated youth in Ohio, nor is it unique to juveniles. In a study of adult male prisoners in Canada, researchers found that early release was unusual but that most inmates anticipated getting it (Zamble and Porporino, 1988).

Eventually all youth are released from juvenile prison—except those few who are serving blended sentences and are ordered to adult prison. When release day comes, parents or guardians usually come to the prison to pick up their sons. Sometimes, when a young man's family cannot or will not come to get him, the state provides a bus ticket home. Marcus's family, for example, did not have a car, so he returned to his home in the western part of the state on Greyhound. In Ohio, youth under the age of twenty-one are not released unless they have an approved home placement. In some cases, this means that youth are held until the age of majority because they have no state-approved home arrangement on the outside. Once they reach the age of twenty-one, social workers provide them with a bus ticket and the address of a homeless shelter in their community.

Ohio does not have an extensive post-release planning program, although the majority of prison social workers at least encourage the youth to think through reentry issues. This somewhat informal system stands in contrast to states with established post-release planning programs. In these programs, social workers help youth to make arrangements for schooling, employment, or various types of community programs. Minnesota, for example, has an extensive furlough program that allows youth nearing their release dates to spend three to five days in the community finalizing their job or education plans. The state also employs ninety-day extended furloughs to help youth adapt to life outside the institution before they are officially placed on parole. Juveniles in Ohio, because of the minimal planning help available and the uncertainty about release dates, have great difficulty making firm plans for their reentry into the community. In one of my Inside Outside classes, for example, I watched two young men apply to college, get accepted, and then not be able to attend as their presumptive release dates came and went.

When I conducted interviews with newly released youth, I always asked them about the day they got out. Without fail, they would describe the excitement of the day and tell me in great detail about all of the people they saw, the food they ate, and the places they went. Incarcerated youth spend a great deal of time fantasizing about getting out, and this causes the first day to take on a special significance. The first day out is unique, however, and youth quickly discover that the outside world is not always so welcoming.

Parole

> It ain't hard for me. Basically, it's like somebody else being your parent. You know. They telling you what time to come in, when to call and check in. Keep a job. Just like an extra mom.
> —Colby

Colby's description of parole would probably please its original framers. Like the idealized role of a parent, parole was intended to help guide ex-prisoners while, at the same time, disciplining and monitoring them. Over the years, however, the treatment side of parole has diminished in importance while the surveillance side has increased (Petersilia, 2003). This is, at least in part, because budgets are tight and caseloads are high. Helping a parolee get work or find an apartment is far more time consuming than having a meeting once a month or administering a drug test. Additionally, public concerns about crimes committed by parolees have pressured parole offices to increase surveillance.

While there is an official set of rules governing each youth's parole, agents have a tremendous amount of discretionary power. They are able to enforce or ignore any particular regulations. They also choose how closely they monitor their caseloads. The youth in this study had a wide range of reactions to their parole agents, largely driven by how restrictive and controlling their agents were. John Irwin (1970) identified three variables that determine parolees' reactions to their agents—two of which relate to the use of power. The first, intensity, refers to the degree to which officers insert themselves in the lives of the parolee. Frequent visits, investigations, and lots of questions indicate a high degree of intensity. The second variable is tolerance. Agents with high tolerance sometimes let rule breaking slide. They might, for example, choose to ignore minor alcohol violations. Finally, agents vary in how "right" they are. Rightness refers to how the agent treats the parolee. An "all right" agent deals with his or her caseload with honesty, dependability, and respect. Not surprisingly, Irwin concludes that most parolees like their agents to be low intensity, highly tolerant, and "all right." Although Irwin's work is dated, his assessment of parolees' views toward parole agents seems to hold true in this study as well. The youth clearly wanted an agent who had low involvement in their lives and who would ignore the small stuff. They also appreciated agents who seemed to want them to succeed.

Sam and I talked at some length about how much he liked his parole agent. His comments reflect the fact that the agent was both low intensity and "all right." He said, "He's real, real nice. . . . I called him every Monday, and he checked up on me a few times. Show me like pictures of him and his family fishing and stuff. And I got like a little bit of brownie points on him. Went fishing. Went to a few meetings." Alex also liked his agent because he treated him with respect, an element of being "all right":

> He's pretty cool, actually. I mean, he stopped over yesterday . . . [and] he tell my ma, he was, "I don't really got to worry about you guys. I mean, evidently, you guys got a stable house, a stable family. You all ain't out here getting in trouble. I mean we got people to worry about with heroin and doing all this stuff around here. And these kids I got to worry about. So I'm going to check in on you just because that's my job." He was like, "But I ain't really worried about you as long as you stay out of trouble. 'Cause, you know what I'm saying, I won't be in your face." And I was like, "I stay out of trouble." So he kind of just leaves me alone, and he checks up on me every week or two, calls me, sees how I'm doing, comes to the house and sees me, you know what I'm saying. He just does all that, but he don't want to be bothered with it. He knows I'm being good.

Sam and Alex were among a small but vocal group of youth who really liked their agents. The majority, however, either felt neutral or negative about them.

One of the reasons that many youth felt so resentful of their agents—and of parole more generally—was that they had given little thought to it prior to their return home. Neither the prison youth culture nor the staff place a great deal of emphasis on parole. Instead of talking about a "parole date" or being "released to parole," juveniles and staff talk about their "release date" or getting "early release." Similarly, youth focus on their minimum sentence, not on the fact that they are technically committed to the system until they are twenty-one. Adult parole is different because it represents a shortening of a sentence, and most adult parolees feel fortunate to receive it. By contrast, juvenile parole usually happens after a minimum release date, and juveniles experience it as a lengthening of their sentence. As a result, many feel deep resentment at the restrictions. I asked Andrew what he thought about parole, and he said, "I couldn't do nothing. I couldn't have a girl over. I couldn't leave the house at certain times. It kinda got on my nerves. I was kinda like bounded, and I hated it." I asked Marcus if anything good had come out of parole. He said yes, but then was unable to come up with any concrete examples. He seemed to think that parole was little more than the system's way to force him to continue the impression management he had perfected in prison: "It gave me limitations on what stuff I can't do. You know. All parole did was made me wait so I could get off parole. Couldn't wait 'til I get off parole. . . . It was like I put on an act or something. . . . I just knew how to work the little system then."

Marcus clearly did not like his parole rules, but youth who were required to attend parole-office classes tended to be even more resentful. These programs were similar to ones offered in prison—anger management and victim awareness were frequent offerings. Being enrolled in these programs required youth to find transportation and be at the parole office at a certain time each week. Even more irksome, however, was that some of the programs they were required to complete were not appropriate for their needs or were repetitions of prison programs. Tom said,

> They kept having me do different things. They had me doing stuff that I ain't need. . . . They had me doing stuff that I was doing at Perry Point, but I had to do it all over again when I got out. I ain't, I ain't never used drugs and they found me not guilty of using drugs here . . . [but the parole office] had me doing substance abuse like ten weeks, and they had me going to victim awareness ten weeks, and they had put me in some other programs and stuff like that. It was just crazy . . . it was like I wasn't even free. It was like I was still locked up.

While parole's restrictions and classes annoy youth like Tom, they generally do not cause their lives significant hardship. At the same time, there are a few parole restrictions that can have potentially serious consequences for a youth's employment. Colby's agent, for example, told him that he was required to participate in a weekly anger management class at the parole office. In order to attend the class, Colby needed to ensure that he was not scheduled to work on Monday nights. Not wanting to lie to the employer, Colby finally confessed that he had to take a class at the parole office. He told me that he felt lucky that the employer kept him on after that. The jobs of two other youth were jeopardized when their parole agents insisted on checking up on them at work. It is likely that these agents chose to come to the youth's work in order to confirm their employment or because work was convenient—I do not think they were purposely trying to cause trouble for the youth. An agent showing up at work, however, alerts an employer to a youth's parole status, which could lead to distrust and increased monitoring. Of additional concern, research has indicated that recidivism is higher for youth with bosses who think that they are "bad kids" (Miller and Ohlin, 1985, 62).

It is difficult to summarize youth's feelings about parole because they can both resent it and appreciate it at the same time. For example, parole can be quite helpful as an excuse to avoid criminal behavior. Four parolees reported that they liked the restriction against drug use because it served as a socially acceptable excuse to abstain. They found it easier to tell friends that they were afraid of violating parole than to admit that they did not want to use drugs. Parole can also be an aid to youth trying to disengage themselves from delinquent friends, because most parolees are required to refrain from all contact with other people on parole. Here is Andrew talking about how he stayed away from old friends:

> ANDREW: It's simple. Don't get in my face, man, 'cause I'm on parole.
> 'Cause my friends are on parole.
> ANNE: So how did you decide which friends to keep and which ones not?
> ANDREW: I really didn't. I just quit hanging out with people on parole.
> ANNE: Oh, yeah? And is that just to stay out of trouble or do you not like them?
> ANDREW: To stay out of trouble and I don't like them that much. 'Cause I don't do drugs anymore.

Of course, not all the youth embraced the restriction against contact with other parolees. Some simply ignored the rule because they wanted to continue hanging out with paroled friends. Complicating matters, some of the siblings and cousins of returning juvenile prisoners are on parole themselves. The no-contact rule, when applied blindly, can significantly upset youth and disrupt family relationships. Eric's cousin, for example, was on parole and, like Eric, worked for his father. It took some tricky maneuvering to ensure that they avoided each other. Fortunately, in this sample of youth, most parole officers recognized this issue and allowed exceptions. For example, Freddie and his brother were incarcerated at about the same time (for different offenses), and the parole agent allowed them to live together once both were released.

Education

Understanding the effect of juvenile prison on education is important. Research has found that education is linked both to an inmate's later employment and to his desistance from crime (Sampson and Laub, 1993; Duguid and Pawson, 1998). To date, however, we have little information about how juvenile prison affects educational outcomes. This study suggests that it can have both positive and negative effects. As described in Chapter 3, all incarcerated juveniles without a GED or diploma are required to attend school. Most of the youth in this study saw attendance at prison school as a real opportunity. The youth who had been alienated from school on the outside were particularly appreciative of a chance to pursue a degree. Even if they were not able to complete their degree while incarcerated, these young men could make substantial progress toward catching up on credits. Those who had been enrolled in school prior to their incarceration also were grateful for a chance to keep up and return to the proper grade level at their community schools.

Some youth found that they were able to re-enroll easily in school when they returned home from prison. Jason, for example, did not lose any credits and was able to finish his degree at his district's alternative school. At the same time, not everyone was as fortunate as Jason was. Two youth in this study returned home only to find that their schools did not want them back. In Sam's case this appeared to be a result of past trouble he had caused in school (and the trouble he caused during the short period after he was released from prison and before his expulsion was finalized). In the other case, however, the expulsion seemed to be linked to the youth's incarceration. It is often impossible to hide a criminal record from a school because forty-four states automatically notify them when one of their students is involved in criminal or delinquent acts—although in some states this only happens with more serious crimes (Snyder and Sickmund, 2006, 109).

Because schools have a vested interest in maintaining order, they want to minimize the number of potentially disruptive students. Criminal justice involvement is used as an indicator of disruptive potential. Ronnie Casella's 2003 study of two high schools (one in New York, one in Connecticut) revealed that they generally refused to readmit youth who had been suspended (or incarcerated), opting instead to send them to alternative high schools or to special afternoon programs for troubled youth. Casella attributed this to fear of violence in the wake of well-publicized school shootings, perceived high levels of juvenile crime, and pressure to fill the spaces in the alternative schools.

Most states have a way to expel or permanently exclude disruptive youth from their schools. In Ohio, policies allow fairly broad discretion to the superintendent to expel students for up to a year or to permanently exclude them from the public school system. Some states and districts send expelled students to alternative schools or programs, but this does not always happen, particularly if a youth is over the age of sixteen. Once a school refuses to re-admit a youth, there are very limited options for finishing a degree. In some states, these youth can try to enroll in a different public school. For example, a study conducted in a mid-Atlantic state found that the majority of youth who returned from prison wanting to attend school were able to enroll in a public school outside their own neighborhood (Balfanz et al., 2003). There are also some Internet school options, but these tend to be expensive and of variable quality, in addition to requiring Internet access.

Sometimes returning youth are allowed to go back to school but, because they have slipped so far behind their grade level, they refuse to re-enroll. This can happen when a youth is bounced around county-level correctional facilities before being assigned to the state correctional agency. It is also possible to fall behind at the prison school because of teacher shortages, failure to do assignments, or behavioral problems that result in being put in isolation. Another way an incarcerated youth can fall behind is by choosing to pursue a GED and then failing to complete it (either because he is released prior to taking the test or because he fails the test). No high school credits are awarded for GED preparation, and if the youth returns to school in the community, he will be behind. When Marcus returned home with no GED and no high school credits, he became angry and resentful and refused to return to school. Two other youth in the study also decided to drop out because they came back below grade level. When I asked Andrew why he was not returning to school, he said, "I would feel like I was stepping way below my sister. My sister's a junior and she's going to be a senior. And I'm stuck a grade below her. I would be in the same grade as my younger sister and it would make me feel stupid."

Like Andrew, Chad and Frank also returned below grade level, but they were more determined to finish their degrees. Both of their school districts strongly suggested that they consider their county's alternative school. I thought that this solution might work—especially for Frank, since his alternative school was intended for overage students. Unfortunately, both of these alternative schools were underfunded, and Chad and Frank got discouraged and dropped out. I interviewed Chad while he was still attending the school and asked him what he thought of it. He said, "It ain't no school to help. I'd think good of it but they just sit and pass you, you know what I'm saying. . . . Playing cards all day. I'm like . . . if this is supposed to be a school, then I ain't supposed to be playing."

In Chapter 7, I discuss some specific policies that could be implemented to improve the school system in juvenile prisons. At the same time, experiences like Chad's and Frank's indicate that change must also happen outside the correctional facility because prison and community schools are inextricably linked. The deficiencies of public schools in impoverished areas have been well documented, but less attention has been given to alternative schools. These schools are often the last resort for youth returning from prison, and they operate at very low levels of funding. It is upsetting to youth, and potentially devastating to their futures, when they return home from substandard prison schools to find that their communities cannot do much better.

Employment

Almost all of the youth in the study told me that their primary post-release goal was to find legitimate employment. This decision seemed to reflect a desire both to "go straight" and to be financially independent. Many of the youth, especially the older ones, told me that they were too old to be dependent on their parents anymore. While this desire for independence is hardly unique to the prison population, some of the youth linked their feelings to having been on their own in prison. For example, Nick and I were talking about how incarceration had changed his life. He told me, "I just feel that I'm grown up now. I need to start doing grown-up things. I need to stop being a kid." When youth like Nick saw themselves as grown-ups, finding a job took on a central importance. As a result, most youth in this study wanted to go directly into full-time work, although eight of the younger men wanted to combine part-time work with finishing high school.

Although newly released young men's internal motivation is often strong enough to encourage them to find a job, external pressures exist that can serve as an additional motivator. The high school graduates (and GED recipients) reported that they were either required to seek work as a condition of their parole or that their parole officer was putting strong pressure on them to do so. The assumption of all the parties—the parole board, the parole agents, and even the youth themselves—was that employment serves as a deterrent to further trouble. There is a strong common-sense perception that employment prevents delinquency, as expressed in the adage "Idle hands are the devil's workshop."

The Unsuccessful Job Hunt

When the youth in this study returned home, all but two sought employment. Most quickly discovered that they were not qualified for any but the most entry-level positions. Job searches were also hampered by the fact that most of the youth did not have a clear idea about what sort of work they would like to do. When I asked them during the first set of interviews about what sort of job they would like, the most common response was that it did not matter as long as it paid well. Without skills, help, or a clear plan, the youth simply applied randomly to jobs in their neighborhood. In general, these jobs were at fast food restaurants like McDonald's or Burger King, or at big-box stores like Target or Wal-Mart. An example of a fairly typical approach to job applications occurred when I took Alex to lunch at Pizza Hut. He was interested in getting a job, and during lunch it occurred to him that he could apply to Pizza Hut. It is likely that the good-looking girl who smiled at him when she took his order made the prospect of working there especially desirable. He did end up requesting an application and came back later to turn it in. His other job applications were equally as spontaneous.

This scattershot approach to job hunting was not terribly effective for Alex or for the rest of the youth. The story they told over and over was that they applied at numerous places (often as many as ten or fifteen) and never got a call back. Sometimes they interviewed but never heard back from the employer. In fact, when I talked to Alex (who was back in prison) at the third interview, he told me he had heard nothing about his application to Pizza Hut. Here is an excerpt from that interview:

ALEX: Been looking for a job. I've been applying everywhere around here.
ANNE: Like where have you applied?
ALEX: I applied at Wendy's, Bob Evans, Big Boy's, Burger King, Taco Bell, McDonald's.
ANNE: What do they tell you?
ALEX: Nothing. They don't call me back. I keep calling them and calling them and calling them. They say, they give me the same thing. We ain't went over your application, or we lost it, or some stupid stuff. But I'll keep calling back. Big Boy's was going to give me a job but then they're like, we be starting in a week and we'll call you back in a couple of days with the details. And then they didn't call me back. I called them back like a week later, I was like, well, you guys said that. And the manager said, well, we don't need you anymore.

Steven talked about the same experience: "They set me up on an interview or they tell me that they have hired somebody already or something. They'll call back and just give me some type of pitiful excuse."

Why did so many of the youth find themselves being rejected or ignored by employers? One important factor involved the job market itself. During the years of this study, unemployment rates for teenagers were quite high.

In 2002, for example, the unemployment rate for youth ages fifteen to seventeen was 21 percent, compared to 5 percent for adults ages twenty-five to fifty-four (Snyder and Sickmund, 2006). This suggests that all teenagers, not only those who had been incarcerated, had difficulty finding work. It is also possible that the youth in this study, because they were not conducting a well-planned job search, put in applications at places where there was no position available.

A weak job market limits the number of positions available to youth, and it also allows employers to be more selective about the people they hire. It is likely that some of the youth's difficulty finding employment was a result of pre-existing characteristics that made them less desirable to employers than youth who had never been to prison. For example, youth who spend time in prison may have fewer job and social skills, and they may be less responsible than youth who do not end up in prison. As a result, they are not appealing as employees. Without any comparison group, my data cannot systematically assess the role of this human capital explanation. My interactions with the youth, however, did indicate that many had traits that might discourage employers from hiring them. A few had tattoos or styles of dress that might have signaled gang involvement to an employer. Others wrote poorly or mumbled badly when they spoke. Other researchers' work supports the idea that these kinds of underlying traits help explain both criminal behavior and difficulty finding and keeping a job. For example, Michael Gottfredson and Travis Hirschi (1990) argue that lack of self-control causes both criminal behavior and employment problems. People who fail to learn self control as children—generally because of poor parenting—have problems throughout their lives because they have difficulty resisting the temptations of crime or laziness.

Although pre-existing differences are important in understanding why unemployment and incarceration appear to be linked, a number of researchers have shown that these differences fail to entirely explain the employment gap between youth who have been incarcerated and those who have not (Sampson and Laub, 1993). As a result, we need to consider other explanations. For example, it is possible that youth who have been to prison fare poorly on the job market because their criminal record discourages employers from hiring them. Research with samples of adult ex-offenders certainly suggests that this is a plausible explanation. Numerous studies have found that having a criminal record decreases a person's chances of employment (Freeman, 1991; Holzer, Raphael and Stoll, 2004, 2007; Pager, 2003, 2007). Deevah Pager (2007) explored this link by sending matched pairs of job seekers to apply for entry-level employment. The pairs were similar in the qualifications they presented, but one reported a criminal record while the other did not. She found that employers are much less likely to hire an ex-offender than a similar person without a record. Notably, this effect is stronger for black applicants. Using a completely different methodology, Harry Holzer, Steven Raphael, and Michael Stoll (2007) surveyed employers about their hiring preferences. Employers reported that they were less willing to hire ex-offenders than other stigmatized groups (e.g., welfare recipients or people who have worked only sporadically). In fact, 40 percent said that they would "probably not" or "definitely not" hire someone with a record (122). Analysis of actual hiring practices revealed that the employers' behavior was generally consistent with their attitudes.

Employers do not want to hire ex-convicts because they see crime and incarceration as a marker of untrustworthiness or instability. Additionally, some are concerned about legal liability if an ex-offender commits a crime at work. Given these fears, it makes sense for employers to avoid hiring ex-offenders if there are other willing workers available. William Sabol's study of employment among ex-offenders in Ohio (2007) provides support for the idea that employers are less likely to hire ex-offenders when unemployment is high. Using data from 1990 to 2000, he found that for every 1 percent decrease in unemployment, ex-convicts' chances of finding employment increased by about 4 percent (258).

In order for criminal records to have a negative effect on employment, it is necessary for employers to have access to, or at least knowledge of, these records. As described in Chapter 1, juvenile records are becoming increasingly available to employers. It is likely that, over time, these records will become a more important factor in hiring. In this study, youth believed that their records were confidential, and none mentioned that their employer got a background check. Aside from background checks, however, there are other ways that employers can find out about the criminal record of a juvenile applying for a job. For example, earlier in this chapter I discussed parole restrictions that are hard to hide from an employer (a required class at the parole office that limits work hours or a parole officer showing up at work). In my previous work with paroled fathers (Nurse, 2002), I identified one other factor that might cause youth to reveal their records to an employer. Job applications usually ask for references, and because many incarcerated youth have had difficulty in school and prior jobs, they have few people from whom to choose. A parole officer is a reputable person in the community who can serve as a job reference. Given the choice of leaving the box blank or listing a parole officer, some youth choose the latter.

There are a number of other ways that employers (especially those in rural areas) can find out about juvenile criminal records. First, people in small towns tend to know each other and talk about local crimes. A youth who goes to prison is the subject of gossip that can easily reach employers' ears. Second, newspapers sometimes publish information about juvenile offenders. For example, Steven told me that everyone in his small town knew he had been arrested and convicted because it was in his local paper. Historically, there was an effort to prevent the media from publishing the names of juvenile offenders. During the 1990s some of these protections were relaxed as forty-seven states limited their confidentiality laws. Today, while laws vary across states, most allow the public and the media to access the identities of juveniles through open hearings. In fourteen states, the media can attend juvenile hearings and publish the youth's names. In thirty states, the media has access to juvenile hearings under certain circumstances (involving the age of the accused and the severity of the crime) and can publish the information. In four states (including Ohio), the media can obtain and publish youth's names if they are granted permission by the court (Snyder and Sickmund, 2006, 109). Additionally, in all states but three, the media can publish youth's names if the information is obtained from sources other than the juvenile justice system (for example, by talking to someone who attended the hearing). This is a result of two Supreme Court hearings in the late 1970s (*Oklahoma Publishing Company v. District Court in and for Oklahoma City* and *Smith v. Daily Mail Publishing Company*) (Snyder and Sickmund, 2006).

The Successful Job Search

Youth in the study were not totally unsuccessful in finding jobs. In fact, most found a job in their first six months out. The jobs they obtained fell into two categories. The first included fast food jobs acquired when a young man walked in and requested an application. The other category included low-skill manual labor jobs (tree trimming, construction, auto detailing, landscaping). The manual labor jobs tended to pay more and have better conditions than the fast food work. As a result, youth stayed at them longer. Notably, virtually every one of the manual labor jobs was obtained through the use of connections. For example, Andrew found a job at an auto body shop owned by his girlfriend's father. Kyle obtained his groundskeeping job at a golf course through his mother. Gabe got a carpentry job working with his uncles and cousins. Kirk had a friend who recommended him to the boss at the printing press where he worked. Jason showed great resourcefulness when his friend came over to complain that he had been fired from his job at a hog farm.

Jason jumped in the car and drove over to offer his services. The farmer, who was desperately trying to feed his pigs by himself, hired him immediately.

It is clear that networks are an effective and important way to locate a job and get hired. This finding correlates with a large number of studies examining how people get jobs (Davern and Hachen, 2006; Lin and Dumin, 1986; Montgomery, 1994). Most relevant for the present research, one study examined employment outcomes of adult males released from prison in Chicago (Visher and Kachnowski, 2007). Of the 30 percent of the sample who were employed four to eight months after release, 48 percent reported that family and friends had helped them obtain the job (90). Additionally, Mark Granovetter showed, in his oft-cited article "The Strength of Weak Ties" (1973), how social connections are an important way to get a job. Importantly, he argued that it is not primary ties like immediate family that are most crucial, but rather secondary ties like friends and neighbors. Because Granovetter was not studying people with a criminal record, however, it is important to be careful about generalizing his findings too broadly. John Hagan (1993) points out, for example, that the social networks of criminal youth may be less helpful than those of noncriminal youth. This is because the people in a criminal youth's network are often involved in crime rather than in the legitimate job market.

Since networks are a vital resource in a job search, it is important to understand how time spent in juvenile prison might affect ties to people who work at conventional jobs. Harry Holzer (2007) argues that prison severs the network ties that potentially connect ex-offenders with jobs. Holzer's study, however, was conducted with adults, and it is not clear that its findings generalize to youth. Most of the youth in this study, for example, were not working prior to incarceration (so they did not lose previous work connections), and the length of their sentences (eight and a half months on average) meant that they were out of their community for a fairly short period of time. As I discuss later in this chapter, it appears that returning youth do not face a lot of stigma from their families and communities (with the exception of small rural communities), suggesting that their social connections are not irreparably harmed. The problem appears to be that youth have few connections or skills prior to their incarceration and prison does not provide them with a chance to improve either. If prison has an effect on employment, it is likely to be a result of time lost in building an education, an employment history, or social connections. Further research should be conducted, however, with youth who are not first-time admissions to the prison system, to see whether repeated incarcerations and longer sentences have a more pronounced impact.

Keeping the Job

Obtaining a job can be difficult, but keeping a job also presents challenges to newly released youth. I was constantly surprised by the rapid job changes—rarely did a youth hold a job for more than a few months. Often their job change was a result of being fired. For example, Marcus got fired from a job stacking boxes because he didn't show up for his shift. Jason lost his hog farm job because he was chronically late. Kyle told me he was fired from the golf course because the boss "said I wasn't putting my best effort in." These cases are all examples of youth losing jobs because of their own negligence at work, but two other youth were fired when they had a run-in with the law. David was working as a dishwasher in a Mexican restaurant and got locked up for a few days for an offense having nothing to do with his job. The following quote was in response to my question about how he had liked the job:

> It was actually pretty good. I was about to get an apartment. . . . I was working 5 days a week, the only day I had off was Monday, and I was doing good. And you got paid every two weeks, and [I got] my every-two-week paycheck, which came anywhere from $420 to $460, so I was actually doing pretty good. I mean, I was putting a lot of hours in though. . . . It was getting to the point where I needed an apartment. And when I went to court, I tried to explain that to the judge, that, look, this is my job. I know I messed up. But if I lose this, then I'm really going to be in a messed-up position. She said she didn't care. Well, she didn't say she didn't care but she said, "That's not up to me, you got in trouble." By the time I did go [back] to court and saw the judge I was already fired from my work.

Like David, Jake lost his job unloading trucks when he was arrested and had to miss work to attend court dates. He told his boss that he had to go to court, but the boss told him that because he had not accrued any vacation days, he could not take any time off.

Most of the youth changed jobs because they were fired, but a significant number moved on because they decided to quit their jobs. The most common reasons for quitting were that the pay was too low or the working conditions were bad. Marcus and Kyle earned six dollars an hour working the grill at McDonald's. They both hated it and decided to quit after several weeks. Darius worked on an assembly line at a factory for eight dollars an hour and left hoping to find better wages and conditions elsewhere. The young men, not surprisingly, desired jobs with decent pay, respect, and the possibility of promotion. I had lunch with Kirk at an Applebee's near his home and asked him where he had applied before finding his current job. His answer illustrates the importance of pay and scheduling:

> Oh, everywhere. I applied here, Kohl's, Staples. I mean, I can look around and every place I see I applied there. . . . A couple people offered me the job, but they were like, oh, we're going to pay you $6.35 an hour, and we're going to work you nights and weekends. I was just going, no. And I got this, I seen this ad in the paper. It was financial adviser, telemarketing, and stuff like that, and whatever, I'd give it a shot. I called them up, had a two-hour over-the-phone interview, and like, well, we'll call you. Okay, I wasn't going to get the job. They're not going to call me. And so they called me, like, two days later, like, do you want to come in for an interview? And I was like, yeah. So they brought me in. They did an interview, and they're like, yeah, 'cause I had past telemarketing experience. . . . And so, they were just like, we'll call you. So now I'm thinking again, okay, they've looked at me. They've seen me, and no, they're not going to call. But then, like, the next day they were like, we want to offer you a position. Do you want to come in? I was like, "Yes, like eight bucks an hour!"

Kirk was excited about earning more than minimum wage and about being able to sit down at work. When I came back and talked to him six months later, however, he was no longer working there. It turned out that the company he had worked for was trying to sell some type of subprime mortgages. Kirk did not completely understand what he was selling, but he quickly realized that the company's practices were questionable on both legal and ethical grounds. He also discovered that eight dollars an hour does not guarantee that management will treat you with respect. He finally quit.

The problem with youth desiring a well-paid, flexible (or at least first-shift) job is that such jobs tend to be inaccessible to them. Most of them live in impoverished urban neighborhoods or, at the opposite extreme, in rural areas. Neither of these locations have many jobs available, especially to youth who do not have cars. The youth are further handicapped by a lack of skills and education. Unfortunately, the entry-level jobs they do find may simply serve to make crime more appealing. Richard Freeman's work (1991), conducted in the 1980s, provides support for this hypothesis, indicating that crime often pays more than a legitimate entry-level job. Additionally, crime allows youth to set their own hours and have some control over the conditions under which they work. When I spoke with Freddie, he talked about how alluring crime looked from the perspective of his fast food job:

FREDDIE: I worked at a Taco Bell at [city name] twice. Then I worked at a
   Burger King over on West 25th.

ANNE: And did you quit or what happened?

FREDDIE: I quit both times. I quit all three times.

ANNE: How come?

FREDDIE: Man, it was just . . . I couldn't see myself doing that for six or
   seven dollars an hour. As soon as I got off of work I turned myself
   around and made some calls—each of them like thirty dollars', fifty
   dollars', sixty dollars' worth. I just quit and started hustling. Dedicated
   myself to it.

Freddie clearly believed that entry-level jobs do not pay enough to make
them worth his time, especially when he could sell drugs much more easily
and lucratively.

Fast food work as an entry-level job is particularly problematic, not
only because of the low pay but because of the lack of respect associated
with it. These youth have seen little respect in their lives: not from their
schools, from employers, or from the correctional system. They come back
from prison having gained some respect as a "tough guy," but it is very difficult to act the image of the tough guy if you are wearing a McDonald's
uniform. And while fast food can be an acceptable job for a teenager who
plans to go on to college or who can use the job as a stepping-stone to
something else, these youth are not in that position—they are looking for
an "adult" job that can provide them with a chance for a living wage. They
recognize that fast food restaurants have few opportunities for promotion
or pay raises. As a result, no youth in the study stayed at a fast food job for
more than six weeks.

Family Relationships Post-release

Oh, it was cool. My mom was like, she ain't take the Christmas tree
down until . . . they release me. I opened my presents and she seemed
all sad, like you don't even seem like you happy, and I'm like, you know
what I'm saying, I'm happy. I ain't just hopping up and down.
   —Chad

Youth nearing their release date have many fantasies about the things
they will do once they get home. Perhaps surprisingly, spending time with
families often tops the list. Some youth have not seen their families for many
months, and most have not seen younger siblings (or their own children)

since their incarceration. The first few weeks at home tend to be marked by fairly harmonious family relationships, in part because both the young men and their families have built high expectations for their return. As described in the previous chapter, the family's hope is often based on promises the youth have made while they were incarcerated. At first, youth try to fulfill these promises by staying at home and abstaining from drugs. When I asked newly released youth about their relationships with their parents, many told me that they were about the same as they were prior to incarceration, but a significant number said that the relationships were better. I asked Marcus how things were with his mother. He said,

> MARCUS: It is better. I talk to her. I stay there. I come home instead of talking to people. Talk about stuff before I got locked up.
> ANNE: And you're there more now? Why is that?
> MARCUS: I don't use drugs no more.

Both Alex and Eric agreed with Marcus that their post-incarceration sobriety had improved their relationships with their mothers. Alex said, "We can talk more now, like, I can sit there and have a conversation with her now, a respectable conversation. 'Cause before I went in jail, I was always high, so you know what I'm saying, so I couldn't really sit there and be stoned talking to my ma." In an interview soon after his release, Nick told me that he felt closer to his grandmother:

> We just connected better now. Like before, you know . . . I was always out and stuff, but in the last couple of months for some reason we just started talking. . . . I'd sit in a room and just talk to her about stuff. And before it wasn't really . . . I mean, like I'd be able to sit there and talk to her, but . . . now I'm holding like an hour-and-a-half conversation about stuff. Like just about life and stuff. Before . . . I never talked to her about life. Like she could tell me what I needed to do. I'd be like, "Yeah." You know what I'm saying? "Whatever. I'm, I'm gonna go." But now like I'll sit and I'll listen to her.

The parents I talked to in the weeks following their sons' homecomings also sounded positive about their relationships. Kyle's mother said, "Yeah, it's more better. It's more better. It's more positive. . . . We've learned how to get along and get along better, with everything that's happening in our lives right now."

While families are hopeful and encouraged by the first weeks post-release, they are also quite aware of the possibility that their sons might again become involved with drugs or crime. The youth reported that their families were more vigilant about their behavior than they had been prior to incarceration. Richard, for example, said that his mother had begun asking him where he was going every time he left the house, something she rarely did before his incarceration. Tom's mother was terrified that he would get rearrested for some minor infraction, and she pleaded with him to stay home as much as possible.

Because I conducted most of the family interviews during the youth's incarceration or immediately after their release, I do not have a lot of information about the family's perceptions of changes in the relationships over the long term. There is evidence to indicate, however, that some families become disappointed as the youth start hanging out more with friends, restart drug use, or reinvolve themselves with crime. I interviewed Nick's grandmother several months after he was released. I asked her what he had been doing recently:

NICK'S GRANDMOTHER: Out on the street, I guess you could say. He ain't going to school or nothing. Just out.

ANNE: And . . . he's living here?

NICK'S GRANDMOTHER: Uh-huh.

ANNE: And how is that for you?

NICK'S GRANDMOTHER: Good. He know he don't have any place else to go so I told him, I said, "You gonna have to get you a job because I'm only let you stay here until the end of the summer." I said, "It would give you a chance to kind of get yourself together, get you a job." I said, "After you gonna have to, you know, you gonna have to move." But . . . [I] let him stay here for free. You know. Kind of go as he please. And he's an adult now, and I don't tell him nothing. He look at me like, okay. You know. Just keep on going. But I'm a crutch, and I'm not gonna be a crutch. Like I said I'd give him a chance to get hisself together. If he don't get a job . . . oh, well. He still got to go.

ANNE: Do you think his time in jail has changed him in any way?

NICK'S GRANDMOTHER: I don't think it has helped him none. I don't think it changed him. It just ain't helping him.

This quote makes it clear that Nick's grandmother was nearing the end of her rope. Kyle's mother, also initially hopeful, became more and more distraught as her son proved unwilling or unable to hold down a job. Ethan's family stopped talking to him after they went on vacation and left the house in his care. When they returned home, they found that it had been trashed. Jake was rearrested several months after his release from the DYS. I asked him how his parents had reacted, and he said, "They were mad. 'Cause I told [them] when I got out of DYS, I wasn't gonna do nothing else dumb."

Because only ten of the youth in this study were fathers, I am not able to draw strong conclusions about the effect of incarceration on relationships with children. For guidance, I turn to my own previous research with 258 fathers paroled from the California Youth Authority (Nurse, 2002). The experience of the California fathers suggests that relationships with children, like those with other family members, tend to be strong during the first few weeks post-release. This is because incarcerated fathers spend a lot of time thinking about their children and want to be actively involved in their lives. Interestingly, the informal culture of the prison is supportive of active fatherhood, and youth often urge each other to be good dads. As a result, many young men promise their children and the children's mothers that they will provide financial and emotional support once they are released. Most parolees make an effort to fulfill these promises but find that reality places many barriers before them. Some return from prison to find children who are uncomfortable around them and are unwilling to obey. Others find it impossible to negotiate relationships with the mothers of their children, complicating efforts to arrange visitation time with their children. As described, many newly released young men also find it difficult to obtain a job and, consequently, are unable to provide the financial support they have promised. While some are successful in maintaining involvement over time, most decrease contact with their children as the months go by.

The preceding paragraphs tell the story that I heard most often from the youth—that they made promises to many members of their families, were welcomed home, tried to keep the promises, and began to fail over time. It is important to note, however, that there were two significant exceptions to this pattern. First, not every parent welcomed his or her son home. Casey's father, for example, was not able to get over his anger about his son's incarceration. Both Casey and his mother reported that when Casey came home, his father avoided him or spent time yelling at him. Similarly, Kirk's incarceration was the last straw for his stepfather, and he made it clear that he did not want Kirk to return to the house. Ultimately, Kirk moved into an apartment, and his mother and his stepfather divorced, in part because they were fighting so much about Kirk. Darius's mother told him she did not want him back and went so far as to sell his clothes. Youth whose families do not want them to come home face unique challenges, especially when parole conditions (or economic conditions) force them to live with resentful family members. A second exception to the pattern—and one that is far more positive—is when youth return from prison and succeed in fulfilling their promises to their families. I discuss these youth at the end of this chapter.

Friendships Post-release

MARCUS: Some things never change. Same old thing. Same thing.
ANNE: So it was like you were never gone?
MARCUS: Never gone. Same thing.

When the youth arrive home, they are surprised to find that little seems to have changed in their absence. Even more surprising, perhaps, is that they find it easy to return to their circle of friends as though they had never been gone. Sometimes close friends treat them with special attention for a short period of time but quickly return to "normal" behavior. The youth in this study found this rather mystifying. Without talking to a wider sample of nonincarcerated youth, it is hard to tell why a youth's absence and return are so unremarkable, but it likely has to do with high rates of incarceration in the neighborhoods from which the prison pulls. Serving time is fairly common, and neighborhoods are used to assimilating returning prisoners.

Only one of the youth reported that incarceration had a negative impact on his friendship circle. He returned home to find that a few of his friends no longer wanted to associate with him, presumably because he had been to prison. The fact that this was so unusual suggests, however, that there is little stigma associated with incarceration. In his research with urban minority youth, Paul Hirschfield (2008) also failed to find a stigma associated with incarceration. My own prior work with paroled fathers in California suggested the same thing (Nurse, 2002). It appears that time spent in prison can actually enhance a youth's reputation—especially if tales of his fighting prowess in the institution reach the streets. Because news travels fast in most communities, youth usually do not have to tell people where they have been because the street networks already know. In a few cases, however, youth in the study tried to play up their DYS experiences in the hopes of impressing people and making new friends. Kenneth told me that he went so far as to show his DYS shower flip-flops to people to prove that he had done time. Unfortunately, friends who are attracted to the DYS reputation often are engaged in criminal activities themselves and do not offer much support to help young men desist from crime. When I asked Ethan whether having been to the DYS changed how his friends viewed him, he said, "I got more demand. You know what I'm saying? It did change that way. Got more popular with some of the known dope dealers. Which wasn't a good thing."

The newly released youth made it clear that they felt considerable pressure and temptation to re-engage with old friends or to spend time with new criminally involved friends. Some youth, however, tried to resist this pressure in order to lessen their chances of going back to crime. Research has found that most delinquents have a mix of delinquent and nondelinquent friends (Haynie, 2001). About half of the incarcerated youth in this study told me that they planned to avoid some of their more delinquent friends in order to increase their own chances of going straight. This was particularly true of the youth who had been addicted to drugs. Sammy told me he wanted to find new friends when he got out of prison. When I asked why he told me, "Because all the friends I hung out with, they did drugs, you know, drank and when I get out I know I gotta problem with alcohol and smoking pot that I can't be around 'em because then it's just gonna be a big temptation."

As it turns out, staying away from old friends can be difficult. Parolees are usually released back into their old neighborhoods, and their delinquent friends often live next door or down the block. Most of the youth said that it was impossible to completely avoid old friends but that it was possible to limit the time they spent with them. None actually told their old friends that they wanted to avoid them—they just gradually gave them the cold shoulder and hoped that the friendship would amicably fade away. As described above, youth also sometimes use parole rules as an excuse to avoid former friends who are also on parole. Going back to the old group of friends is a continuous temptation however. When I interviewed John the first time, he told me he intended to stay away from his old crowd. Once he was released, however, it proved to be too difficult to stay away from the neighborhood youth. From adult prison, John told me, "I got out, start messing with the same people, end up with another charge. That's what happened. . . this time, too. Started drinking, chill with the same people, end up with this charge I got now."

Prison Friendships: Do They Last?

In Chapter 4, I discussed friendship formation in prison, arguing that while it may be somewhat superficial, it does occur in the more private spaces in the prison. This leads to the question of whether these friendships continue past incarceration. When I asked the youth about this possibility, they were clear that prison friendships are not lasting. The parole rule forbidding parolees from contact with other parolees does serve as a deterrent for some of the youth, but more important, the youth themselves are distrustful of their prison friends, recognizing that the people they knew on the inside might not act the same on the outside. Freddie came home from prison and hoped that the close friend he made while incarcerated could be an ally on the outside as he tried to go straight. Notable about the story is Freddie's caution in reestablishing contact on the outside:

I called him from a pay phone because I didn't want him to know my cell phone. . . .'Cause, you know, it's different when you're in jail with a person than when you get out. So I was just trying to see where he was at. . . . They'll be your friend while you're in here . . . and when they come to jail they put up roles or something. Some of them just don't want to get in trouble. But when they hit the streets they go buck wild, you know. That's why. 'Cause Joel was real cool. He was like, we was like, we was like brothers in there. We argued and stuff like we were brothers. . . . But he just went back to the same thing. . . . If he had some money in his pocket, he'd probably be the same person. But money changes people. He starts using that stuff [drugs] and robbing, stealing.

Alex also had a close friend in prison. One day the friend just showed up at his house. Alex was angry because it was a potential parole violation for both of them.

Out of nowhere he just pulled up at my house one day. And I'm like, 'cause I told him you know where I live and everything, when I was in there, and he pulled up to my house and was sitting on my porch. I'm like, yeah, right. And then, he was like, "What you been up to?" And I was like, "Nothing." And then I say, "Why you down here? You ain't allowed down here. You live in Marion. You're on parole." He's like, "I mean, I just ran away." I said, "Well, get the hell away from me."

Youth in prison often have a sophisticated understanding of impression management. They understand that the institution encourages youth to act in ways they might not normally, with some putting on a facade of wanting to change and others acting more tough and violent as a means of self-protection. As a result, youth do not trust that the "friends" they have inside the institution will be the same once they emerge from the institution. In this study, only one prison friendship lasted beyond a few letters or phone calls.

Relationships with Girlfriends Post-release

Most of the youth in this study (thirty-one of forty) reported that they were dating someone at the time of their incarceration. Few had faith that these young women would wait for them, and for the most part, they were right. Thirteen of the young women either broke up with their incarcerated boyfriends or got involved with someone else and allowed word of it to reach the prison. Another four relationships ended when the incarcerated youth themselves broke it off. By the time the youth in this study were released, only ten reported that they were still involved with their girlfriends. Of these ten, only six couples lasted more than a few weeks past the young men's release.

Couples who stayed together for the duration of the study, not surprisingly, were those who had been together the longest and were most enmeshed in each other's lives. Jake had been with his girlfriend for a year and a half when he was arrested for the offense that brought him to the DYS. His girlfriend had become part of his family and developed a particularly close relationship with his mother. Jake was nervous about whether she would stay faithful, but he was also happy that she seemed willing to try. When he was released, the couple moved in together, and within weeks she became pregnant. Both Frank and Dion were together with their girlfriends for a relatively long time prior to their incarceration (two years and one and a half years, respectively), and their girlfriends seemed extremely committed to the relationship, writing to them daily. Anthony and his girlfriend had the longest relationship (six years) of any in the study. Richard had also been involved in a long-term relationship, meeting his girlfriend three years before incarceration. Just prior to his arrest, they had become engaged and had been planning to move in together. It was these long-term relationships that were able to survive incarceration and release.

Because I did not interview the young men's girlfriends, I cannot report on why they choose to stay with incarcerated boyfriends. In her research with the wives and girlfriends of adult inmates, Megan Comfort (2008) found that women stay with incarcerated men because they are hopeful that the men's criminal or abusive behavior will change and because the prison provides a controlled environment in which men tend to be both attentive and remorseful. She notes that women are frequently disappointed when the men return home and cannot or will not live up to their promises. Similarly, when youth come home from prison and try to resume relationships with girlfriends, they face significant challenges. As I described in *Fatherhood Arrested* (2002), young women often become more independent in the young men's absence. This is hard for a youth to accept since he assumes he will return to the central position he played in the girlfriend's life prior to incarceration. In this study, Richard told me that his fiancée was a different person when he got back—more grown up and more independent. As a result, they struggled to find a new way to be together. Like families, girlfriends are sometimes nervous that their boyfriends might return to their criminal ways. When some do go back to prison, the girlfriends tend to be extremely disappointed. During the course of this study, Ethan returned to crime and went back to prison. He reported that his girlfriend (who was also the mother of his child) was furious and disappointed.

The relationships that survived prison but ended soon after the young men's release were different from the ones that survived long term in that they were of shorter duration and the couples did not know each other well. It is likely that these relationships outlasted incarceration, at least in part, because they were in the early stages and seemed to hold great promise and excitement. The couples were able to build a fantasy relationship through letters, but they could not sustain this fantasy in person. Casey, for example, had just met his girlfriend when he was locked up. She promised to stay faithful, and they wrote loving letters. The truth, however, was that she and Casey hardly knew each other, and they broke up almost immediately upon his release. Similarly, Joshua started dating his girlfriend two months prior to his incarceration. The relationship survived three months after his release until he concluded that she was not stable and left her. Kenneth's relationship also disintegrated when he was released. He and his girlfriend had dated casually eight months prior to his arrest but drifted apart while he was gone. Dan's relationship was the only one with a substantial history that came to an end once he was released. He had dated his girlfriend for about a year and returned home from prison to a new baby that had been conceived just prior to his incarceration. He and the baby's mother tried to give the relationship a go, but she decided she could not trust him and ended things.

Conclusion

The period immediately following the youth's release from prison is filled with hope, expectation, and excitement, but with few definite plans. Although they return to a world that seems little changed, the echoes of prison can be felt in their social relationships and in their attempts to get an education or a job. In the area of education, some are able to earn the high school degree they had assumed, prior to prison, was out of reach. Others, however, fall behind in school or are prevented from returning to public school. The echoes of prison may resonate even further as juvenile records become increasingly available to educational institutions. It is likely that those youth who have college aspirations may see their hopes dashed when institutions of higher learning are able to access their records. Failing to get a high school degree or being blocked from college are significant barriers to later employment and earning.

It does not appear that time served in juvenile prison has a strong impact on immediate employability in the low-level jobs that youth are generally eligible for. Prison does not train youth for higher-level jobs, nor does it contribute to a youth's work history. This serves to make the young men less desirable to potential employers. Parole restrictions and lax regulations about the confidentiality of juvenile records, in some cases, can also interfere with employment. In most cases, prison does not appear to harm the willingness of social networks to link youth to jobs. In rural areas, however, social network damage tends to be much more extensive because gossip and a greater stigma associated with incarceration combine to make it harder for rural youth to escape their pasts.

Perhaps the area where youth feel the most change from their pre-incarceration lives is in their relationships with their families and girlfriends. High initial expectations from families mean that the first few weeks out are hopeful and relationships feel close. This closeness and hope appears to decrease over time as many youth are unable to live up to the expectations that they helped to build from prison. Their continuing inability to find or hold a job upsets many families as does the fact that some youth return to drugs or crime. As described, few romantic relationships outlast the youth's prison terms. The youth sometimes told me that prison caused the break-ups, but it is likely that most of their relationships—like most adolescent relationships—would have ended regardless of their incarceration. In fact, it is likely that prison lengthened some of the relationships as it allowed the youth to build a fantasy relationship through the mail. Relationships that survived incarceration were challenged by girlfriends' new independence and by their high expectations for their boyfriends' behavior.

Further research on reentry topics is of critical importance since this study does not follow youth long enough to assess prison's long-term impact. I do, however, have information about the youth at the conclusion of this study, two and a half years after it began. Four young men—Tom, Ben, Caleb, and Nelson—were still being held on their original charges. Not surprisingly, these youth were among the most deeply troubled of the group. Nelson, for example, came to the DYS having already acquired an institutional mindset during several periods of incarceration at his county-level detention home. In conversations with me, he loved to brag about his position in the prison hierarchy and the amount of fighting he did. He told me that he had spoken with his mother once or twice at the beginning of his sentence, but by the end of this study, he was in full hard-timing mode and had no outside contact. Although his minimum sentence was twelve months, he kept getting assigned additional time. Tom, Ben, and Caleb were not as institutionalized as Nelson, but all were extremely angry and had been involved in numerous violent incidents during their incarcerations. It is likely that these four young men will have significant problems reintegrating to life outside prison.

At the opposite end of the spectrum, there was a group of youth who returned home from prison and quickly got their lives back on track. Most of these young men had very limited criminal histories and strong support systems outside prison. Gabe, for example, was released from the DYS to a minimum-security drug treatment facility. During the six months he spent there, he received training in life and job skills in addition to drug treatment. He returned home, moved in with his girlfriend and baby, and immediately found a stable carpentry job. Similarly, Richard returned to his mother and stepfather's home and secured a job at a package delivery company. His family monitored him closely and supported his efforts to desist from crime. Sam and Kenneth were two of the youngest study participants, and both spent relatively little time at the DYS. They returned from prison and were quickly accepted back into their high schools. At the conclusion of the study, they seemed to be doing well and told me (fairly convincingly) that they had dramatically cut back any criminal involvement.

While it is clear that some youth are able to successfully reenter society after incarceration, this was not the most common path followed by the youth participating in this study. Instead, most returned home and encountered serious problems with school, employment, and family relationships. A significant number returned to criminal involvement. Six young men, including Nick, Alex, and Jason, were released to parole, committed new crimes or technical violations, and were incarcerated again by the end of the study period. Another two (Jamal and Tyrell) went AWOL from parole and were likely to be reincarcerated when located. These young men represent a 22 percent recidivism rate for my study group. It is likely that, over time, this rate could easily approach or surpass the DYS's published three-year rate of 53 percent (Ohio Department of Youth Services, 2008).

At the time of the third interviews, it was not hard for me to see which youth were at high risk of recidivism or other problems like depression or drug addiction. Marcus, for example, had returned to dealing drugs after a long period of unsuccessful job hunting. He assured me, in carefully guarded language, that he'd gotten better at dealing drugs and would not be caught this time. Steven had a few minor brushes with the law and could not seem to find employment. Kyle refused to conduct a serious job search and instead spent his time hanging out and fighting with his mother. These young men were directionless and unhappy, and unless something dramatic happened, they were at high risk of continued unemployment and later incarceration. As of February 2009, at least six of them were under the supervision of the adult correctional system.

After following these youth for two and a half years, this study had to come to a close. My own private and professional life made it difficult to continue the arduous schedule that interviewing required. I also began to lose track of youth as they got off parole, moved, and went through multiple cell phone numbers. During the final interviews, I reminded the young men that this would be the last time I contacted them for an official meeting. Although a few looked relieved, most took the opportunity to say that they had enjoyed the study and looked forward to the completion of the book. I was surprised by the number who expressed hope that the project might be used to create public policies that would make the experiences of future generations of youth better than their own.

Chapter 7

Policy Directions

In the first six chapters we followed forty young men through their experiences with the juvenile justice system. In this chapter, I step back from the chronological account of these youth's lives to ask what their stories contribute to our theoretical understanding of juvenile detention and to our policy debate about the correctional system. The chapter concludes with thoughts about further research and about the future of the juvenile justice system.

Impression Management in Prison: Navigating Impossible Demands

The term "impression management" refers to the ways in which people, consciously or unconsciously, try to influence the impression others form of them (Goffman, 1959). Impression management is a process that all of us engage in throughout our lives. In a sense, we put on a performance any time we are with others—although some acts feel more natural and real to us than others. Prison life presents some unusual challenges to impression management because youth are subject to conflicting requirements and expectations. This study indicates that prison culture requires young men to appear tough, violent, successful with females, poor in social class, rich in possessions, and well connected. At the same time, as described in Chapter 3, the formal organization demands an act of remorse and compliance to authority—qualities that are the opposite of toughness and masculinity.

Youth are often already familiar with contradictory impression management requirements when they arrive at prison. Elijah Anderson (2000) found that changing acts was common among youth in the poor urban neighborhood he studied. Youth had to accomplish this as they moved from the impression management demands of street life to those of their families. In prison, however, two contradictory acts need to occur simultaneously since the youth who demand a tough act and the staff who require remorse and compliance are both in the same living space, the same anger management group, and the same recreation yard. The price of failure is high—those who do not fulfill the requirements of the staff may find their release date moved back, while those who fail to fulfill the expectations of their fellow inmates can find their status and safety in jeopardy. The youth who are most successful in prison are those who become masters of code switching.

Every time I teach my Inside Outside class, I spend two sessions talking about impression management. While all the students seem to enjoy this topic, the inside students respond with special enthusiasm. It is clear that they find impression management to be a particularly useful way to understand and explain their day-to-day lives. They also seem to find it cathartic to talk about the complex and exhausting acts they feel required to maintain. The youth in this study, although they had never heard a lecture on it, were well aware of the ideas of impression management. Sam, for example, told me about the need to put on an act in the presence of prison staff. He said, "Sometimes you might, like, have to fake it to make it. Say you going along and you acting like you really gonna change. Fool the social worker just to get out. And sometimes you might have to do that." Impression management, often unconscious outside of prison, becomes highly conscious and calculated once youth are incarcerated.

The rigidity of the impression management requirements and the need to code switch encourages incarcerated youth's tendency to distrust others. Because it is necessary to play their acts consistently and rigorously, most youth come to see everyone as an actor, and it becomes hard to accept anyone's presentation of self as "real." The youth told me that endless time is spent analyzing the acts of others in prison. This is illustrated by a quote from my third interview with Marcus. The interview took place just after he had been paroled. Musing about prison he said, "I ain't never go and talk to nobody. I was always sitting down chilling and looking. Looking around. Watching everybody. Learning everybody. You know, so when they characterize their talk . . . you have to know all about talk. Who's, who's for real. You know. Who's fake. You know what I'm saying? You pinpoint all that. That's how you take control." Here Marcus shows a sophisticated understanding of the game of impression management in prison. The public nature of the contact between youth requires them to maintain a constant facade of toughness and masculinity. Personal information about others becomes valuable because it can be used to uncover who the other youth "really are."

The informal culture of the prison demands that youth maintain a front that is emotionally exhausting and promotes an unhealthy environment.

Changing this culture, however, will not be easy. Research suggests that small facilities with well-trained and caring staff tend to have the most success fostering a healthy informal culture (Bortner and Williams, 1997; Feld, 1981). At the same time, larger institutions may be able to make positive changes through a manipulation of the status system. This technique is not a new idea—in the past, prisons have tried to reduce violence by closing particularly unhealthy routes to status. For example, the DYS periodically tries to discourage or break up area code affiliations. This strategy has not been terribly effective, however, perhaps because no other routes to status were put in its place. In an environment with so few opportunities for status or respect, youth cling to the existing system. Rather than simply eliminating this system, the prison should instead alter the informal culture by adding new mechanisms for status attainment.

One way for prison staff to open additional routes to status would be to allow more activities in the prison (sports tournaments other than basketball, music groups, drawing clubs). A second way would be to follow the lead of another residential youth institution—the military academy—and create institutionally sanctioned routes to prestige and respect. While military academies have their own sets of institutional problems, Murray Milner (2004) points out that they are successful in promoting a status system based on time spent in the academy. Prisons could make use of similar techniques. Privileges are bestowed on cadets as they rise through the ranks, and those at low ranks can easily see the privileges they will gain as they advance. Most important, cadets buy into the system because it gives them solidarity and guarantees them benefits with time spent in the institution. Same-status cadets spend time together, support each other, and are invested in helping each other.

Ohio juvenile prisons currently have a behavioral ranking system, but it is not systematic and does not encourage inmates of the same rank to see each other as allies. It might be possible to change this mentality by setting up military-style "entering classes" that are meant to support each other. Youth who enter the prison during the same month (or perhaps who have similar release dates) could be put into support groups and encouraged to work together to move through ranks. Such a system would give youth an immediate group identity and lessen the need to quickly affiliate with an area code. This change would require a fundamental reworking of some of the assumptions currently operating in the system, but it could potentially result in a far healthier environment for all involved. In terms of status, it would give youth another mechanism for ordering themselves, one that is not based on possessions or hegemonic masculinity.

While making changes in the prison's informal culture is most pressing, states should also think carefully about their formal impression management requirements. In Chapter 3 I described how youth are required to prove that they have been rehabilitated through a "proper" display of remorse and through public self-revelation. In an environment where a youth's personal safety is at stake if he does not act masculine enough, it is simply not fair to base release decisions on a show of submission and remorse. Research suggesting that there is variation in norms regarding the expression of remorse across racial/ethnic groups also calls into question its use as a marker of rehabilitation (Everett and Nienstedt, 1999). Prisons will need to continue to use institutional behavior as a way to make decisions about release dates and rewards, but impression management should be de-emphasized.

Fostering Hatred in the Juvenile Prison

Chapter 4 illustrated the central role that hatred (or at least the appearance of it) plays in the culture of the juvenile prison. The expression of hatred based on race, sexual orientation, and gender is a way for youth to gain status and to ensure their own safety. Given the large number of young people who pass through our nation's prisons, it is surprising that we know little about the long-term effects associated with time spent in such a racist, homophobic, and misogynist environment. For example, there has been very little research on the question of incarceration's effects on individual racial attitudes (and even less on attitudes toward gender or sexual orientation). Researchers have focused more on group dynamics—examining, for example, the conditions under which racial groups will have more or less antagonism toward each other. The results of the few (and quite dated) studies that have been conducted conclude that the racial attitudes of adult inmates become more negative during their incarceration (Bugansky, 1958; Irwin, 1980). While this study was not specifically designed to measure racial attitudes over the course of juvenile incarceration, it does support the idea that prison can intensify racial hatred, at least among whites.

During the first and second round of interviewing, I talked with each young man about his feelings toward both whites and blacks. I also asked if he felt incarceration was changing any of his racial attitudes. About half of the white youth told me that incarceration was causing them to develop more negative feelings toward blacks. Ben, for example, said, "When I first got locked up, I was thinking, I even told somebody else, like, man, this, me coming to jail makes me want, not want to like black people." When I asked these young men to describe how their feelings were changing during their incarceration, most said that they had come to see blacks as "domineering" and "aggressive." A few said that prison had reinforced their image of blacks as violent and dangerous. One of the factors driving the whites' negative views was jealousy—the youth who expressed the most negative views were quick to complain about blacks' perceived monopoly on power and status in the institution. Blacks were less likely than whites to express negative sentiments about the other racial group and few said that incarceration was changing earlier attitudes toward whites (although three youth commented that they had come to see white youth as "weak"). This lack of reported change is consistent with research indicating that blacks are less likely than whites to change racial attitudes in response to intergroup contact (Tropp and Pettigrew, 2005). It is probably not surprising that blacks expressed little hostility toward whites since they believed themselves to be the culturally dominant group in the prison and generally did not feel threatened by other racial/ethnic groups.

The question of the long-term effects of prison on racism, homophobia, and sexism calls for further work. The ideal research would be longitudinal, allowing researchers to identify whether attitude change occurs during incarceration and whether any new attitudes persist past release. If we find that prison increases racism (or homophobia or sexism), we need to be concerned about the implications for society. Regardless of the answers to these long-term questions, however, states have a responsibility to stem the violence and fear that racism, homophobia, and sexism create inside the institution. One solution, as described in the previous section, may be to increase the number of routes to status so that youth do not have to rely on the expression of hatred as a way to gain respect. Staff also need extensive training in diversity issues so that they are given the confidence and understanding necessary to help create a safe environment.

A few states have begun to work on even more targeted reforms to decrease hate. In 2006, for example, Hawaii settled a lawsuit that had been filed by the American Civil Liberties Union on the behalf of three youth. The suit alleged verbal and physical harassment of juvenile prison inmates on the basis of sexual orientation and gender identity. Hawaii settled the lawsuit and is now in the process of implementing a number of programs and safeguards (Magin, 2006). In 2007, the state of California went a step further when it passed SB 518, the Juvenile Justice Safety and Prevention Act. This law prohibits discrimination against and harassment of incarcerated youth based on their sexual orientation or gender identity. Finally, in 2007, New York adopted sweeping new guidelines prohibiting discrimination and improving conditions for incarcerated gay, lesbian, and transgender youth. All states need to evaluate their policies involving the expression of racism, sexism, and homophobia in juvenile prisons. If states are not willing to make changes for ethical and moral reasons, the legal system may soon intervene. The success of the lawsuits in Hawaii and California suggests that other states will be forced to implement new policies if they do not do so on their own.

Trust, Legitimacy, and Citizenship

Every time I listen to this study's interview tapes, I am struck by the anger and helplessness the young men expressed about their experiences in the correctional system. While some youth were just angry in general, my coding of the data revealed that there were several experiences that caused distress across the group. While I describe these experiences elsewhere in the book, it is worthwhile to consider them together. They include unclear release dates, a lack of respect by authorities, inconsistency in rule enforcement, and favoritism by staff. This list indicates that youth become most upset when they feel out of control, discriminated against, or disrespected.

Tom Tyler's work on procedural justice helps to explain why experiences with unfairness or inconsistency are so distressing to incarcerated youth (see, for example, Tyler and Lind, 2001). Tyler argues that people's feelings about encounters with the legal system are based largely on the procedures employed. People want to feel that they are playing on a level field and that they have an opportunity to be heard. They also want to be treated with respect. Looking specifically at the legal system, Tyler finds that these kinds of procedural justice issues are important predictors of how a person will feel about his or her trial at its conclusion—even more important than the trial's outcome. Given this finding, it is hardly surprising that the youth in this study were upset about policies that seemed arbitrary and beyond their control. It is useful to examine three of these policies in more detail: indeterminate sentencing, parole, and child support.

During the interviews, I quickly learned that asking a youth about his release date was a sure way to upset him. The young men simply did not have a firm idea of when they would be able to go home, and they did not understand how their release dates were calculated. One day in an Inside Outside class, I asked whether anyone could explain the process of determining release dates. Several young men raised their hands and started off confidently but then realized that they were confused. The entire class finally started laughing, and a staff member stepped in to give a semicoherent explanation. It became obvious that indeterminate sentences are not clearly explained to incarcerated youth or to their families. As a result, the youth in this study were often completely confused about early release dates, minimum dates, and presumptive dates. They did not fully understand how a presumptive release date was calculated, nor did they understand the criteria for extra time. This left the youth frustrated and angry when extra time was assigned. Some told me they felt as if the prison system was toying with them.

Programming requirements were another aspect of indeterminate sentences that violated youth's sense of procedural justice. Indeterminate sentences allow the correctional agency to hold a youth until he completes an assigned set of programs (like victim awareness or drug treatment). There are not always good screening mechanisms to assign youth to these programs. As a result, a young man with a drug violation might be required to complete an irrelevant anger management program before he is released. This problem is compounded by the fact that the youth think that some of the required programs are stupid and useless. Perhaps the most unfortunate circumstance is when programs are full or are offered infrequently and a youth is not given an opportunity to complete them before his release date, ensuring an extension of his sentence. This is a waste of young men's time and taxpayers' money.

When implemented fairly and clearly, indeterminate sentences are an important tool in maintaining order in prison and encouraging youth to participate in rehabilitative programming. Indeterminate sentences are also potentially good for public safety as staff can assess whether youth would be a danger to others if released. At the same time, states need to think about procedural justice in the implementation of these sentences. Release should not be based on program completion unless these programs are offered in a timely manner and are shown to be effective, and unless screening mechanisms are implemented to ensure that only youth who need the programs are required to take them. Most important, indeterminate sentences must be clearly explained to youth and their families at the time of sentencing.

Parole was a second policy that the youth felt violated their procedural justice. The young men in this study did not understand what parole was, and more important, they did not understand that their "release date" referred to a release to parole, not to freedom. As a result, parole felt like a second punishment. This problem is not difficult to fix—it is simply a matter of changing the language used by the correctional system, from "minimum time to release" to "minimum time to parole." Institutional caseworkers should start talking to youth about parole as soon as they are admitted so that they understand its purpose and duration. All families should receive information about parole long before their sons return home.

A final policy the youth in this study identified as procedurally problematic was child support. As described, the arrival of a child-support order came as a surprise to three of this study's youth and to their families. This was largely because Ohio does not have a consistent policy—some families receive child-support orders and others do not. Because I was confused about the rules, I called a number of child-support enforcement agencies in Ohio to ask about the policies regarding juvenile incarceration and child support. The responses I received—even when I pushed for more information—were bewildering and contradictory. Given this, it is not surprising that youth and their families were confused and believed these orders were unfairly implemented. It is clear that Ohio (and other states) needs to develop a uniform policy across counties and publicize it widely.

Changing and clarifying sentencing, parole, and child-support policies could go a long way toward making incarcerated and paroled youth less angry and resentful of the system. If we are serious about improving procedural justice, however, larger-scale change is needed. Today most states, like Ohio, employ high levels of situational control in their juvenile prisons. According to researchers, situational control involves very close monitoring of inmate behavior, limitations on movement, and restrictions on privileges (Sparks, Bottoms, and Hay, 1996). The operative assumption for the use of this type of control is that inmates will engage in "disruptive" behavior if given the opportunity. The effort is made, therefore, to control the prison environment so closely that these opportunities are minimized. Social control—the other end of the spectrum—is when prison staff attempt to create a social environment that is conducive to order by encouraging close relationships between inmates and guards, allowing prisoners to be involved in policy creation, and bestowing privileges on well-behaved inmates. The assumption behind social control is that inmates act rationally and will modify their behavior in response to their environment. In other words, prisoners who feel respected will treat others in a similar way.

Moving our juvenile prisons closer to a model of social control would improve procedural justice in prison policies. For example, it would allow youth to participate in some aspects of decision making in the institution. This has the potential to teach valuable skills in negotiation, compromise, and respect. It is also likely to result in a decrease in violence (Feld, 1981; Bortner and Williams, 1997). Importantly, it also could give youth the sense that they have a voice in making real decisions. This policy suggestion, however, can only be implemented in small facilities (or within units of larger institutions). Staff need to ensure that any power they give to youth is real power—not just the power to rubber-stamp the current policies. To accomplish a situation of true social control, staff will need to be given intensive training and support. Previous experiments with moving toward social control suggest that it is difficult for staff to move to a new model that, at first glance, appears to diminish their power (Bortner and Williams, 1997).

In the short term, improving procedural justice in institutional and sentencing policies has the potential to relieve distress and anger among youth and their families. It may also provide long-term societal benefits. Tyler (1998) finds that people who experience low levels of procedural justice are more likely to distrust authority and to resist complying with rules. Given that the goal of our nation's juvenile correctional system is to rehabilitate youth and return them to society as productive citizens, we need to be very concerned about the possibility that we are instead creating distrustful and noncompliant people through violations of basic procedural justice.

Thinking about the Life Course: The Impact of Juvenile Prison

Life course theorists direct our attention to the timing and order of life transitions. They argue that any particular transition can have a profound impact on other transitions, shaping the trajectory of people's lives. Given the large numbers of young people who pass through our nation's prisons, it is important to learn about the effect that serving time in a juvenile prison has on later life transitions, particularly education, employment, and recidivism. This study, with its limited time frame and lack of a comparison group, cannot provide comprehensive answers to these questions. It does, however, provide some important insights into prison's effects.

Education

Two years ago, I was invited to attend the high school graduation ceremony at Oak Hill, one of the two prisons where I interviewed youth. I was excited to go to the ceremony, but having been to a lot of graduations, I figured that this one would be much the same. As it turned out, the setting was typical, but the level of emotion was not. I was surprised to see mothers, fathers, and many of the graduates crying with joy throughout the ceremony. The graduates who addressed the audience could barely contain their emotion as they talked about what their degree meant to them. It was clear that these youth received far more than a diploma that day; they received a level of respect and validation rarely bestowed upon juvenile prisoners. In addition, research indicates that diplomas increase young people's future chances of higher wages and greater job stability (Elman and O'Rand, 2004).

While the Oak Hill graduation represented a triumph for a small group of incarcerated youth, we know little about how juvenile prison affects educational outcomes more broadly. Chapter 3 suggested that the answer is complex, for prison appears to have both positive and negative repercussions on youth's educational trajectories. Youth who drop out of school prior to incarceration but manage to complete their degree during their stay in prison benefit the most. Because dropouts are overrepresented in prison, the positive impact of prison educational programming should not be understated. At the same time, it appears that youth who are enrolled in (and actually attending) school prior to incarceration suffer mostly negative effects— especially if they are not able to finish a degree before their release date. As described in Chapter 6, youth who leave prison interested in returning to school may not be allowed to re-enroll or may be channeled into low-quality alternative schools. Other youth fall behind in credits and are too ashamed to return to school below their grade level.

This study suggests several ways prisons could improve their schools to help youth move on to postsecondary education or to stable employment. First, a number of the young men in this study chose to work toward a GED rather than a high school diploma because it seemed easier and quicker. Research suggests, however, that a GED does not have the same positive effect on wages as does a diploma. In fact, one study found that a GED had little effect on the later wages of adult prisoners, with only a small positive effect until the two-year mark for nonwhites and no effect for whites (Tyler and Kling, 2007). Another study on the same question drew similar conclusions (Visher and Kachnowski, 2007). In addition, GED preparation focuses on a limited range of skills, making GED recipients less prepared for the workforce than high school graduates (Murnane, Willett, and Boudett, 1995). For these reasons, it is tempting to recommend that only high school classes be offered to incarcerated youth. There are compelling reasons to keep both paths open, however. First, there is some evidence pointing to beneficial effects associated with a GED. For example, one study found that a person with a GED does somewhat better in the job market than a person who drops out of high school (Murnane, Willett, and Boudett, 1995). Another study found that a GED appears to be linked to a reduced chance of recidivism (Wilson, Gallagher, and MacKenzie, 2000). It is possible that GEDs have these positive effects because they facilitate entry into job-training programs and the military.

Given the potential benefits of a GED, it makes sense that juvenile prisons continue to help older youth prepare to take the test—especially those with short sentences. At the same time, youth should be encouraged to pursue a diploma whenever possible. Ohio seems to be moving in this direction as they recently increased the age for GED preparation from sixteen to seventeen. Washington State provides a different solution. There, youth can apply to take a GED course when they are within a couple of months of completing their sentence. This course takes place during one period of the academic day. Participating youth take regular high school classes during the rest of the day. This allows them to stay on track with a high school diploma in case their sentences are extended or they decide to complete a diploma after they are released. Interestingly, even those youth who acquire their GED are required to keep attending academic classes until they leave the facility or turn eighteen.

In those states where youth can choose between a GED and a high school diploma, prisons could encourage incarcerated youth to stay in high school by improving the quality of classes. The chaos and busy work found in many prison classrooms is not a selling point for youth who want to receive a quality education in a safe environment. The education youth receive in today's prison high schools also makes it difficult, if not impossible, for them to successfully transition to college. Incarcerated youth leave prison well versed in filling out workbook pages but ill prepared to write a paper, take an essay exam, or engage in an academic debate. Offering higher-quality classes in the institution is one way to give youth the tools they need to succeed once they are released.

Employment

With McDonald's being the second largest private employer in the United States, it is probably not surprising that it played a central role in this study. At least ten of the paroled youth applied to work there, and five went on to accept jobs. Many of the interviews for this study were conducted at a McDonald's, and the restaurant served as a theme in quite a few discussions. The youth seemed to see McDonald's—with its minimal wages, unattractive uniforms, and low status—as the archetype of the undesirable job. The fact is, however, that the youth's lack of work history and job skills made them ill prepared for other types of work, and all too often, they were forced to fall back on McDonald's. Chapter 6 of this book described this cycle—a scattershot job hunt, an occasional low-wage job, and a firing or resignation.

There are many possible explanations for the youth's difficulties finding and holding jobs. The youth's age, related immaturity, and lack of work history probably played a role. It is also likely that some of the black youth faced racial discrimination in hiring. This study suggests that the youth's incarceration may also have been a factor. The Ohio prisons in this study did not provide comprehensive vocational training or post-release planning, and as a result, youth left prison with few job skills and no reasonable plan for obtaining employment. Additionally, the time the youth spent in prison was time not spent building an employment history or making network connections. This can be a handicap for all incarcerated youth, but it is particularly problematic for youth who are locked up for long periods of time or are older when they are released (in some states, youth can be held in juvenile prison until the age of twenty-four). It is important to point out, however, that contact with the correctional system also appears to have some positive effects on post-release employment—it enables some youth to finish a high school degree, giving them access to better jobs, job-training programs, or the military. Parole also provides an incentive to get a job, and parole agents are sometimes a resource in locating employment.

Research with adults suggests that one reason ex-convicts have difficulty obtaining employment is the stigma associated with incarceration. Adults must report felony records, and employers have access to adult criminal background checks. This study suggests, however, that juveniles are generally shielded from stigma when confidentiality provisions prohibit employers from accessing juvenile records. The youth in this study knew that they did not have to report their criminal histories, and there was no evidence to suggest that employers were able to obtain their records. Confidentiality protections are an important way that the juvenile system allows youth a chance to start their lives fresh when they are released. This is consistent with the juvenile justice system's historic emphasis on rehabilitation. Without these laws, it is unlikely that newly released youth—such as those in this study—would be able to obtain jobs at all. As described, research clearly shows that, if given a choice, most employers refuse to hire people with criminal records (Holzer, Raphael, and Stoll, 2004; Pager, 2003).

In recent years states have begun to reduce juvenile confidentiality protections, opening juvenile records to employers, schools, and adult courts. Support for these changes is based on a number of different arguments. Some proponents believe that the juvenile system should be more punitive and that youth should not be allowed to hide their criminal histories. Others argue that when an adult commits a crime, it is in the interest of public safety to allow the court to consider the person's juvenile records in their assessment of prior history. Sometimes proponents focus on the rights of employers to know the full criminal history of potential employees.

In addition to public safety and rights issues, academics have put forth a powerful argument in favor of opening all criminal records. They believe that when these records are unavailable, employers make hiring decisions based on their best guess about past criminality. This results in a situation where employers become reluctant to hire whole categories of people they believe are likely to have records. Because black males often serve as the stereotype of the criminal, employers discriminate most against them. In a number of papers, Harry Holzer and his colleagues present evidence for this spillover effect, showing that when employers do conduct background checks, they are more likely to hire black workers. (Holzer, Raphael, and Stoll, 2006; Holzer, Offner, and Sorenson, 2005). To date, there is no research on whether this spillover effect operates at the juvenile level. The fact that employers are denied access to reliable background information for juveniles, however, suggests that the effect might be pronounced.

It is important that we find a solution to the confidentiality issue that acknowledges the strong arguments on both sides. Here I suggest two ways this could be done, but there are surely other solutions. First, we could seal records for some criminal offenses and not others. For example, we could seal all first-time offenders' records or seal records when they involve minor offenses. Alternately, or additionally, we could seal records after a set period of time. This would allow a juvenile record to be sealed after some number of years (like two) if the youth remains conviction-free during this time. England already has policies at the adult level similar to both of these suggestions (Petersilia, 2003). It should be acknowledged that neither of these solutions is ideal because they will result in reduced employment opportunities for some newly released youth. They do, however, acknowledge public safety and employer-rights concerns while potentially reducing the employment spillover effect that black males currently experience.

This study indicates that a stay in a juvenile prison can have an effect on a youth's employment in the short term, but that this effect is fairly limited. Most youth are unemployed (or are unstably employed) prior to incarceration and return home to the same situation. It should be kept in mind, however, that this study only included youth who had fairly short sentences because they were first-time admissions to the DYS. It is likely that youth who spend longer periods of time in prison suffer more negative effects on their employment trajectory. Additionally, because this study took place over two and a half years, it was not possible to assess the long-term impact of the youth's prison experience on employment. Prison may have little short-term impact, but it is conceivable that disadvantage accrues over time. Work conducted by other researchers suggests that this may be the case. For example, one study found that people who served time in juvenile prison were 5 percent less likely to be employed five years after their release than people without a juvenile record (Western and Beckett, 1999, 1048). Another study found that people who served terms in juvenile prison had less continuity of employment and less attachment to work when they were in their late twenties (Sampson and Laub, 1993).

Recidivism

One of the most discouraging facts about our nation's juvenile correctional system is its high recidivism rate. In states like California, Texas, and Ohio, more than 50 percent of youth return to prison in the three years following their release (Juvenile Justice Digest, 2006; Texas Youth Commission, 2003; Ohio Department of Youth Services, 2008). The rates in most other states are not much better. Of course, youth return to prison for many different reasons, often having little to do with the correctional system itself. At the same time, we know that the prison and parole systems can and do play a role in recidivism. For example, prison may socialize inmates in ways that make it difficult for them to function in the outside world (Clemmer, 1940/1958). The stigma of a criminal record can close doors to legitimate jobs and noncriminal social networks, pushing ex-convicts into crime (Goffman, 1961).

This study highlights three ways that juvenile corrections can exert some limited influence over recidivism rates. These include institutional programming, post-release support services, and parole rules. Although we do not have reliable findings on all the programs offered in prisons, several types of programming have been shown to reduce recidivism and increase employment after incarceration. Those programs include academic training, vocational training, and substance abuse treatment (Wilson, Gallagher, and MacKenzie, 2000; Petersilia, 2003). Interestingly, although youth in this study were generally disparaging about prison programs, they were surprisingly enthusiastic about the opportunity to participate in educational programming and drug treatment (Ohio had only limited vocational training opportunities at the time of this study). It was clear that these programs gave the youth pride and the tangible rewards of a high school education and sobriety.

Given the benefits associated with education and drug treatment, prisons need to concentrate their limited budgets in these areas. One way to improve these programs is to raise teacher salaries to make teaching in prison a more attractive option. Teachers also need to be better trained and provided with the resources they need to teach this challenging population. Prison schools must be funded at a level that allows them to develop individualized education programs (IEPs) for all special education students. Also, while high school education should be the first priority, vocational education needs to be improved. All training should be assessed to make sure that it teaches skills relevant for the current job market. Community-prison partnerships are one way this can be accomplished.

In terms of drug treatment, research suggests that therapeutic communities are the most effective way to help addicts achieve long-term sobriety (CASA/Columbia University, 1998; Pearson and Lipton, 1999). The large size of juvenile facilities makes it difficult to implement quality therapeutic communities, but specific dorms can be converted. If we moved toward the Missouri cottage model, it would be even easier to designate some cottages as drug treatment communities. This will, however, require training staff and increasing funding to treatment services. No matter what type of drug treatment is provided, it needs to be made available in a timely manner so that youth do not end up serving extra time to complete the program.

If states are looking to achieve the maximum benefit from prison programming, it should be paired with post-release services. As Chapter 6 illustrated, many of the youth in this study came home determined to stay out of prison but were tested by criminal friends, repeated job rejections, and readily available drugs. While some states have fairly intensive support services for returning youth, many (like Ohio) provide little in the way of help. Several of the youth in this study told me they were upset about the lack of support services outside prison. Ethan, for example, told me that he got out of prison committed to changing his life but found that there was no support:

> They should have fucking gave—they didn't even tell me how to do anything. You now what I'm saying? I asked for independent living skills and all that shit. . . . They just left me out to dry. You know what I'm saying? Oh, yeah, we're gonna do this, we'll do that for you. But my out day came and they left me dry. You know what I'm saying? You're eighteen now, you go out . . . go home and do your stuff. Like I said, all I knew was the streets. That's what I went back to.

Nick's grandmother was also upset that there were no support services available for her struggling grandson. She commented, "I would like for him to be in some kind of training and to get his GED. So he can get a GED plus some kind of training all at the same time. Give him something to occupy his time with. You know. That's what I would like him to do. . . . To me it seems that they are not trying to help 'em. They just letting them get out, putting them back in."

Both Nick and Ethan arrived home interested in pursuing a noncriminal life, but after a couple of months, they became discouraged and went back to their criminal pursuits. It is likely that both youth could have benefited from support services provided immediately upon release. Follow-up drug treatment is particularly important as research shows that aftercare significantly increases the chances that youth will remain sober once they return to their communities (CASA/Columbia University, 1998; Hiller, Knight, and Simpson, 1999). The findings of research on other types of post-release services, however, is somewhat mixed (see MacKenzie, 1997, for a review of the literature). Further research should be conducted to determine what sorts of services are the most effective in reducing recidivism.

Institutional and post-release programming are two important ways that states can reduce recidivism. States can also control recidivism through the design and implementation of their parole systems. Parole, by its very nature, has the potential to cause recidivism. Because youth on parole have special restrictions (like curfews and work requirements) that do not apply to youth in the general population, they may be more likely to commit acts that result in being returned to prison. Parolees are also more closely supervised than other youth, making it more difficult for them to commit crimes without detection. States are able to choose how closely they supervise parolees and how willing they are to revoke parole. Some states, like Connecticut, rarely revoke parole, while others, like Wisconsin, do so far more frequently. States can also choose the restrictions that they place on parolees.

This study suggests that parole restrictions make a difference in determining which youth return to prison. For example, the requirement that youth refrain from contact with other parolees put those with paroled family members in a difficult situation. At the same time, this rule allowed some young men to use parole as an excuse to avoid delinquent friends. In this study, one of the more typical parole requirements was that youth find employment. Common sense suggests that this should have a negative effect on criminal involvement—employed youth should be too busy or too committed to their work to commit crimes. Research conducted in the past twenty years has provided some limited support for this idea. In 1993, researchers reanalyzed longitudinal data collected between 1940 and 1965 to compare the adult outcomes of delinquent and nondelinquent youth (Sampson and Laub, 1993). Their analysis indicated that crime (or lack thereof) was fairly stable across the life course but that a significant number of delinquent youth did end up "going straight." The researchers found that two factors, marital attachment (a variable measuring the quality of marriage relationships) and job stability (finding and maintaining a job over time), largely explained why some youth ceased criminal behavior and others did not. Another study on the relationship between crime and shifts in life circumstances (including employment, school, living with a partner, and probation or parole) provided additional support for the deterrent effects of employment on crime (Horney, Osgood, and Marshall, 1995).

It is tempting to conclude from these studies that parole systems should push newly released youth to find jobs as quickly as possible. Unfortunately, there is little evidence that employment has the same deterrent effect for juveniles that it does for adults. For example, Christopher Uggen's (2000) study of the relationship between employment, recidivism, illegal earnings, and age failed to find evidence of work's deterrent effect among youth. Using data gathered by the National Work Demonstration Project, he examined whether low-wage employment served as a turning point in criminal involvement. His conclusion was striking—work was associated with lowered recidivism and illegal earnings but only for people over the age of twenty-six. It appears that marginal employment (the type most young parolees obtain) does not encourage youth to desist from crime. Surprisingly, some studies even conclude that under certain circumstances, working increases youth's delinquent behavior. This is partly a result of selection bias, but it also appears that employment can lead to delinquency through decreased social support, reduced school commitment, and increased exposure to delinquent peers (Bachman and Schulenberg, 1993; Ploeger, 1997; Wright, Cullen, and Williams, 1997).

Given the weak findings on the deterrent effect of work, parole officers and juvenile correctional personnel should, whenever possible, encourage youth to stay in school and finish their degrees instead of getting a job. There is strong evidence that remaining in school is related to decreased criminal involvement (Thornberry, Moore, and Christenson, 1985). We also know that finishing a high school or college degree leads to higher wages and more job stability across the life course. Importantly, it appears that obtaining a degree may have a greater impact on later earnings when it is completed at a normative age. One study found that people who complete a college degree in their early twenties see greater earning gains than people who return to school to complete a degree at a later age (Elman and O'Rand, 2004). For this reason, we need to encourage paroled youth to stay on track with their educations, and parole offices should provide all youth with information about high school and college options in their communities. Parole boards should emphasize school over employment in setting parole requirements.

While education should be the clear first choice for newly released youth, it will not be appropriate for everyone. Some parolees will be unwilling or unable to return to school. These youth should be encouraged to find employment. Employment may not lead them to desist from crime, but it can provide income, a sense of purpose, references for later jobs, and connections in the community. It may also lead to better labor market outcomes later in life (Mihalic and Elliott, 1997). As described, however, the low-wage, low-skill jobs most newly released youth obtain provide only limited help in these areas. For this reason, youth who are not in school should be encouraged to think in terms of a career and plan their job search carefully. Young men who take a scattershot approach to job hunting find themselves changing jobs frequently because of low wages, difficult schedules, and poor conditions. Thus, they do not build up skills or experiences that will help them in the future. Parole officers should resist the temptation to rush youth into the first available job, instead working with them to find interesting entry-level jobs that promise a possibility of skills and promotion.

Impact of the Juvenile Prison on Families

One of the strongest themes running through this study's interviews was the importance of family. Almost all of the young men had close ties with at least a few members of their families, especially their mothers. While in prison, they worried about their parents, siblings, and children and longed to be reunited with them. The youth believed that their incarceration was hard on their families but that it would ultimately bring them closer. In visiting hours, phone calls, and letters, youth talked about what their lives would be like after prison and made promises about starting anew.

The period of incarceration generally did seem to bring youth closer to their families. The youth were sober and willing to talk to their families about serious topics. At the same time, the youth wanted contact to go well and were hesitant to describe problems in the facility or negative thoughts about the future. Part of the reason was that contact was so difficult and expensive for families that youth felt guilty if the visit or phone call did not go well. If conditions for contact were improved, families would be able to have more contact and that contact might be more natural, truthful, and conducive to realistic planning for the future. To accomplish this, the current reliance on collect-call systems must be changed. As described, collect calls from prison phones are extremely expensive, and the limits on who can receive them also make them impractical. States should consider implementing a calling-card arrangement so youth or their families can buy minutes ahead of time. Calling cards can also be used to reach people in hospitals and others who have restrictions on their phones. If states insist on keeping collect-call systems, rates should be kept to a reasonable level. Once these new policies are in place, states could help youth to have positive communication with their families by increasing the privacy available to them during phone calls. Because personal information about others is a valuable commodity in the prison culture, youth are motivated to listen in on others' calls. Phones could be arranged in a way that precludes this from happening. A new phone arrangement could also help reduce the high noise levels that currently make communication difficult.

Visiting hours offer another opportunity for the state to help youth maintain healthy family relationships. One particularly vital change would be to open visiting hours to youth's children. Most of the fathers plan to resume relationships with their children after incarceration. To help them do this successfully, it is important to allow them to build and maintain bonds during their time in prison. When this does not happen, youth return home as strangers to their children and have difficulty rebuilding a relationship (Nurse, 2002). It is not enough to simply open visiting hours to children, however. As described, visiting hours are difficult for children when they are expected to sit still for long periods of time. States should investigate the possibility of installing small children's areas in the visiting space. Many adult prisons have already moved in this direction, creating play areas stocked with books and toys. Such areas allow inmates to have more natural interactions with children, as there is an activity for them to share. Once states make it possible and comfortable for youth to see their own children, it should be fairly easy to extend the same visiting privileges to young siblings.

Visiting hours are extremely important to incarcerated youth and their families. Each state should review its visiting schedule to ensure that parents who work weekends or third shifts have options for coming to the facility. It will be more difficult to solve transportation problems. Ideally, state justice systems will move toward community-based facilities, reducing the distance between families and their incarcerated children. In the meantime, however, it might be possible to provide bus service from major cities to juvenile institutions. This could be provided by the state (as New York does at the adult level) or by nonprofits. It might also be possible for a nonprofit to set up a ride-share board on the Internet, enabling families to carpool to the prison.

In Chapter 5, I described some of the challenges that families face once they arrive at visiting hours. For example, parents or other visitors are sometimes denied entry because their clothes do not meet the dress code. The dress code policy must be made clear to families before they arrive, but facilities should also keep a limited number of shirts, skirts, and pants available to lend. This clothing box could be stocked and maintained by a local nonprofit, and a sign asking for donations could be posted at the facility. The same nonprofit might also be willing to donate some small games for families to engage in during visiting hours. Having decks of cards or board games available for families would make communication less strained and ease the pressure to sustain conversation over several hours. Whenever possible, prisons should encourage privacy by providing sufficient visiting space.

The youth in this study returned home from prison anxious to reunite with their families. At first, this homecoming was joyful, but as the weeks went by, the youth came under increasing pressure to live up to promises they had made to their families from prison. A group of youth in this study successfully managed this transition and went back to school or started a job. Many, however, returned to crime or drugs, and their families became increasingly distraught. Ultimately, the youth's time in prison appeared to leave their relationships with their families much as they were before incarceration. Although the design of this study precluded exploration of this topic, I suspect that families did feel more anger and despair (both at their sons and at the prison system) once their hope that incarceration would help their sons faded away. To help these families, it would be useful to provide them with information about typical problems that newly released youth face. Families also need to be offered support services during the post-release period. Although states probably cannot fund family counseling, all parole officers should provide parents with information about low-cost family counseling available in the community.

Further Research

During the course of this study, I encountered several interesting research questions that were impossible to answer because of time constraints or research design issues. I mentioned a number of these topics throughout the text. Here I briefly discuss a few other areas that warrant investigation. One important question involves the impact of incarceration on racial identity development. Research suggests that, as the dominant group in society, whites tend to see themselves as raceless (Frankenberg, 1993; McKinney, 2003). Comments made to me by white youth during this study, however, suggested that the racial heterogeneity and antagonism they encountered in prison forced them to see whiteness as a marker of their identity. This is not surprising given similar findings in multiracial high schools, but we know little about how racial identity develops in the unique prison context (Perry, 2001). We also lack information about the impact of incarceration on minorities' racial identity development. Social psychological research outside prison indicates that the discrimination and prejudice these youth face causes them to go through a process of racial/ethnic identification (Cross, 1978; Tatum, 2004; Phinney, 1989). It is not clear, however, how life in prison affects this process. This study was unable to address these questions, but it is a worthy area for future research.

As with any complex topic, there remains much to be learned about juvenile incarceration and reentry. In particular, more work needs to be done to understand the unique experiences of females in the juvenile justice system. Females today constitute about 15 percent of the juvenile prison population, but it appears that their numbers are growing (Snyder and Sickmund, 2006, 207). Similarly, Latinos compose a large and growing segment of many state juvenile prison populations. Because of Ohio's small Latino population, this study was unable to explore their experiences or the impact of their presence inside prisons. Further research should concentrate on Latinos, as well as on other racial/ethnic groups such as Asians and Native Americans. Finally, this study, with its focus on youth, did not include the voices of prison staff. These individuals play a key role in the institution, and their actions and attitudes can have a profound impact on youth's experiences. Research conducted with staff could help us find ways to reduce turnover, improve conditions, and enhance training.

Prison research is important and compelling, but we need to be careful to pair it with research on reentry and parole. It is difficult to study the large and complex parole system, but research in this area has significant public policy implications. Parole systems are expensive, and if researchers find that they have little effect on youth's lives, then the government should find more productive uses for taxpayers' money. Specific research topics should include the effect of parole on employment, education, and criminal involvement. It would also be useful to know whether various styles of parole are associated with different youth outcomes. Researchers need to study both the effects of parole supervision and the effects of support services provided during parole. While this study provided an overview of the reentry issues youth face, there is still a need to study the impact of incarceration on youth's employment prospects and family relationships.

A final area in need of further research involves alternatives to incarceration. In this study, a number of the youth were low-level offenders and did not pose a threat to public safety. They were sentenced to the DYS, at least in part, because their counties lacked other options. If we decide to develop more noncustodial options, we will need to increase our research efforts to determine which types of programs are most effective.

The Future of the Juvenile Justice System

In recent years, there have been calls to abolish the juvenile justice system and place offenders into the adult system. The arguments used to support this position range from the punitive ("adult time for adult crime") to the pragmatic (the two systems are already similar, and it would be less expensive to merge them). There are a number of compelling reasons, however, to maintain two separate correctional systems. Most important, research suggests that adolescents are developmentally different from adults.

Thus, they are more likely to commit crime during adolescence, more likely to desist from crime over time, and more likely to respond to rehabilitation. For example, adolescents appear more likely to commit crime because they have a higher tolerance for risk, less ability to reason in stressful situations, and more focus on short-term rewards than on long-term consequences. Teenagers are at the height of developing their own identities and, as a result, are more likely to experiment with risky behaviors and be influenced by their peers (Scott and Steinberg, 2008). In addition to these psychological differences, adolescents are also financially dependent and have little power in society. The fact that they are not as well integrated and invested in society as adults makes them more willing to engage in crime (Hirschi, 1969).

As adolescents age, they move into new developmental stages, and by the age of eighteen, they are psychologically similar to adults. Social differences also begin to disappear as youth get jobs, get married, and begin families. Related to these changes, many youth age out of crime by the time they are twenty-five. Specifically, research suggests that both crime and drug use peak in late adolescence and decline dramatically by the time people are in their mid-twenties (Chen and Kandel, 1995; Farrington, 1986; Sampson and Laub, 1993). The fact that many youth age out of crime is an important argument for keeping a separate juvenile justice system. It is simply not a wise use of money or human capital to incarcerate youth for the kind of extended sentences the adult system assigns. The separate juvenile justice system, with its shorter indeterminate sentences, allows us to acknowledge and account for developmental differences that lead to teenage crime and later desistence.

Society benefits from a separate juvenile justice system because it allows us to address the unique needs of incarcerated adolescents. The system's historic emphasis on rehabilitation, combined with public support of rehabilitative efforts for juveniles, provides an opening for innovative programming (Petersilia, 2003). This is especially exciting because research indicates that high-quality programming is more effective with juveniles than adults (Aos et al., 2001). Housing juveniles separately from adults allows us to provide targeted and intensive programs that are most likely to be successful.

At the same time, our current system does not exploit its potential to change young people's lives. One reason is that we lock up too many youth in large residential centers. We need to reduce the number of youth we incarcerate, reserving secure detention for violent or dangerous youth. Many of the youth we lock up, particularly those with drug addictions, are not dangerous. Drug addiction is a medical disorder that can and should be treated outside of prison. California has already moved in this direction, allowing all first-time drug offenders to get treatment services in lieu of prison. It is also possible to treat other types of first-time and low-level offenses with community diversion programs or other nonresidential options. In this study, Gabe and Richard were examples of extremely low-risk offenders whose cases could have been more successfully handled through these kinds of community programs. In fact, research suggests that when treatment is provided in the community, it has a higher rate of success than when it is provided inside a residential facility (Andrews et al., 1990; Lipsey, 1992).

When residential placement is the only option, youth should be housed in small facilities in their own communities. Smaller facilities have much better success at controlling violence, providing effective programming, and building a healthy informal culture. Research indicates that living spaces should be small, preferably with ten or fewer youth sharing space (Parent et al., 1994). In order to decrease violence levels, rooms should be double or single occupancy. This enables youth to have more private space. As described in Chapter 4, double-occupancy rooms have the advantage of allowing youth to develop friendships without group pressures. At the same time, roommates do not always get along, and violence happens more easily in double-occupancy than single-occupancy rooms (McCain, Cox, and Paulus, 1980; Krisberg, 2003).

Missouri provides a model for states to follow. Starting in the 1970s, they began to move away from large institutions and toward a cottage-based model where youth receive intensive rehabilitation and training. Today, Missouri does not have any large juvenile facilities. Instead, there are over thirty residential programs, each housing no more than thirty-five youth. These facilities do not resemble traditional juvenile prisons—youth wear their own clothes, and facilities have couches and carpets. Because there are so many facilities, it is possible to house youth near their homes, usually within fifty miles. This makes it easy for parents to visit and also enables them to participate in therapy. In addition to residential programs, Missouri also employs a number of lesser sanctions, including day-reporting centers. Although the way Missouri calculates its recidivism rates is different from many states, it appears that they are achieving notable rehabilitative success (Missouri Department of Social Services, 2003).

States should investigate ways to replicate the Missouri model. It is important, however, to move slowly in this direction because it will take time to develop and staff high-quality community centers. States will also have to think hard about how to provide services for the small subset of extremely violent youth. When less-secure community facilities are not appropriate, states may need to place these youth outside their communities in special high-security facilities. Over time, it may be possible to move them into community-level facilities, but that can only happen after intensive and secure treatment options are in place. Ultimately, the goal should be to close large state facilities and to house youth who need residential placement in small state- and county-funded facilities in or near their own communities.

Conclusion

Fifteen years ago I found my way into juvenile corrections research when one of my graduate school advisers offered me a job evaluating a new parolee education program. That job led to my dissertation research on juvenile incarcerated fatherhood and to my long-term commitment to juvenile justice issues. Over the years, I have had the opportunity to develop many close relationships with both incarcerated youth and with prison staff members. It has become increasingly clear to me that there are no winners in our current juvenile justice system—youth and staff live and work in oppressive and unhealthy environments, taxpayers see little return on their money, and families and communities suffer the absence of too many of their youth.

The failures of our juvenile correctional system are costly. When we do not provide proper rehabilitation and education to incarcerated youth, we simply shift the problem to the social welfare system or to the overburdened adult prison system. This crisis is frustrating because we know that focused, high-quality prison or community rehabilitation programming can be effective, especially at the juvenile level. The finding that juvenile rehabilitation can be effective means that the correctional system has enormous potential to positively influence the lives of incarcerated youth. If we choose to harness this potential, it can bring both financial and social benefits to all of us.

As we move forward with juvenile justice reform, the secrecy surrounding the system must come to an end. In a hidden system, we put our youth at risk of abuse and neglect. Additionally, an uninformed public cannot exert necessary oversight of the system or make educated decisions about legislation involving juvenile offenders. There are simply too many of our young people in the system to continue pretending that juvenile prisons do not exist or that they house only "bad guys." It is my hope that this book—and the experiences of the youth whose voices form the heart of it—can be a contribution to the public dialogue about the future of the juvenile justice system.

Sources Cited

Abeyratne, S., Sowards, B., and Brewer, L. (1995). *Youths incarcerated in ODYS institutions who have children and youths incarcerated in ODYS institutions who are children of teenage parents.* Columbus: Ohio Department of Youth Services, Office of Research.

Adler, P., and Adler, P. (1998). *Peer power: Preadolescent culture and identity.* New Brunswick, NJ: Rutgers University Press.

Alaska Division of Juvenile Justice. (2009). *McLaughlin Youth Center parent/guardian orientation brochure.* Retrieved February 15, 2009, from *health.hss.state.ak.us/djj/facilities/myc/MYC_orientation.pdf.*

Alltucker, K. W., Bullis, M., Close, D., and Yovanoff, P. (2006). Different pathways to juvenile delinquency: Characteristics of early and late starters in a sample of previously incarcerated youth. *Journal of Child and Family Studies, 15,* 479–92.

American Correctional Association. (1983). *The American prison: From the beginning, a pictorial history.* College Park, MD: American Correctional Association.

Anderson, E. (2000). *Code of the streets: Decency, violence and the moral life of the inner city.* New York: W. W. Norton.

Andrews, D. A., Zinger, I., Hoge, R. D., Bonta, J., Gendreau, P., and Cullen, F. T. (1990). Does correctional treatment work? A clinically relevant and psychologically informed meta-analysis. *Criminology, 28,* 369–404.

Aos, S., Phipps, P., Barnoski, R., and Lieb, R. (2001). *The comparative costs and benefits of programs to reduce crime.* Seattle: Washington State Institute for Public Policy.

Arizona Department of Juvenile Corrections. (2009). *Family Handbook.* Retrieved February 15, 2009, from *www.juvenile.state.az.us/handbooks.htm.*

Armstrong, G. S., and MacKenzie, D. L. (2003). Private versus public juvenile correctional facilities: Do differences in environmental quality exist? *Crime and Delinquency, 49,* 542–63.

Associated Press. (2010). Report: Sex abuse high at 13 juvenile centers. *New York Times,* January 7. Retrieved January 8, 2010, from *www.nytimes.com.*

Austin, J., and Irwin, J. (2001). *It's about time: America's imprisonment binge* (3rd ed.). Belmont, CA: Wadsworth.

Bachman, J. G., and Schulenberg, J. (1993). How part-time work intensity relates to drug use, problem behavior, time use, and satisfaction among high school seniors: Are these consequences or merely correlates? *Developmental Psychology, 29,* 220–35.

Balfanz, R., Spiridakis, K., Curran, R., and Neild, N. L. (2003). Deconstructing the pipeline: Using efficacy, effectiveness, and cost-benefit data to reduce minority youth incarceration. In J. Wald and D. J. Losen (Eds.), *Deconstructing the school-to-prison pipeline* (pp. 71–89). San Francisco: Jossey-Bass.

Bartollas, C., Miller, S., and Dinitz, S. (1976). *Juvenile victimization: The institutional paradox.* New York: John Wiley and Sons.

Beck, R., and Fernandez, E. (1998). Cognitive-behavioral therapy in the treatment of anger: A meta-analysis. *Cognitive Therapy and Research, 22,* 63–74.

Benekos, P. J., and Merlo, A. V. (2008). Juvenile justice: The legacy of punitive policy. *Youth Violence and Juvenile Justice, 6,* 28–47.

Berk, B. B. (1977). Organizational goals and inmate organization. In R. G. Leger and J. R. Stratton (Eds.), *The sociology of corrections.* New York: John Wiley and Sons.

Bernard, T. (1992). *The cycle of juvenile justice.* New York: Oxford University Press.

Binder, A., Geis, G., and Dixon, B. (2001). *Juvenile delinquency: Historical, cultural and legal perspectives* (3rd ed.). Cincinnati: Anderson.

Bishop, D. M., and Frazier, C. E. (1996). Race effects in juvenile justice decision-making: Findings from a state-wide analysis. *Journal of Criminal Law and Criminology, 86,* 392–414.

Bishop, D. R. (1997). Juvenile recordhandling: Policies and practices of the Federal Bureau of Investigation. In *National conference on juvenile justice records: Appropriate criminal and noncriminal justice uses* (NCJ-164269). Washington, DC: Bureau of Justice Statistics. Retrieved January 5, 2009, from *www.ojp.usdoj.gov/bjs.*

Bortner, M. A., and Williams, L. M. (1997). *Youth in prison.* New York: Routledge.

Bosworth, M. (2009). *Explaining U.S. Imprisonment.* Thousand Oaks, CA: Sage Publications.

Bottoms, A. E. (1999). Interpersonal violence and social order in prisons. *Crime and Justice, 26,* 205–81.

Bridges, G. S., and Steen, S. (1998). Racial disparities in official assessments of juvenile offenders: Attributional stereotypes as mediating mechanisms. *American Sociological Review, 63,* 554–70.

Bugansky, A. (1958). *Certain factors in prejudice among inmates of three ethnic groups within a short-term penal institution.* Ph.D. diss., Department of Sociology, New York University.

Bureau of Justice Statistics. (2008). *Direct expenditures by criminal justice function, 1982–2006.* Retrieved July 12, 2009, from *www.ojp.usdoj.gov/bjs.*

Bushway, S., Briggs, S., Taxman, F., Thanner, M., and Van Brakle, M. (2007). Private providers of criminal history records: Do you get what you pay for? In S. Bushway, M. Stoll, and D. Weiman (Eds.), *Barriers to reentry? The labor market for released prisoners in post-industrial America* (pp. 174–200). New York: Russell Sage Foundation.

California Department of Rehabilitation and Correction. (2008). *About CDCR: Ward per capita cost.* Retrieved October 15, 2009, from *www.cdcr.ca.gov/Reports_Research/wardcost_0405.html.*

California Youth Authority. (1995). *Office of Criminal Justice Planning Juvenile-Justice and Delinquency Prevention Program project summary.* Sacramento: CYA.

Callahan, V. (2004). *Feeding the fear of crime: Crime-related media and support for three strikes.* El Paso, TX: LFB Scholarly Publishing.

Carroll, L. (1974). *Hacks, blacks, and cons: Race relations in a maximum security prison.* Prospect Heights, IL: Waveland Press.

CASA (Center on Addiction and Substance Abuse)/Columbia University. (1998). *Behind bars: Substance abuse and America's prison population.* Retrieved December 15, 2008, from *www.casacolumbia.org/.*

Casella, R. (2003). High-poverty secondary schools and the juvenile justice system: How neither helps the other and how that could change. In J. Wald and D. J. Losen (Eds.), *Deconstructing the school-to-prison pipeline* (pp. 55–70). San Francisco: Jossey-Bass.

Cheesman, F. L., and Waters, N. L. (2008). Who gets a second chance? An investigation of Ohio's blended juvenile sentence. Washington, DC: National Center for State Courts. Retrieved October 20, 2008, from *www.ssrn.com.*

Chen, K., and Kandel, D. B. (1995). The natural history of drug use from adolescence to the mid-thirties in a general population sample. *American Journal of Public Health, 85,* 41–47.

Christmon, K., and Lucky, I. (1994). Is early fatherhood associated with alcohol and other drug use? *Journal of Substance Abuse, 6,* 337–43.

Cillessen, A. H. N., and Mayeux, L. (2004). From censure to reinforcement: Developmental changes in the association between aggression and social status. *Child Development, 75,* 147–63.

Claes, M., and Simard, R. (1992). Friendship characteristics of delinquent adolescents. *International Journal of Adolescence and Youth, 3,* 287–301.

Clausel, L. E., and Bonnie, R. J. (2000). Juvenile justice on appeal. In J. Fagan and F. E. Zimring (Eds.), *The changing borders of juvenile justice: Transfer of adolescents to the criminal court* (pp. 181–206). Chicago: University of Chicago Press.

Clemmer, D. (1940/1958). *The prison community.* New York: Holt, Rinehart, and Winston.

Cloward, R. (1960). *Theoretical studies in social organization of the prison.* New York: Social Science Research Council.

———. (1977). Social control in the prison. In R. G. Leger and J. R. Stratton (Eds.), *The sociology of corrections: A book of readings* (pp. 97–109). New York: John Wiley and Sons.

Cocozza, J., and Skowyra, K. (2000). Youth with mental health disorders: Issues and emerging responses. *Office of Juvenile Justice and Delinquency Prevention Journal, 7,* 3–13.

Cohen, F. (2008). *Final fact-finding report S.H. v. Stickrath*. Retrieved October 18, 2008, from *www.dispatch.com/wwwexportcontent/sites/dispatch/local_news/ stories/2008/03/09/dys_factfinding.pdf*.

Cohen, L. E., Felmlee, D., Nurse, A., and Will, S. (1997). *Second year report to the California Youth Authority: Positive parenting program* (October). Sacramento, CA: California Office of Criminal Justice Planning.

Coie, J. D., Dodge, K. A., and Coppotelli, H. (1982). Dimensions and types of social status: A cross-age perspective. *Developmental Psychology, 18* (4), 557–70.

Comfort, M. (2008). *Doing time together: Love and family in the shadow of the prison*. Chicago: University of Chicago Press.

Connell, R. W. (1987). *Gender and power*. Stanford, CA: Stanford University Press.

Cressey, D. (1959). Contradictory directives in complex organizations: The case of the prison. *Administrative Science Quarterly, 4*, 1–19.

Crewe, B. (2006). Codes and conventions: The terms and conditions of contemporary inmate values. In A. Liebling and S. Maruna (Eds.), *The effects of imprisonment* (pp. 177–208). Devon, UK: Willan.

Cross, W. E., Jr. (1978). The Cross and Thomas models of psychological nigrescence. *Journal of Black Psychology, 5*, 13–19.

Crouch, B. M., and Marquart, J. W. (1989). *An appeal to justice: Litigated reform of Texas prisons*. Austin: University of Texas Press.

Curry, G. D., Howell, J. C., and Roush, D. W. (2000). *Youth gangs in juvenile detention and corrections facilities: A national survey of juvenile detention centers* (Research Report). Washington, DC: Office of Juvenile Justice and Delinquency Prevention.

Cutting, C., Bartolotta, R., Mason, L., Wilson, M., and Leone, P. (2004). Analysis of education policies in juvenile corrections. Paper presented at the TECBD Annual Conference, Tempe, AZ, November 18–20. Retrieved October 13, 2008, from *www.edjj.org/Publications/presentations/12-21-04c.ppt*.

Darroch, J. E., Landry, D. J., and Oslak, S. (1999). Pregnancy rates among U.S. women and their partners in 1994. *Family Planning Perspectives, 31* (3), 122–26.

Davern, M., and Hachen, D. S. (2006). The role of information and influence in social networks. *American Journal of Economics and Sociology, 65*, 269–93.

DePanfilis, D., and Zuravin, S. J. (2002). The effect of services on the recurrence of child maltreatment. *Child Abuse and Neglect, 26*, 187–205.

Department of Labor Occupational Employment Statistics. (2002). 2002 employment and wage estimates (occupation profiles). Retrieved January 28, 2009, from *www. bls.gov/oes/2002/oes_stru.htm*.

DiIulio, J. J. (1987). *Governing prisons: A comparative study of correctional management*. New York: Free Press.

Duguid, S., and Pawson, R. (1998). Education, change, and transformation: The prison experience. *Evaluation Review, 22*, 470–95.

Eder, D. (1995). *School talk: Gender and adolescent culture*. New Brunswick, NJ: Rutgers University Press.

Elman, C., and O'Rand, A. M. (2004). The race is to the swift: Socioeconomic origins, adult education and wage attainment. *American Journal of Sociology, 110*, 123–60.

Elster, A. B., Lamb, M. E., and Tavare, J. (1987). Association between behavioral and school problems and fatherhood in a national sample of adolescent youths. *Journal of Pediatrics, 111*, 932–36.

Everett, R. S., and Nienstedt, B. G. (1999). Race, remorse, and sentence reduction: Is saying you're sorry enough? *Justice Quarterly, 16*, 99–122.

Farrington, D. (1986). Age and crime. *Crime and justice: An annual review of research, 7*, 189–250.

Federal Bureau of Prisons. (2000). *TRIAD drug treatment evaluation final project report of three year outcomes: Executive summary.* Washington, DC: U.S. Department of Justice, September. Retrieved January 21, 2009, from *www.bop.gov/news/research_reports.jsp#drug.*

Feinstein, R., Greenblatt, A., Hass, L., Kohn, S., and Rana, J. (2001). *Justice for all? A report on lesbian, gay, bisexual and transgendered youth in the New York juvenile justice system.* New York: Urban Justice Center.

Feld, B. C. (1981). A comparative analysis of organizational structure and inmate subcultures in institutions for juvenile offenders. *Crime and Delinquency, 27*, 336–63.

———. (2000). Juvenile court. In M. Tonry (Ed.), *The handbook of crime and punishment* (pp. 509–41). Oxford, UK: Oxford University Press.

Ferguson, A. A. (2001). *Bad boys: Public schools in the making of black masculinity.* Ann Arbor: University of Michigan Press.

Flynn, E. F. (1976). The ecology of prison violence. In A. K. Cohen, G. F. Cole, and R. G. Bailey (Eds.), *Prison violence* (pp. 110–33). Lexington, MA: D. C. Heath.

Foucault, M. (1980). *Power/Knowledge: Selected interviews and other writings.* New York: Knopf.

Frankenberg, R. (1993). *White women, race matters: The social construction of whiteness.* Minneapolis: University of Minnesota Press.

Freeman, R. B. (1991). Crime and the employment of disadvantaged youths. Working Paper #387, National Bureau of Economic Research, Cambridge, MA.

Gaboury, M. T., Sedelmaier, C. M., Monahan, L. H., and Monahan, J. J. (2008). A preliminary evaluation of behavioral outcomes in a corrections-based victim awareness program for offenders. *Victims and Offenders, 3*, 217–27.

Gender, E., and Players, E. (1989). *Race relations in prison.* Oxford, UK: Oxford University Press.

Glueck, S., and Glueck, E. (1934/1965). *One thousand juvenile delinquents: Their treatment by court and clinic.* New York: Kraus Reprint.

Goffman, E. (1959). *The presentation of self in everyday life.* New York: Doubleday.

———. (1961). *Asylums: Essays on the social situation of mental patients and other inmates.* Garden City, NY: Anchor.

Gottfredson, M. R., and Hirschi, T. (1990). *A general theory of crime.* Stanford, CA: Stanford University Press.

Gottschalk, M. (2006). *The prison and the gallows: The politics of mass incarceration in America.* New York: Cambridge University Press.

Granovetter, M. S. (1973). The strength of weak ties. *American Journal of Sociology, 78,* 1360–80.

Griffin, P., Torbet, P., and Szymanski, L. (1998). Trying juveniles as adults in criminal court: An analysis of state transfer decisions. Office of Juvenile Justice Delinquency and Prevention, December. Retrieved June 15, 2009, from *ojjdp.ncjrs. org/pubs/tryingjuvasadult/transfer2.html.*

Hagan, J. (1993). The social embeddedness of crime and unemployment. *Criminology, 31* (4), 465–91.

Hairston, C. (1991). Family ties during imprisonment: Important to whom and for what? *Journal of Sociology and Social Welfare, 18* (1, March), 87–104.

Harper, C. C., and McLanahan, S. (2004). Father absence and youth incarceration. *Journal of Research on Adolescence, 14,* 369–97.

Harvey, J. (2005). Crossing the boundary: The transition of young adults into prison. In A. Liebling and S. Maruna (Eds.), *The Effects of Imprisonment* (pp. 232–54). Devon, UK: Willan.

Hayes, L. M. (2009). Characteristics of juvenile suicide in confinement. *Juvenile Justice Bulletin* (Office of Juvenile Justice and Delinquency Prevention), February.

Haynie, D. (2001). Delinquent peers revisited: Does network structure matter? *American Journal of Sociology, 106* (4), 1013–57.

Hemmens, C., and Marquart, J. W. (1999). The impact of inmate characteristics on perceptions of race relations in prison. *International Journal of Offender Therapy and Comparative Criminology, 43,* 230–47.

Henderson, M. L., Cullen, F. T., Carroll, L., and Feinberg, W. (2000). Race, rights, and order in prison: A national survey of wardens on the racial integration of prison cells. *Prison Journal, 80,* 295–308.

Hill Collins, P. (2006). New commodities, new consumers: Selling blackness in a global marketplace. *Ethnicities, 6,* 297–317.

Hiller, M. L., Knight, K., and Simpson, D. D. (1999). Prison-based substance abuse treatment, residential aftercare and recidivism. *Addiction, 94,* 833–42.

Hirschfield, P. (2008). The declining significance of delinquent labels in disadvantaged urban communities. *Sociological Forum, 23* (3), 575–601.

Hirschi, T. (1969). *Causes of delinquency.* Berkeley: University of California Press.

Holzer, H. (2007). Collateral costs: The effects of incarceration on the employment earnings of young workers. Institute for the Study of Labor Discussion Paper 3118. Retrieved December 18, 2009, from *papers.ssrn.com.*

Holzer, H. J., Offner, P., and Sorensen, E. (2005). Declining employment among young black men: The role of incarceration and child support. *Journal of Policy Analysis and Management, 24,* 329–50.

Holzer, H. J., Raphael, S., and Stoll, M. (2004). Will employers hire former offenders? Employer preference, background checks and their determinants. In M. Patillo, D. Weiman, and B. Western (Eds.), *Imprisoning America: The social effects of mass incarceration* (pp. 205–46). New York: Russell Sage Foundation.

———. (2006). Perceived criminality, criminal background checks and the racial hiring practices of employers. *Journal of Law and Economics, 49,* 451–80.

————. (2007). The effect of an applicant's criminal history on employer hiring decisions and screening practices: New evidence from Los Angeles. In S. Bushway, M. Stoll, and D. Weiman (Eds.), *Barriers to reentry? The labor market for released prisoners in post-industrial America* (pp. 117–50). New York: Russell Sage Foundation.

Horney, J., Osgood, D. W., and Marshall, I. H. (1995). Criminal careers in the short-term: Intra-individual variability in crime and its relation to local life circumstances. *American Sociological Review, 60,* 655–73.

Howells, K., and Day, A. (2003). Readiness for anger management: Clinical and theoretical issues. *Clinical Psychology Review, 23,* 319–37.

Hubner, J. (2008). *Last chance in Texas: The redemption of criminal youth.* New York: Random House.

Huizinga, D., and Elliot, D. (1987). Juvenile offenders: Prevalence, offender incidence, and arrest rates by race. *Crime and Delinquency, 33,* 206–23.

Hunt, G., Reigal, S., Morales, T., and Waldorf, D. (1998). Changes in prison culture: Prison gangs and the case of the "Pepsi Generation." In T. J. Flanagan, J. W. Marquart, and K. G. Adams (Eds.), *Incarcerating criminals: Prisons and jails in social and organizational context* (pp. 118–26). New York: Oxford University Press.

Illinois Department of Juvenile Justice. (2007). *IDJJ News: State and Macon County program helps divert young offenders from prison,* August 24. Retrieved July 25, 2009, from *www.idjj.state.il.us/subsections/news/archive/archive. asp?article=2007\20070824-State%20and%20Macon%20County%20program%20 helps%20divert%20young%20offenders%20from%20prison.htm.*

Inciardi, J. A., Martin, S. S., and Butzin, C. A. (2004). Five-year outcomes of therapeutic community treatment of drug-involved offenders after release from prison. *Crime and Delinquency, 50,* 88–107.

Irwin, J. (1970). *The felon.* Englewood, NJ: Prentice-Hall.

————. (1980). *Prisons in turmoil.* Glenview, IL: Scott and Foresman.

————. (2005). *The warehouse prison: Disposal of the new dangerous class.* Los Angeles: Roxbury Press.

Irwin, J., and Cressey, D. (1977). Thieves, convicts, and inmate culture. In R. G. Leger and J. R. Stratton (Eds.), *The sociology of corrections: A book of readings* (pp. 133–47). New York: John Wiley and Sons.

Jewkes, Y. (2002). *Captive audience: Media, masculinity and power in prisons.* Portland, OR: Willan.

Johnston, N. (2000). *Forms of constraint: A history of prison architecture.* Chicago: University of Illinois Press.

Jonson-Reid, M., and Barth, R. P. (2000). From placement to prison: The path to adolescent incarceration from child welfare supervised foster or group care. *Children and Youth Services Review, 22,* 493–516.

Juvenile Justice Digest. (2006). California: Youth recidivism is 70 percent. Retrieved February 20, 2009, from *findarticles.com/p/articles/mi_qa3985/is_200609/ ai_n17195432?tag=content;col1.*

Kazdin, A. E., Esveldt-Dawson, K., French, N. H., and Unis, A. S. (1987). Problem-solving skills training and relationship therapy in the treatment of antisocial child behavior. *Journal of Consulting and Clinical Psychology, 55*, 76–85.

Keeley, J. L. (2004). The metamorphosis of juvenile correctional education: Incidental conception to intentional inclusion. *Journal of Correctional Education, 55*, 277–95.

Kempf-Leonard, K. (2007). Minority youths and juvenile justice: Disproportionate minority contact after nearly 20 years of reform efforts. *Youth Violence and Juvenile Justice, 5*, 71–87.

Kerman, B., Wildfire, J., and Barth, R. P. (2002). Outcomes for young adults who experienced foster care. *Children and Youth Services Review, 24*, 319–44.

King, M., and Szymanski, L. (2006). *National overviews: State juvenile justice profiles.* Pittsburgh, PA: National Center for Juvenile Justice. Retrieved July 23, 2009, from *www.ncjj.org/stateprofiles/.*

Kreider, R. M. (2007). Living arrangements of children, 2004. *Current Population Reports,* 70–114.

Krisberg, B. (2003). *General corrections review of the California Youth Authority.* Sacramento, CA: California Youth Authority. Retrieved November 13, 2008, from *www.nccd-crc.org/nccd/pubs/cya_report_2003.pdf.*

———. (2006). Stopping sexual assaults in juvenile corrections facilities: A case study of the California Division of Juvenile Justice. Testimony before the National Prison Rape Elimination Commission, Boston, June 1. Retrieved March 5, 2009, from *www.nccd-crc.org/nccd/pubs/2006_NPREC_testimony.pdf.*

Lee v. Washington. (1968). 390 U.S. 333.

Leiber, M. J. (2002). Disproportionate minority confinement (DMC) of youth: An analysis of state and federal efforts to address the issue. *Crime and Delinquency, 48*, 3–45.

Leone, P. E., Meisel, S. M., and Drakeford, W. (2002). Special education programs for youth with disabilities in juvenile corrections. *Journal of Correctional Education, 53* (2), 46–50.

Lerman, R. I., and Ooms, T. J. (1993). *Young unwed fathers: Changing roles and emerging policies.* Philadelphia: Temple University Press.

Levine, M., and Levine, A. (1970). *A social history of helping services: Clinic, court, school, and community.* New York: Appleton-Century-Crofts.

Lewin, Tamar. (2001). Class time and not jail time for anger, but does it work? *New York Times,* July 1. Retrieved October 17, 2008, from *query.nytimes.com/gst/fullpage.html?res=9C02EFDE1339F932A35754C0A9679C8B63.*

Liebling, A. (2004). *Prisons and their moral performance: A study of values, quality, and prison life.* Oxford, UK: Clarenden Press.

Lin, N., and Dumin, M. (1986). Access to occupations through social ties. *Journal of Social Networks, 8*, 365–85.

Lipsey, M. W. (1992). Juvenile delinquency treatment: A meta-analytic inquiry into the variability of its effects. In T. Cook, H. Cooper, and D. Cordray (Eds.), *Meta-analysis for explanation: A casebook* (pp. 83–128). New York: Russell Sage Foundation.

Liptak, A. (2008). Inmate count in the U.S. dwarfs other nations. *New York Times,*

April 23. Retrieved June 30, 2009, from *www.nytimes.com/2008/04/23/ us/23prison.html.*

Livsey, S., Sickmund, M., and Sladky, A. (2009). *Juvenile residential facility census, 2004: Selected findings.* Washington, DC: Office of Juvenile Justice and Delinquency Prevention. Retrieved December 20, 2009, from *www.ojjdp.gov.*

Lochman, J. E. (1992). Cognitive-behavioral intervention with aggressive boys: Three-year follow-up and preventive effects. *Journal of Consulting and Clinical Psychology, 60,* 426–32.

Macaulay, L. J., and Kane, E. W. (1993). Interviewer gender and gender attitudes. *Public Opinion Quarterly, 57,* 1–28.

MacKenzie, D. L. (1997). Criminal justice and crime prevention. In L. Sherman, D. Gottfredson, D. MacKenzie, J. Eck, P. Reuter, and S. Bushway, *Preventing crime: What works, what doesn't, what's promising; A report to the United States Congress.* Retrieved May 20, 2009, from *www.ncjrs.gov/works/.*

————. (2000). Evidence-based corrections: Identifying what works. *Crime and Delinquency, 46,* 457–71.

Magin, J. L. (2006). Hawaii agrees to broad changes in procedures for incarcerated gay youths. *New York Times,* February 13. Retrieved December 18, 2009, from *www. nytimes.com.*

Mann, J., and Mann, J. (2007). Anger dynamics in prison inmates. Paper presented at the annual meeting of the American Society of Criminology, Atlanta, Georgia, November 14. Retrieved October 10, 2008, from *www.allacademic.com/meta/ p200160_index.html.*

Martinson, R. (1974). What works? Questions and answers about prison reform. *Public Interest, 35,* 22–52.

Massey, D. S., and Denton, N. A. (1993). *American apartheid. Segregation and the making of the underclass.* Cambridge: Harvard University Press.

Maurer, M. (2002). Mass imprisonment and the disappearing voters. In M. Mauer and M. Chesney-Lind (Eds.), *Invisible punishment: The collateral consequences of mass imprisonment* (pp. 50–58). New York: New Press.

McCain, G., Cox, V. C., and Paulus, P. B. (1980). *The effect of prison crowding on inmate behavior.* Washington, DC: National Institute of Justice.

McEwen, C. A. (1978). *Designing correctional organizations for youths: Dilemmas of subcultural development.* Cambridge: Ballinger.

McGuire, B., and Booth, C. (1998). *Oregon Youth Authority: 1995–1997 Biennial Report.* Salem, OR: Oregon Youth Authority. Retrieved January 24, 2009, from *www.oregon.gov/OYA/docs/OYA_95_97BiennRpt.pdf.*

McKinney, K. D. (2003). I feel "whiteness" when I hear people blaming whites: Whiteness as cultural victimization. *Race and Society, 6,* 39–55.

McShane, M. D., and Williams, F. P. (2007). *Youth violence and delinquency: Monsters and myths.* Westport, CT: Greenwood.

Meisel, S., Henderson, K., Cohen, M., and Leone, P. (1998). Collaborate to educate: Special education in juvenile correctional facilities. In *Building Collaboration between Education and Treatment for At-Risk and Delinquent Youth* (pp. 59–72).

Richmond: National Juvenile Detention Association, Eastern Kentucky University.

Mihalic, S. W., and Elliott, D. (1997). Short- and long-term consequences of adolescent work. *Youth and Society, 28*, 464–98.

Miller, A. D., and Ohlin, L. E. (1985). *Delinquency and community: Creating opportunities and controls.* Beverly Hills, CA: SAGE.

Milner, M. (2004). *Freaks, geeks, and cool kids: American teenagers, schools, and the culture of consumption.* New York: Routledge Press.

Minnesota Department of Corrections. (2009). *Thistle Dew residential intake packet.* Retrieved February 15, 2009, from *www.thistledewprograms.com/wordpress/ wp-content/uploads/2009/12/residentintake.pdf.*

Missouri Department of Social Services. (2003). *Annual report: Fiscal year 2002.* Jefferson City, MO: Division of Youth Services. Retrieved March 13, 2009, from *www.dss.mo.gov/re/pdf/dys/dysfy02.pdf.*

Missouri Youth Services Institute. (2009). Home page. Retrieved July 23, 2009, from *www.mysiconsulting.org/.*

Monahan, L. H., McNahan, J. L., Gaboury, M. T., and Niesyn, P. A. (2004). Victims' voices in the correctional setting: Cognitive gains in an offender education program. *Journal of Offender Rehabilitation, 39*, 21–33.

Montana Department of Corrections. (2008). *Inmate phones.* Retrieved February 15, 2009, from *www.cor.mt.gov/Facts/inmatephones.mcpx.*

Montgomery, J. D. (1994). Weak ties, employment, and inequality: An equilibrium analysis. *American Journal of Sociology, 99*, 1212–36.

Moon, M. M., Sundt, J. L., Cullen, F. T., and Wright, J. P. (2000). Is child saving dead? Public support for juvenile rehabilitation. *Crime and Delinquency, 46*, 38–60.

Moore, S. (2009). Missouri system treats juvenile offenders with lighter hand. *New York Times,* March 26. Retrieved July 23, 2009, from *www.nytimes. com/2009/03/27/us/27juvenile.html?_r=1&scp=3&sq=Moore%20Missouri%20 System&st=cse.*

Mulcahy, C., and Leone, P. E. (2006). Nationwide analysis of state-level education policies in juvenile corrections. Paper presented at the American Society of Criminology, Los Angeles, November 1.

Murnane, R. J., Willett, J. B., and Boudett, K. P. (1995). Do high school dropouts benefit from obtaining a GED? *Educational Evaluation and Policy Analysis, 17*, 133–47.

Murphy, D. E. (2004). California settles lawsuit on juvenile prisons. *New York Times,* November 17. Retrieved November 20, 2008, from *www.nytimes.com/2004/11/17/ national/17calif.html?_r=1&scp=1&sq=California%20settles%20lawsuit%20on%20 juvenile%20prisons&st=cse.*

National Center for Juvenile Justice. (2006). Oldest age for original juvenile court jurisdiction in delinquency matters as of the end of the 2005 legislative session. Retrieved July 21, 2009, from *www.ncjj.org/stateprofiles/.*

National Center for Victims of Crime. (1996). *National victim services survey of adult and juvenile corrections and parole agencies, final report.* Arlington, VA: National Center for Victims of Crime.

Novaco, R. W., Ramm, M., and Black, L. (2001). Anger treatment with offenders. In C. Hollin (Ed.), *The essential handbook of offender assessment and treatment* (pp. 201–96). West Sussex, UK: John Wiley and Sons.

Nurse, A. (2002). *Fatherhood arrested: Parenting from within the juvenile justice system.* Nashville: Vanderbilt University Press.

Office of Juvenile Justice and Delinquency Prevention. (2008a). *Juvenile justice reform initiatives in the states, 1994–1996: Ohio sharing responsibility for administration of juvenile justice.* Retrieved November 5, 2008, from *ojjdp.ncjrs.org/PUBS/reform/.*

———. (2008b). *OJJDP statistical briefing book.* Retrieved June 10, 2009, from *www.ojjdp.ncjrs.gov/ojstatbb/.*

Ohio Department of Youth Services. (2008). *RECLAIM Ohio statistics.* Retrieved March 12, 2009, from *www.dys.ohio.gov/dnn/Community/ReclaimOhio/ RECLAIMOhioStatistics/tabid/144/Default.aspx.*

Ohio Department of Youth Services. (2009). *Statistics: Fiscal year 2002.* Retrieved December 15, 2009, from *www.dys.ohio.gov/dnn/.*

Owen, B. A. (1988). *The reproduction of social control: A study of prison workers at San Quentin.* New York: Praeger Press.

Pager, D. (2003). The mark of a criminal record. *American Journal of Sociology, 108,* 937–75.

———. (2007). Two strikes and you're out: The intensification of racial and criminal stigma. In S. Bushway, M. Stoll, and D. Weiman (Eds.), *Barriers to reentry? The labor market for released prisoners in post-industrial America* (pp. 151–73). New York: Russell Sage Foundation.

Palm, G. F. (2003). Parent education for incarcerated parents: Understanding "what works." In V. L. Gadsden (Ed.), *Heading home: Offender reintegration into the family* (pp. 89–122). Lanham, MD: American Correctional Association.

Parent, D. G., Leiter, V., Kennedy, S., Livens, L., Wentworth, D., and Wilcox, S. (1994). *Conditions of confinement: Juvenile detention and corrections facilities; Research summary.* Washington, DC: Office of Juvenile Justice and Delinquency Prevention.

Parke, R., and Clarke-Stewart, K. A. (2002). Effects of parental incarceration on young children. Paper presented at the Department of Health and Human Services conference, Washington, DC, January 30–31. Retrieved January 22, 2009, from *www.ncjrs.gov/App/Publications/abstract.aspx?ID=202994.*

Parkhurst, J. T., and Hopmeyer, A. (1998). Sociometric popularity and peer-perceived popularity: Two distinct dimensions of peer status. *Journal of Early Adolescence, 18* (2), 125–44.

Pearson, F. S., and Lipton, D. S. (1999). A meta-analytic review of the effectiveness of corrections-based treatments for drug abuse. *Prison Journal, 79,* 384–410.

Peek, C. (2003). Breaking out of the prison hierarchy: Transgender prisoners, rape and the Eighth Amendment. *Santa Clara Law Review, 44,* 1211–48.

Perry, P. (2001). White means never having to say you're ethnic: White youth and the construction of 'cultureless' identities. *Journal of Contemporary Ethnography, 30,* 56–91.

Petersilia, J. (2003). *When prisoners come home: Parole and prisoner reentry.* New York: Oxford University Press.

Peterson-Badali, M., and Koegl, C. J. (2002). Juveniles' experiences of incarceration: The role of correctional staff in peer violence. *Journal of Criminal Justice, 30,* 41–49.

Pfefferbaum, A., and Dishotsky, N. I. (1981). Racial intolerance in a correctional institution: An ecological view. *American Journal of Psychiatry, 138,* 1057–62.

Phillips, C. (2008). Negotiating identities: Ethnicity and social relations in a young offenders' institution. *Theoretical Criminology, 12,* 313–31.

Phinney, J. S. (1989). Stages of ethnic identity development in minority group adolescents. *Journal of Early Adolescence, 9,* 34–49.

Ploeger, M. (1997). Youth employment and delinquency: Reconsidering a problematic relationship. *Criminology, 35,* 659–75.

Pope, C., and Feyerherm, W. (1993). *Minorities and the juvenile justice system: Research summary.* Washington, DC: Office of Juvenile Justice and Delinquency Prevention.

Pratt, T. C., and Maahs, J. (1999). Are private prisons more cost-effective than public prisons? A meta-analysis of evaluation research studies. *Crime and Delinquency, 45,* 358–71.

Putnins, A. L. (1997). Victim awareness programs for delinquent youths: Effects on moral reasoning maturity. *Adolescence, 32,* 709–32.

Puzzanchera, C., and Sickmund, M. (2008). *Juvenile Court Statistics 2005.* Pittsburgh, PA: National Center for Juvenile Justice.

Ramos-Zayas, A. Y. (2007). Becoming American, becoming black? Urban competency, racialized spaces, and the politics of citizenship among Brazilian and Puerto Rican youth in Newark. *Identities: Global Studies in Culture and Power, 14,* 85–109.

Rider-Hankins, P. (1992). Juvenile correction education: A review of the current literature. *Technical Assistance Bulletin, 7.* Chicago: American Bar Association.

Robertson, J. E. (2006). Foreword: "Separate but equal" in prison: *Johnson v. California* and common sense racism. *Journal of Criminal Law and Criminology, 96,* 795–848.

Rothman, D. (1971). *The discovery of the asylum: Social order and disorder in the New Republic.* Boston: Little, Brown.

Sabol, W. (2007). Local labor market and post prison employment: Evidence from Ohio. In S. Bushway, M. Stoll, and D. Weiman (Eds.), *Barriers to reentry? The labor market for released prisoners in post-industrial America* (pp. 257–303). New York: Russell Sage Foundation.

Sampson, R. J., and Laub, J. H. (1993). *Crime in the making: Pathways and turning points through life.* Cambridge: Harvard University Press.

Santos, M. G. (2004). *About prison.* Belmont, CA: Wadsworth Press.

Schlossman, S. (1995). Delinquent children: The juvenile reform school. In D. Rothman, (Ed.), *The Oxford History of the Prison* (pp. 363–90). Oxford, UK: Oxford University Press.

Schuman, H., and Kalton, G. (1985). Survey Methods. In G. Lindzey and E. Aronson

(Eds.), *Handbook of social psychology*, vol. 1, *Theory and method* (3rd ed., pp. 635–97). New York: Random House.

Scott, E., and Steinberg, L. (2008). *Rethinking juvenile justice*. Cambridge: Harvard University Press.

Sheridan, Richard. (2007). Paying for adult and juvenile corrections, FY 2008– FY 2009. *State Budgeting Matters, 3* (32, October 31). Cleveland: Center for Community Solutions. Retrieved November 20, 2008, from *www.communitysolutions.com/store/index.asp?DEPARTMENT_ID=38*.

Sherman, L. W., Gottfredson, D. C., MacKenzie, D. L., Eck, J., Reuter, P., and Bushway, S. D. (1998). *Preventing crime: What works, what doesn't, what's promising; A report to the United States Congress*. Washington, DC: National Institute of Justice.

Sickmund, M. (2003). Juveniles in Court. *Juvenile Offenders and Victims Bulletin: National Report Series*. Washington, DC: U.S. Department of Justice. Retrieved June 6, 2009, from *www.ncjrs.gov/pdffiles1/ojjdp/195420.pdf*.

Simon, J. (2007). *Governing through crime*. New York: New York University Press.

Skiba, R., and McKelvey, J. (2000). *Anger management: What works in preventing school violence*. Safe and Responsible Schools Project, Indiana University. Retrieved February 12, 2009, from *www.indiana.edu/~safeschl/AngerManagement.pdf*.

Slosar, J. A. (1978). *Prisonization, friendship, and leadership*. Lexington, MA: Lexington Books.

Snyder, H. N., and Sickmund, M. (2006). *Juvenile offenders and victims: 2006 national report*. Washington, DC: U.S. Department of Justice, Office of Justice Programs, Office of Juvenile Justice and Delinquency Prevention.

Sparks, R., Bottoms, A., and Hay, W. (1996). *Prison and the problem of order*. Oxford, UK: Oxford University Press.

Stone, M., and Brown, B. (1999). Identity claims and projections: Descriptions of self and crowds in secondary school. *New Directions for Child and Adolescent Development, 84* (Summer), 7–20.

Stouthamer-Loeber, M., and Wei, E. H. (1998). The precursors of young fatherhood and its effect on delinquency of teenage males. *Journal of Adolescent Health, 22*, 56–65.

Suedfeld, P. (1980). Environmental effects on violent behavior in prisons. *International Journal of Offender Therapy and Comparative Criminology, 24*, 107–16.

Sykes, G. M. (1958). *The society of captives: A study of a maximum security prison*. Princeton, NJ: Princeton University Press.

Sykes, G. M., and Messinger, S. (1960). The inmate social system. In R. A. Cloward, D. R. Cressey, G. H. Grosser, R. McCleery, L. E. Ohlin, G. M. Sykes, and S. L. Messinger (Eds.), *Theoretical studies in the social organization of the prison* (pp. 5–19). New York: Social Science Research Council.

Tatum, B. D. (2004). Family life and school experience: Factors in the racial identity development of black youth in white communities. *Journal of Social Issues, 60*, 117–35.

Teasley, D., and Doyle, C. (2003). Juvenile justice: Opening juvenile records, pro and con. In L. V. Moore (Ed.), *Juvenile crime: Current issues and background* (pp. 85–107). New York: Nova Science Publishers.

Teplin, L. A., Abram, K. M., McClelland, G. M., Dulcan, M. K., and Mericle, A. A. (2002). Psychiatric disorders in youth in juvenile detention. *Archives of General Psychiatry, 59,* 1133–43.

Texas Youth Commission. (2003). *2003 review of agency treatment effectiveness.* Austin: Texas Youth Commission. Retrieved February 18, 2009, from *www.tyc.state.tx.us/archive/Research/TxmtEffect03/index.html.*

Thornberry, T. P., Moore, M., and Christenson, R. L. (1985). The effect of dropping out of high school on subsequent criminal behavior. *Criminology, 23,* 3–18.

Thornberry, T. P., Wei, E. H., Stouthamer-Loeber, M., and Van Dyke, J. (2000). *Teenage fatherhood and delinquent behavior.* Washington, DC: Office of Juvenile Justice and Delinquency Prevention.

Toch, H. (1992). *Living in prison: The ecology of survival* (Rev. ed.). Washington, DC: American Psychological Association.

Travis, J. (2005). *But they all come back: Facing the challenges of prisoner reentry.* Washington, DC: Urban Institute Press.

Travis, J., and Lawrence, S. (2002). *Beyond the prison gates: The state of parole in America.* Research Report (November) Washington, DC: Urban Institute Justice Policy Center.

Tropp, L. R., and Pettigrew, T. F. (2005). Relationships between intergroup contact and prejudice among minority and majority status groups. *Psychological Science, 16,* 951–957.

Tyler, J. H., and Kling, J. R. (2007). Prison-based education and reentry into the mainstream labor market. In S. Bushway, M. Stoll, and D. Weiman (Eds.), *Barriers to reentry? The labor market for released prisoners in post-industrial America* (pp. 222–56). New York: Russell Sage Foundation.

Tyler, J. L., Ziedenberg, J., and Lotke, E. (2006). *Cost effective corrections: The fiscal architecture of rational juvenile justice systems.* Washington, DC: Justice Policy Institute.

Tyler, T. (1998). Trust and democratic governance. In V. Braithwaite and M. Levi (Eds.), *Trust and governance* (pp. 269–94). New York: Russell Sage Foundation.

Tyler, T., and Lind, A. (2001). Procedural justice. In J. Sanders and V. Lee Hamilton (Eds.), *Handbook of justice research in law* (pp. 65–92). New York: Kluwer Academic/Plenum.

Uggen, C. (2000). Work as a turning point in the life course of criminals: A duration model of age, employment, and recidivism. *American Sociological Review, 67,* 529–46.

University of South Carolina. (2006). *Juvenile detention in South Carolina.* School of Law, Children's Law Office. Retrieved February 20, 2009, from *childlaw.sc.edu/.*

U.S. Census Bureau. (2000). Total population by age, race and Hispanic or Latino origin for the United States, 2000. *Census 2000 brief.* Retrieved February 25, 2009, from *www.census.gov/population/.*

———. (2004). Detailed living arrangements of children by race, Hispanic origin and age, 2004. Retrieved January 25, 2009, from *www.census.gov/population/www/socdemo/children.html.*

U.S. Department of Justice. (2008). *Statewide CRIPA investigation of Texas state schools.* Retrieved January 15, 2009, from *www.justice.gov/crt/split/documents/TexasStateSchools_findlet_12-1-08.pdf.*

U.S. National Institute of Corrections. (2004). *Corrections-based services for victims of crime.* Longmont, CO: U.S. Department of Justice, National Institute of Corrections Information Center. Retrieved November 8, 2008, from *www.nicic.org/pubs/2004/019947.pdf.*

Ventura, S. J., Martin, J. A., Curtin S. C., Menacker, F., and Hamilton, B. E. (2001). Births: Final data for 1999. *National Vital Statistics Reports, 49* (1). National Center for Health Statistics, Hyattsville, MD.

Visher, C., and Kachnowski, V. (2007). Finding work on the outside: Results from the "Returning Home" project in Chicago. In S. Bushway, M. Stoll, and D. Weiman (Eds.), *Barriers to reentry? The labor market for released prisoners in post-industrial America* (pp. 80–114). New York: Russell Sage Foundation.

Wacquant, L. (2000). The new "peculiar institution"? On the prison as a surrogate ghetto. *Theoretical Criminology, 4*, 377–89.

Wald, J., and Losen, D. (2003). Defining and redirecting a school-to-prison pipeline. In J. Wald and D. Losen (Eds.), *Deconstructing the school-to-prison pipeline* (pp. 9–15). San Francisco: Jossey-Bass.

Ways, N., Cowal, K., Gingold, R., Pahl, K., and Bissessar, N. (2001). Friendship patterns among African American, Asian American, and Latino adolescents from low-income families. *Journal of Social and Personal Relationships, 18* (1), 29–53.

Wener, R., and Olsen, R. (1980). Innovative correctional environments: A user assessment. *Environment and Behavior, 12*, 478–93.

Western, B., and Beckett, K. (1999). How unregulated is the U.S. labor market? The penal system as a labor market institution. *American Journal of Sociology, 104*, 1030–60.

Western, B., Petit, B., and Guetzkow, J. (2002). Black economic progress in the era of mass imprisonment. In M. Mauer and M. Chesney-Lind (Eds.), *Invisible punishment: The collateral consequences of mass imprisonment* (pp. 165–80). New York: New Press.

White, B. (2009). Youth prison model sets high bar. *Wall Street Journal*, October 12. Retrieved December 13, 2009, from *online.wsj.com/.*

Wilson, D. (2006). Steep phone rates cut off youth offenders from home. *Columbus Dispatch*, October 22.

Wilson, D. B., Gallagher, C. A., and MacKenzie, D. L. (2000). A meta-analysis of corrections-based education, vocation, and work programs for adult offenders. *Journal of Research in Crime and Delinquency, 37*, 347–68.

Winoker, K. P., Blankenship, J., Cass, E., and Hand, G. (2003). *An evaluation of the Florida Department of Juvenile Justice's Impact of Crime Curriculum.* Tallahassee, FL: Justice Research Center.

Wright, J. P., Cullen, F. T., and Williams, N. (1997). Working while in school and delinquent involvement: Implications for social policy. *Crime and Delinquency, 43,* 203–21.

Zamble, B., and Porporino, F. J. (1988). *Coping, behavior, and adaptation in prison inmates.* New York: Springer-Verlag.

Acknowledgments

This book was, in so many ways, a team effort. The most important contribution was that of the forty young men whose voices, experiences, and ideas appear throughout. They gave generously of their time even though they understood that they would receive little for their efforts. During my research, several staff members at the Ohio Department of Youth Services—including administrators, social workers, and parole officers—provided invaluable help, far beyond anything I could have expected. I would also like to thank the George Gund Foundation for their funding of the last stage of interviewing.

I wrote the bulk of this book during a year of research leave from The College of Wooster. I am deeply grateful for that time and for the College's willingness to support my project with faculty development funds. From the College staff, Di Springer helped me tremendously by carefully and cheerfully transcribing what seemed like an endless number of muffled interviews. My mother, Pam Nurse, assisted with copyediting, as well as providing outstanding feedback and encouragement. Numerous colleagues helped me think through the material for this book. Mary Bosworth, Peggy Giordano, Patrick Carr, and Heather Fitz Gibbon were particularly helpful with early drafts. Chuck Hurst provided a number of crucial references, and Christopher Uggen helped me to think more deeply about the confidentiality of juvenile records. Megan Comfort gave me incredibly insightful and detailed feedback on the manuscript. I am extremely grateful for her efforts. Michael Ames at Vanderbilt University Press helped to shape the original direction of this manuscript and provided support along the way. Jessie Hunnicutt, also at Vanderbilt, provided thoughtful and thorough copyediting, improving the manuscript considerably. I also greatly appreciate the valuable reactions and suggestions of the anonymous reviewers of both this manuscript and earlier article submissions based on the same research.

On a more personal note, my ability to write this book hinged on unfailing support from both family and friends. Among the friends, I would especially like to thank Deborah, Eva, Heather, Pam, Shirley, and Susie. They were a source of encouragement and advice, as well as providing a frequently needed sense of humor. You are an extraordinary group of women. I am also deeply grateful to my parents. No matter the circumstances, they have always been there for me.

I am exceedingly fortunate to live with four amazing people who are my ongoing support, and who have put up with me during the research and writing of this book. Every day I give thanks that, many years ago, I had the sense to accept a blind date with the ex-boyfriend of a friend's friend. The man who showed up that day eventually became the best friend and partner imaginable. Our three sons—Alexander, Jacob, and Gabriel—are also an endless source of joy. The boys were much involved with the writing of this book, providing commentary on my ideas and asking questions. Proudly I can now answer one of the most persistent of those questions. Yes, Jakie, mommy is FINALLY done with that book.

Index